NATURAL RESOURCES OF HIMALAYA

Himalaya Past and Present Series

NATURAL RESOURCES OF HIMALAYA

Editor
K. S. Gulia

ISHA BOOKS
DELHI-110009

Natural Resources of Himalaya

ISBN : 81-8205-4087

Published in 2007 in India by:
ISHA Books
B-63, Ist Floor, New Gupta Colony,
Near DDA Market, Delhi-110009
Phone: 9212142040
Email: ishabooks@hotmail.com

Laser Type setting by: Tact Computer Graphics, Delhi
Printed at: Salasar Imaging System, Delhi

Contents

Introduction

Indigenous knowledge as applied to Himalayas is a very broad term that comprises all aspects of life - food, farming, and hunting, medicine preparation and treatment, arts, crafts and technologies used by indigenous cultures. What distinguishes this knowledge from western knowledge systems is its integration in the culture and cosmology as a whole. Each aspect of this knowledge is but one strand of knowledge, intricately interwoven and inextricably linked to the whole web of existence in the Himalayas. In contrast, western technology prides itself of its detached and analytical mode of thinking, an abstract model that separates the observer from the observed and thus creates an artificial model of reality in which each part can be examined in isolation as if it had no bearing on the whole. Scientists believe that this is a more advanced and superior method of investigating natural phenomenon. However, ever since this mode of analyzing and interpreting nature first appeared on the horizon of human consciousness it has deluded us, making us belief that because we understand a particular component of a living system we therefore can control the entire system, and, not only that, but also derive at conclusions about other systems that might demonstrate the same particular characteristic or component.

Hence the common theory that what works or doesn't work on rat's must have the same or similar effect on humans etc. Indigenous knowledge on the other hand seeks to comprehend the interwoven aspects of its ecosystem by means of identification rather than by abstraction. The healer knows that he or she will learn precious little about a plant or tree by burning its leaves and analysing the ashes. Instead, he or she identifies with it and its spirit, seeking to know its essential nature and thus learns about its healing potential. The same goes for all aspects that make up the ecosystem of which we humans are but a part. Thus, indigenous knowledge is based on a cosmology of relationships between the observer and the observed and both are aspects of an integrated wholeness.

In recent years scientists have increasingly been turning to the keepers of indigenous knowledge, realizing that their age-old systems have managed to preserve an ecological balance or that their medicine might have tremendous potential for the development of modern drugs. But the indigeous people does not always welcome this renewed interest. Having been exploited for centuries and their rights abused too many times by those who claim to come as friends, they are now often rather reserved and suspicious and unwilling to share what they consider a sacred aspect of their culture. Pharmaceutical companies in particular have already demonstrated that they have no respect for the cultural or intellectual property of others, but cheerfully engage in acts of biopiracy, stealing biological materials as well as the knowledge that goes with it to take out patents that will benefit only themselves.

The debate surrounding biopiracy, intellectual and cultural property rights and benefits sharing has been raging for a long time, and still no satisfactory solution has been found, though at least the international community has acknowledged the problems and is engaged in a process of finding a solution that involves representatives of the indigenous communities concerned. It is a difficult task, but for the sake of our future as human family it is vital that we resolve these issues fairly and responsibly.

Over the last decade or so ethnobotany has assumed a scientific prominence previously denied it. It is endorsed by institutions with a high international profile (the Royal Geographical Society, WWF, UNDP, UNESCO), has a market value placed upon it by foresters, agronomists, development advisors and pharmacologists. At the same time it has become pivotal in preserving the cultural identity and knowledge of indigenous people whose traditional way of life is under threat. Ethnobotanical knowledge has, therefore, become an economic commodity. This is particularly true with respect to the plant knowledge of people of Himalayas.

Traditional knowledge can make a significant contribution to sustainable development. Most indigenous and local communities are situated in areas where the vast majority of the world's plant genetic resources are found. Many of them have cultivated and used biological diversity in a sustainable way for thousands of years. However, the contribution of indigenous and local communities to the conservation and sustainable use of biological diversity goes far beyond their role as natural resource managers. Their skills and techniques provide valuable information to the global community and a useful model for biodiversity policies. Furthermore, as on-site communities with extensive knowledge of local environments, indigenous and local communities are most directly involved with conservation and sustainable use. Some however do get sucked into the vortex created by interested groups who want to exploit this diversity for their own ends.

In our book comprising 17 chapters, we have taken up Himalayan Forests, Economic Geology of Himalayas, Ethnobotany of Eastern Himalayas, Medicinal Plants of Himalayas, Lepcha Medico botany, Ethnobotany of Darjeeling Himalayas, Bon Medicine among Monpas and many more subjects concerning the Himalayas.

In Chapter One, Himalayan Forests have been discussed. The nature and type of any forests depends upon the prevailing climatic conditions, altitude and biotic influences. There are varied types of forests in the Himalayas, starting from Jammu region to Sikkim, Arunachal Pradesh and beyond. All these forests, their subdivisions, the type of trees and shrubbery that grows in there, have been discussed here with detail; the effects of climate on their growth has also been discussed in detail.

As far mineral wealth of Himalayas is concerned, this range is considered to be poor in that respect. There are deposits of salt, slates, sapphires, aquamarine and semi-precious stones. Till now not much efforts has been put in to exploit these deposits. Accessibility of the terrain is one of the reasons. The Government on a continuous basis has undertaken geographical surveys. This has been discussed in chapter Two.

In Chapter Three Ethnobotany of the Himalayas has been discussed. This is also the main subject of our book. Humans interact amongst themselves. They interact with environmental matrices, which are systems or conglomeration of systems. On such related subject of biological ecology of human ecosystems is based the study of ethnobotany. Human ecological research without details of ethnobotany of a given area remains incomplete.

In Chapter Four we discuss the medicinal plants of the Himalayas. The use plants in healing and treating diseases has been evolved from the time of man's earliest social and cultural groupings. The age-old medical system prevailing in whole of the northern India is known as Ayurveda. It is embedded in distinct cultural premises and symbols. As one goes along Himalayas from Jammu along the upper ranges of Himalayan Sikkim and Arunachal Pradesh, flora and fauna keep on changing. The inhabitants of the area have known for ages, where a flower or an herb fits in the cultural stream.

Chapter Five is on Lepcha medico botany. More than any other people of Sikkim, the Lepchas are familiar with the medicinal properties of numerous plants which ground around them, which the use to treat their own ailments and those of their cattle.

Chapter Six discusses ethnobotany of Darjeeling area. The Himalayan ecosystem is known or its richness in biodiversity. The flora of this region not only maintains ecological balance but serves essential medicinal uses too. While there are several plants, which contain curative principles, several other species are very lethal to human beings. But even such species can be put to use. This has been detailed in this chapter.

The entire existence of Monpas, their knowledge and practise, cognition and construction is suffused and coloured by the experience of the spiritual. The hallmark of the Bob supernatural geography overlaps the holistic phenomenology of illness and the structure of the triad cosmos corresponds to the spiritual arrangement of the therapeutic intervention and expertise of specialists. The worship of the mountain is the core concept of bonpo practise of healing. This is a complicated process of medicine and healing, which discussed in Chapter Seven.

Chapter Eight also discusses healing. It is among the Gaddis of Himachal. Gaddis have been relatively isolated and autonomous group. They have their own cultural and medical system and are one of the important systems of their society. In tribal societies, system of cure is not only based on magico-religious means but also of plants. Tribal people have developed pharmacopoeia and some rudimentary knowledge of medical techniques at individual and also at community level. These technique are used either together or separately to cure sick. This magico-religio-plant system has been detailed in this chapter.

Chapter Nine discusses Endangered and Gymospermic Medicinal Plants in Kumaun. Kumaun hills are abode of innumerable medicinal plants many of which are on the verge of extinction. As among Gaddis in Himachal, tribal people also use magico-religio-plant system for healing. There are many plants in Kumaon, which can heal cancer and other dreaded diseases. Indiscrimate exploitation by the local people in connivance with some pharmaceutical companies has taken these plants to the verge of extinction. These are the plants, which the Kumaonese have been using with their magico-religious rituals to treat diseases of their tribes.

Chapter Ten discussed medicinal plants in Northwest Himalayas. It is the general belief of the planners that medicinal plants could be the potential resources for socio-economic uplifting of the northwestern State of Jammu & Kashmir. Excellent findings are reported on developing agro-technology of several important Himalayan medicinal herbs. People's participation in medicinal plant cultivation and its commercialization could lead to fruitful outcomes.

In the Northeast and Sikkim farmer families cultivate and grow crops. To subsidise their incomes, they rear cattle, yaks, goats, sheep, pigs and poultry depending on their economic strength. They also utilize the forests to certain products for their day-to-day needs. In Chapter Eleven, measures taken by the government agencies for betterment of the families are discussed.

Chapter Twelve deals with rural economy of the Eastern Himalayas. The needs of the hill people are biomass based. Their requirements have increased many folds over the years due to the rise in population. This has led to a rapid depletion of the reserve forests. In the Himalaya, degradation of forests has also come about due to over use, beyond the capacity of the forests to regenerate, through too much felling, lopping and grazing. This has been discussed in this chapter.

Chapter Thirteen deals with Environment and Economic Development. The Eastern Himalayas is considered among the principal hotspots for biodiversity. The region is repository to a richness of flora and fauna unrivalled on the face of the planet. It also happens to be economically the poorest region with in the country. The unique microclimate of the region which ranges from the tropical to the alpine over varied ecosystems combines with fine human resources that are aptly suited to the rugged mountain area, and in fact have great economic potential.

The rapid growth in forest industries has necessitated an increased cut from the Himalayan forests. Along with the communications network came the contractor whose job was to transport the produce to be processed by large-scale industries in the private sector. Everybody was exploiting the forests. More crucial was the willful neglect of the local population in the extraction and processing of forest produced. All this has played havoc with the eco system of Himalayas. In

Chapter Fourteen, measures have been suggested, which if taken would to some extent put a stop to this exploitation.

Chapter Fifteen deals with Industry and Minerals in Himalayas. During the old days trade and industry in Uttarakhand hill region were limited to sale and purchase of Borax, Shilajeet, Wool, Ghee, Carpets Hone, Herbs and some other products produced by hill people. With the availability of technology and efforts being put in by the State Government and its development agencies, the area is poised for a big leap in production in small-scale industry. Though because of accessibility there is not much scope for medium scale industry.

Chapter Sixteen deals with traditional methods of water management in the Himalayas. In the central Himalayas, a rich heritage of traditional methods for water conservation and management exists. A whole range of indigenous methods is in practise to store and use water for irrigation and other household purposes. These methods are cost-effective and involve the use of locally available material and human skill to construct the water harvesting structure. The methodology have been discussed elaborately.

Chapter Seventeen reviews settlement-fuel wood equation in the Darjeeling Himalayas. With the leasing out of wastelands by the British after 1857, the seeds of forestry policy in India evolved under the consultancy of German forester Dietrich Brandis. He was perhaps the first Conservator of Forests in India. This Chapter discusses in details the steps that been taken by the British and later on by Government of India and under its guidance by the State Government.

1
Himalayan Forests

The nature and type of forests found in a particular locality depends upon the prevailing climatic conditions, altitude, aspect, topography, soil and biotic influences. The Himalayan mountain chain bears rich forests that are comprised of over a thousand different species of trees, shrubs, herbs and climbers.

The following forest groups have been recognized in the Himalaya by Puri (1960), Champion and Seth (1968), Negi (1985) and Negi (1989). These groups are based on altitude and climate.

Sub-tropical Semi-desert Forest

Around Jammu the area is barren with gravelly soil. This group of forests is found in these foothills. It is made up of forests occurring along river beds in the foothills of Jammu and western Himachal Pradesh. Scrub type of vegetation is predominant. Shisham (Dalbergia sissoo), Khair (Acacia catechu), *Prosopis*, and *Zizyphus* are the main species.

These forests are typical of the south-facing slopes of the western Himalaya drier conditions prevail in that area.

Montane Sub-tropical Forest

This group of forests occurs roughly between an altitude of 500 to 1500 mts. Immediately above the sub-tropical semi-desert forests. Summers are very hot and the mercury may rise to over 40°C. Though bulk of the total annual precipitation is from the SW monsoons, winter rains are also received. The following three subdivisions are prominent:

1. Sub-tropical broad-leaved hill forests they are comprised of the east Himalayan sub-tropical wet hill forest (8B/C2) of Champion and Seth. It is dominated by *Alnus nepalensis, Betula* sp. and *Quercus* sp.

2. Sub-tropical pine forests these forests are dominated by the lower or Siwalik Chir pine forest of Champion and Seth. The main species is *Pinus roxburghii.*
3. Sub-tropical dry evergreen forests these occurs in the terai bhabar tract, Siwalik hills and the foothills of the lower Himalaya.

Montane Wet Temperate Forest

Champion, Seth and Negi (1989) classed the following forest. These form a part of this belt:

1. Northern wet temperate forests occurring between 1800 and 3000 mts in the Darjeeling hills and Arunachal Pradesh.
2. East Himalayan wet temperate forests consist of lower and upper oak forests and lauraceous forests of the eastern Himalaya. The principal species found in these forests are:

Acer campbellii	*Betula* sp.
Castanopsis sp.	*Cinnamomum* sp.
Machilus sp.	*Quercus* sp.

Himalayan Moist Temperate Forest

This group of forests is well distributed usually between an elevation of 1500 and 3300 mts. All over the Himalayas the following are the main forest types that form a part of this group:

1. Lower western Himalayan temperate forest in which the following are included—(1) *Ban oak forest* with *Quercus leucotricophora,* deodar and *Rhododendron.* (2) *Moru oak forest* bearing *Q. dilatata, Q. leucotricophora, Q. semecarpifolia;* fir, spruce, deodar, blue pine, *Rhododendron,* chestnut, walnut, *Betula* and *Acer.* (3) *Moist deodar forest* that is extensively developed in the western Himalaya and in parts of Nepal. (4) *Western mixed coniferous forest* comprising of fir, spruce and deodar. (5) *Moist temperate deciduous forest* usually found in moist shady depressions and comprising of *Acer, Carpinus, Betula* and *Fraxinus.* (6) *Low level blue pine forest* in which pure patches of blue pine are occasionally mixed with fir and spruce.
2. Upper Himalayan temperate forest in which the following forests are included—(a) Kharsu oak forest; (b) Western Himalayan upper oak-fir forest, and
3. East Himalayan mixed temperate forest consisting of the following forests—(a) East Himalayan mixed coniferous forest; and (b) *Abies delavayi* forest.

Himalayan Dry Temperate Forest

In the rain shadow areas of the higher and trans-Himalayas this group of forest occurs. There is less precipitation from rain and more in the form of snow. The following forests form a part of this group (Champion and Seth 1968, and Negi 1989).

1. Dry broad-leaved and coniferous forest dominated by *Pinus gerardiana.*
2. Dry temperate coniferous forest—Neoza pine forest; and Dry deodar forest.
3. West Himalayan dry temperate forest.
4. West Himalayan high level blue pine forest.
5. West Himalayan dry juniper forest.
6. East Himalayan dry temperate coniferous forest.
7. East Himalayan dry juniper forest.

Sub-alpine Forest

This group of forests occupies a position between the alpine meadows and the temperate forests. This usually lies near the snowline in all parts of the Himalaya *Betula, Abies, Junipers* and *Rhododendrons* are the main species. This region represents the uppermost limit of tree growth. Typical arctic conditions prevail. Heavy snowfall occurs all through the long winter season and the ground is covered by a thick blanket of snow for several months at a stretch. The growing period available to the plants is very short. They tend to develop a vast network of roots, which helps to sustain them during the cold season. The biomass below the ground is more than that above it. The main forests forming a part of this group are:

West Himalayan sub-alpine birch/fir forest, and

East Himalayan sub-alpine birch/fir forest are the main forests forming a part of this group.

Moist Alpine Scrub

Moist alpine meadows occur just below the snowline in the moister tracts of the Himalaya. Moist alpine scrub usually occur above an elevation of 3500 mts. The following scrub forests form a part of this group:

1. Birch-Rhododendron scrub forest.
2. Deciduous alpine scrub.
3. Alpine pastures.

Dry Alpine Scrub

Dry alpine scrubs meadows occur near the snowline in the drier part of the Himalaya; usually in the inner dry valleys of the higher Himalayan and in the trans-Himalayan zones. Vegetation is xerophytic.

Western Himalaya

Forests of the eastern Himalaya differ from those found in the western Himalaya. Forests of Nepal have been found to be a transition between the two regions. The western Himalayan forests are diverse, both in extent and composition. The main forest types (based on Champion and Seth 1968 and Negi, 1989) found in this region are:

Moist Sal Forest

Siwalik hills and Himalayan foothills form the eastern extremity of Sirmur district in Himachal Pradesh to the lower hills of Kumaun where Extensive and almost pure forests of sal occur. By and large, sal forests are dominated by one gregarious species—*Shorea robusta.* Sal is more aggressive and dominating than any of its associates because of the following reasons:

— High adaptability to edaphic and site conditions.
— High coppicing power.
— Ability to regenerate under burnt and grazed conditions.
Sal constitutes upto 90 per cent of the top canopy.

Sal is semi-evergreen in habit with a short leafless period of 10 to 15 days at the beginning of the summer season. The shade offered by the new foliage keeps these forests cooler in contrast to other deciduous forests. Its height may be upto 35 mts or even more.

Most of these shrubs are semievergreen and fires lead to their replacement by grass species. Climbers are also commonly found in these forests. A dense undergrowth is common in sal forests. Bamboos and canes are other associates of sal. The following types occur in the western Himalaya.

Moist Siwalik Sal Forest

The average maximum temperature where this forest is found may be in the region of 40°C. This forest is commonly found in the Siwalik hills usually upto an elevation of about 1000 mts. Rainfall is more than 200 cms per year with upto 90 per cent of the total annual precipitation being received from the monsoon rains. Winter rains are experienced in January and February. Frost may also occur during this period. This forest is best developed in the Dehradun and Paonta areas and near Ramnagar, extending to moist depressions on southern aspects.

Main species are:

I.	*Adina cordifolia*	*Anogeissus latifolia*
	Bridelia retusa	*Garuga pinnata*
	Lagerstroemia parviflora	*Shorea robusta*
	Terminalia tomentosa	
II.	*Aegle marmelos*	*Butea monosperma*
	Cassia fistula	*Gardenia turgida*
	Grewia elastica	*Litsea glutinosa*
	Mallotus philippensis	*Miliusa velutina*
	Randia dumetorum	*Zizyphus xylopyrus*
III.	*Clerodendron viscosum*	*Murraya koengii*
IV.	*Chrysopogon fulvus*	*Heteropogon contortus*

Moist Bhabar-Dun Sal Forest

This is a medium to good quality sal forest found in the bhabar and dun tract of Paonta area in Himachal Pradesh. This is also found along the southern zone of Garhwal and Kumaun. Its main constituents are:

I.	*Adina cordifolia*	*Kydia calycina*
	Shorea robusta	*Stereospermum sp.*
	Terminalia bellerica	*T. tomentosa*
II.	*Mallotus philippensis*	*Meliusa velutina*
	Eugenia oojeinensis	*Schleichera oleosa*
III.	*Ardisia solanacea*	*Clerodendron viscosum*
	Glycosmis pentaphylla	*Moghania chappar*
IV.	*Imperata cylindrica*	*Themeda gigantea*
V.	*Butea parviflora*	

Lower Himalayan Sal Forest

Lower Himalyan Sal forest is found on the lower slopes of the Himalaya up to an elevation of 1000 mts in Garhwal and Kumaun. The main species are:

Albizzia lebbeck	*Anogeissus latifolia*
Shorea robusta	*Terminalia bellerica*
Terminalia tomentosa	

Dry Siwalik Sal Forest

Where conditions are relatively dry, these forests are found. Usually they are found on the hot and exposed slopes of the Siwalik hills. The quality varies from medium to good with sal being the dominant species. Biotic pressure is very heavy and hence regeneration is deficient. Winter frost leads to the dying back of the new shoots. Found in the drier tracts of Dehradun and Paonta. The consituents of this forest are:

I. *Acacia catechu* — *Dalbergia sissoo*
Diospyros tomentosa — *Schleichera oleosa*
Shorea robusta — *Terminalia tomentosa*

II. *Cassia fistula* — *Emblica officinalis*
Zizyphus xylopyrus

III. *Colebrookia oppositifolia* — *Indigofera pulchella*

IV. *Heteropogon contortus*

V. *Bauhinia vahlii*

Dry Mixed Deciduous Forest

Champion and Seth (1968) have referred to this forest northern dry mixed deciduous forest by Champion and Seth (1968) and as dry deciduous forest in many working plans. It is found in the drier parts of the foothill zone. The forest is open and made up of poor quality trees of different species. Biotic pressure is very heavy. The average annual rainfall varies from 100 to 150 cms. This forest is well developed in the lower hills of Hamirpur, Una, Kangra, Bilaspur, Solan, Kotdwara and Haldwani areas. The soil is deficient, shallow and at times severely eroded. Main species are:

I. *Acacia catechu* — *Aegle marmelos*
Anogeissus latifolia — *Ehretia laevis*
Feromia limonia — *Flacourtia indica*
Kydia calycina — *Lannea cormomandelica*
Mitragyna parviflora

II. *Dendrocalamus strictus* — *Mallotus philippensis*
Nyctanthes arbortristis

III. *Adhatoda vasica* — *Carissa opaca*
Dodonea viscosa — *Woodfordia fruticosa*

IV. *Acacia caesia* — *Bauhinia vahlii*

Dry Bamboo Brakes

Champion and Seth have termed them as the dry bamboo brakes. This forest is found in the foothill tract of the western Himalaya. *Dendrocalamus strictus* is the main species. There occur a number of shrubs that are also a part of the dry deciduous forests discussed above.

Khair-Sissoo Forest

Champion and Seth have referred to this forest as the khair-sissoo forest by. This is a dry deciduous forest found either as a major riverine succession in the sal-chir pine tract of the Siwalik hills and lower Himalaya or as a major forest type in the drier foothills of Himachal Pradesh in Nurpur, Una, Hamirpur and Bilaspur areas. Both khair *(Acacia catechu)* and sissoo *(Dalbergia sissoo)* are found in almost equal proportions. The canopy is open but generally fairly complete with sissoo trees attaining a height of 15 mts or more. Pure patches of khair may occur on extremely rocky outcrops or on almost pure sandy soils.

The older forests have a fairly dense, deciduous, shrubby undergrowth. However, even in this case, a large proportion of the sandy soil remains exposed. The summer months are very hot and dry in tracts where khair and sissoo occur. Bulk of the precipitation is received from the monsoons though winter rains are also fairly heavy. Winter frost is common. Water supply is available up to moderate depths. Soil conditions are very peculiar in this forest type. The upper layers of the soil are almost entirely devoid of humus and highly porous.

There are three variations of this forest—(a) mixed khair-sissoo forest; (b) pure sissoo forest with occasional trees of khair; and (c) pure khair forest with occasional trees of sissoo.

The main composition of this forest type is:

I.	*Acacia catechu*	*Dalbergia sissoo*
	Tamarix dioica	*Tiliacora acuminata*
II.	*Acacia farnesiana*	*Ehertia laevis*
	Albizzia lebbek	*Holoptelea integrifolia*
	Zizyphus mauratiana	
III.	*Adhatoda vasica*	*Calotropis procera*
	Helicteres isora	*Murraya koengii*
	Pogostemon	
IV.	*Cassia tora*	*Chrysopogon fulvus*
	Chrysopogon gryllus	*Erianthus munja*
	Saccharum munja	*S. spontaneum*
	Vetiveria zizanodies	
V.	*Millettia* sp.	*Vallaris* sp.

Moist Mixed Deciduous Forest

These forest include include the Gangetic tropical moist mixed deciduous riverine forest and west Gangetic moist mixed deciduous forest of Champion and Seth. These forests are associates of the sal, khair, sissoo and even chir pine forests occurring in the Siwalik hills and the lower Himalayan tracts.

This forest has a number of dominant species that are intimately mixed together. It is a fairly closed one. Individual trees may attain a height of upto 30 mts. The second storey is also well developed. It includes a number of evergreen species. Climber growth is heavy. The main species constituting this forest type are:

I.	*Adina Cardifolia*	*Albizzia procera*
	Bauhinia retusa	*Bombax ceiba*
	Dalbergia sissoo	*Ficus sp.*
	Lannea coromendelica	*Madhuca indica*
	Mitragyna parviflora	*Terminalia arjuna*
	T. bellerica	*T. tomentosa*
II.	*Bauhinia vahlii*	*B. variegata*
	Cassia fistula	*Colebrookia oppositifolia*
	Garuga pinnata	*Kydia calycina*
	Mallotus philippensis	*Moghania* sp.
III.	*Dendrocalamus strictus*	
IV.	*Adathoda vasica*	*Clerodendron viscosum*
	Helicteres isora	*Strobilanthes*
V.	*Barleria strigosa*	*Costus speciosus*
VI.	*Aphanamixis polystachya*	*Bischofia* sp.
VII.	*Combretum decandrum*	*Dioscorea* sp.

Dry Scrub Forest

The dry and exposed slopes of the Siwalik hills and the lower Himalaya contain these forests. They may be of the following types.

Dry scrub– The dry scrub forests are of three kinds:

1. Tree scrub containing a fair proportion of tree growth. Individual trees may attain a height of about 20 mts.
2. Tree scrub consisting of a small proportion of tree growth and a comparatively open undergrowth of brushwood species.
3. Scrub forest containing very little tree growth and very open undergrowth of brushwood species.

The main constituents of the dry scrub forest are:

Acacia catechu	*Albizzia lebbek*
Anogeissus latifolia	*Diospyros* sp.
Lannea grandis	*Limonia crenulata*
Stephagyne parvifolia	

Dry deciduous scrub

This is dominated by shrubs of a height between 3 and 6 mts with occasional trees and bamboos. There is a heavy grazing pressure on these forests. The main constituents of this forest are:

Acacia catechu	*Aegle marmelos*
Carissa opaca	*Dodonea viscosa*
Euphorbia sp.	*Gardenia turgida*
Nyctanthes sp.	*Zizyphus* sp.

Sub-tropical Pine Forest

There is virtually no other species in the top canopy. The soil is covered by a growth of perennial and annual grasses. The mean annual temperature varies between 15°C and 20°C with the average maximum temperature being over 35°C. Winter temperatures may drop to 20°C or even lower. The sub- tropical pine forests occur in the very heavy rainfall tract with annual precipitation being over 200 cms.The forest is more or less a pure association of chir pine *(Pinus roxburghii).*

The sub-tropical pine forests are of the following two types.

Lower (Siwalik) Chir Pine Forest

Champion and Seth have referred to this forest type as lower or Siwalik chir pine forest. Mohan also refers to it as lower pine forest. It is a pure forest of chir pine occurring on the Siwalik hills, usually above an elevation of 1000 mts, all along the western Himalaya from Jammu to the Siwalik hills of Haldwani area. This tract experiences a hot and dry summer. Frost commonly occurs in winter. The main constituents of this forest type are:

I.	*Pinus roxburghii*	
II.	*Acacia catechu*	*Albizzia lebbek*
	Emblica officinalis	*Mallotus philippensis*
	Pyrus pashia	*Syzygium cumini*
	Terminalia chebula	
III.	*Carissa opaca*	*Colebrookia* sp.
	Crataegus crenulata	*Dodonea viscosa*
	Flacourtia sp.	*Indigofera pulchella*
	Murraya koengii	*Myrsine africana*
	Rubus ellipticus	
IV.	*Cymbopogon* sp.	*Dichanthium annulatum*
	Heteropogon contortus	*Themeda anathera*
V.	*Rosa moschata*	

The following variations of this forest type were recognised by Mohan and Puri (1956)

— Chir-Carissa-grass with *Terminalia chebula, Lannea* etc.
— *Chir-Carissa-Indigofera*-grass with abundant pine regeneration.
— *Chir-Quercus leucotricophora* with *Berberis, Myrsine* and grass.
— *Chir-Acacia catechu* with grass, *Mallotus* and *Lannea.*
— Chir- *Wendlandia-Dodonea-Carissa.*
— Chir-*Carissa-Flacourtia-grass.*

Upper (Himalayan) Chir Pine Forest

Champion and Seth have termed these as the upper or Himalayan chir pine forest. This is an almost pure forest of chir pine with individual trees attaining a height of over 25 mts. These forests are found upto an elevation of about 1800 mts in the lower Himalaya of Jammu hills, Himachal Pradesh, Garhwal and Kumaun. Well developed on sandstones, quartzites and granites. The average maximum temperature ranges from 38°C to 40°C. Rainfall varies from 90 cms to 250 cms.

Frequent fires and heavy resin tapping has taken a toll on the chir pine forests. They are in various stages of degradation. The main species constituting this forest type are:

I. *Pinus roxburghii*

II. *Coriaria nepalensis*, *Crataegus crenulata*, *Ficus roxburghii*, *Lyonia ovalifolia*, *Myrica sapida*, *Quercus leucotricophora*, *Rhododendron arboreum*, *Syzygium cumini*

III. *Aechmanthera tomentosa*, *Flemingia fruticulosa*, *Glochidion velutinum*, *Indigofera dosua*, *Leptodermis lanceolata*, *Rubus ellipticus*, *Viburnum coriaceum*

IV. *Anaphalis* sp., *Artemisia vulgaris*, *Arundinella intricata*, *Desmodium parvifolium*, *Eulalia mollis*, *Plectranthus strictus*, *Heteropogon contortus*, *Sporobolus elongatus*

V. *Rosa moschata*

Lower Temperate Forest

Moru Oak Forest: This forest is dominated by moru oak *(Quercus dilatata)*. These are found between an elevation of 2200 and 2400 mts. Moru oak forests form one of the best temperate broad-leaved forests with individual trees attaining a height of over 20 mts. This forest type occurs under cooler conditions than the ban oak forests discussed above. Heavy snowfall occurs during the winter months and it may lie on the ground for several days at a stretch.

Moru oak forests are well developed in Chamba, Dalhousie, Shimla, Rohru, Rajgarh, Tons valley, Mayali, Kausani and Pithoragarh tracts of the western Himalaya. Main species are:

I. *Abies pindrow* — *Acer caesium*
Betula alnoides — *Carpinus viminea*
Quercus dilatata — *Q. leucotricophora*
Q. semecarpifolia

II. *Euonymus pendulus* — *Eurya acuminata*
Fraxinus micrantha — *Litsea umbrosa*
Lyonia ovalifolia — *Pyrus lanata*
Rhamnus purprens — *Rhododendron arboreum*
Toona ciliata — *Taxus baccata*

III. *Berberis* sp. — *Daphne canabina*
Desmodium sp. — *Indigofera gerardiana*
Rosa macrophylla — *Sarcococca saligna*

IV. *Geranium wallichianum*

V. *Clematis montana* — *Hedera nepalens*

Bank Oak Forest: This forest is dominated by *Quercus leucotricophora (Q. incana)*. They are found between an elevation of 1700 mts and 2200 mts occupying the lower most zone of the western Himalayan temperate belt. Mean annual temperature ranges from 22°C to 24°C and total annual rainfall varies from 150 to 200 cms. These forests are found on sheltered slopes and moist shady depressions. Biotic pressure is very heavy and hence these forests are severely degraded.

Well developed in Kangra, Shimla, Rajgarh, Mussoorie and Nainital areas. The main constituents of this forest type are:

I. *Carpinus viminea* — *Lyonia ovalifolia*
Quercus leucotricophora — *Rhododendron arboreum*
Toona serrata

II. *Betula alnoides* — *Euonymus pendulus*
Ilex dipyrena — *Lindera pulcherrima*
Litsea umbrosa — *Myrica sapida*
Rhus semialata

III. *Berberis lycium* — *Boenning hausenia*
Desmodium hausenia — *Deutzia staminea*

	Indigofera gerardiana	*Lonicera* sp.
	Myrsine africana	*Viburnum* sp.
IV.	*Agrimonia* sp.	*Hedera* sp.
	Myriactis sp.	*Peridium aquilium*
	Smilax parvifolia	

Temperate Mixed Coniferous Forest: This forest has been referred to as western mixed coniferous forest by Champion and Seth. This is an attractive Himalayan forest having a mixture of temperate conifers viz., deodar, blue pine, fir and spruce. In many tracts, broad-leaved deciduous trees are also mixed with the conifers. Individual trees may attain a height of over 40 mts. Patches of open grassy meadows occur sporadically within this forest. There is a heavy biotic pressure, and regeneration is a problem.

The temperate mixed coniferous forest is found between an elevation of 2400 and 3000 mts or even higher. Snowfall accounts for a substantial part of the total annual precipitation. The first snowfall of the season may occur as early as in mid-November. Winter temperatures remain below the freezing point. Summers are mild and warm with the average maximum temperatures seldom exceeding 32°C.

This forest type is best developed in the Kashmir valley, Chamba, Kulu, Chopal, Kinnaur, Tons valley, Mandakini valley and Pithoragarh areas. The main species constituting the temperate mixed coniferous forest are:

I.	*Abies pindrow*	*Cedrus deodara*
	Picea smithiana	*Pinus wallichiana*
II.	*Acer acuminatum*	*A. caesium*
	A. pictum	*Betula alnoides*
	Euonymus lacerus	*Quercus dilatata*
	Q. leucotricophora	*Q. semecarpifolia*
	Taxus baccata	*Thamnocalamus spathiflorus*
III.	*Deutzia corymbosa*	*Ribes rubrum*
	Skimmia sp.	*Viburnum nervosum*
IV.	*Adinatum venustum*	*Aspidium aculeatum*
	Fragaria sp.	*Petridium* sp.
V.	*Clematis barbellata*	*Hedera nepalensis*
	Schizandra grandiflora	

Moist Deodar Forest: This is an almost pure forest of deodar with occasional conifers like blue pine, fir and spruce. The canopy is more or less closed with individual trees attaining a height of over 40 mts. The trees have long, clean boles and present a majestic appearance. The altitudinal range of this forest type is from 1700 mts to 2500 mts.

Generally low temperatures prevail throughout the deodar tract with temperatures falling below the freezing point in winter. Snow lies on the ground for several days. It aids in the establishment of natural regeneration. Total annual rainfall is over 150 cms.

The moist deodar forest is very well distributed in Kashmir valley, on the slopes of the Pir Panjal; in Chamba, Dalhousie, Kulu, Manali, Parvati valley, Shimla, Rohru, Chopal, Rajgarh, Tons valley, Kedarnath, Kausani and Pithoragarh tracts. The main constituents of the moist deodar forest are:

I.	*Abies pindrow*	*Cedrus deodara*
	Picea smithiana	*Pinus wallichiana*
II.	*Quercus dilatata*	*Q. leucotricophora*
	Rhododendron arboreum	
III.	*Berberis lycium*	*Deutzia staminea*
	Lonicera angustifolia	*Rosa macrophylla*
	Strobilanthes wallichiana	
IV. & V.	*Clematis montana*	*Hedera nepalensis*
	Jasminum officinale	*Lastraea* sp.
	Vitis himalayana	*C. semicordata*

Temperate Secondary Scrub: 1 These are low scrub forests consisting of small-sized evergreen trees and shrubs. 2 Shrubby growth occurs all round the year but is abundant during the monsoons. 3 Thorny species are more dominant on hot, dry exposed slopes.

The mean annual temperature varies from 20°C to 28°C. The summer is warm and dry. The annual precipitation is both in the form of rain and snow. Winters are very severe with sub-zero temperatures being common.

This is a secondary forest that is found on localities that are under a heavy biotic pressure. Its main constituents are:

Berberis lycium	*Cotoneaster bacillaris*
Carissa opaca	*Dodonea viscosa*
Indigofera gerardiana	*Olea cuspidata*
Pistacia sp.	*Prinsepia utilis*
Pyrus pashia	*Rosa macrophylla*
Spirarea canescens	

Temperate Moist Mixed Deciduous Forest: Champion and Seth have named this forest as the moist temperate deciduous forest. It is a mixed deciduous high forest with individual trees attaining a height of about 20 mts. This forest type is found on sites suited for the occurrence of moist temperate forests. The elevation at which this forest occurs ranges from 1800 mts to 2750 mts. It is common in moist shady depressions and along streams and rivers.

A substantial part of the precipitation is in the form of snow that may lie on the ground for several days at a stretch. Winter temperatures fall to levels below the freezing point. Summers are warm with the average maximum temperature being about 33°C. There is heavy biotic pressure on these forests.

These forests are well developed in the Kashmir valley, Bhadrawah, Chamba, Kelatop, Manali, Parvati, Shimla, Rajgarh, Yamuna valley, Mandakini valley and Pithoragarh areas. Its main constituents are:

I.	*Acer caesium*	*A. pictum*
	A. villosum	*Aesculus indica*
	Betula alnoides	*Carpinus* sp.
	Cettis australis	*Fraxinus micrantha*
	Juglans regia	*Prunus cornuta*
	Pyrus lanata	*Ulmus* sp.
II.	*Arundinaria* sp.	*Cornus* sp.
	Corylus colurna	*Euonymus tingens*
	Rhus sp.	*Taxus baccata*
III.	*Aconitum* sp.	*Impatiens* sp.
	Polygonatum sp.	*Spiraea aruncus*
	Spiraea vestita	
IV.	*Hedera nepalensis*	*Vitis lanata*
V.	*V. semicordata*	

Upper Temperate Forest

Kharsu Oak Forest: This forest occupies the highest elevation amongst the three Himalayan oaks. This is an almost pure forest dominated by kharsu oak (*Quercus semecarpifolia*). Altitudinal range is from 2500 mts to 3500 mts. The canopy is dense with individual trees attaining a height of about 20 mts or more. The upper storey may be shared by other conifers and broad-leaved species though their proportion as compared to kharsu oak is low.

These forests are under a heavy biotic pressure. Very heavy snowfall occurs in this tract. Sub-zero temperatures are common in winter. Hailstorms may occur in April and May. These are developed in the upper reaches of the western Himalaya. The main constituents of this forest are:

I.	*Acer caesium*	*Betula alnoides*
	Meliosoma sp.	*Pyrus lanata*
	Querus floribunda	*Q. semecarpifolia*
II.	*Arundinaria jaunsarensis*	*Betula utilis*
	Prunus padus	*Rhododendron arboreum*
	R. barbatum	*Sorbus foliolosa*
	Taxus baccata	
III.	*Cotaneaster* sp.	*Ribes glaciale*
	Rosa macrophylla	*Rosa sericea*
	Sarcococca saligna	*Skimmia laureola*
	Strobilanthes sp.	
IV.	*Fragaria vesca*	*Polygonum speciosum*
	Valeriana hardwickii	*Viola* sp.
V.	*Clematis montana*	*Vitis himalayana*

Oak-fir Forest: Champion and Seth have named them as the west Himalayan upper oak-fir forest. It occurs between an elevation of 2600 and 3400 mts. Conifers and broad-leaved species are intricately mixed together. Heavy snowfall is received in winters. The temperature falls below the freezing point. Summers are warm and dry. The soil is rich in humus, well-aerated and moderately deep. The main constituents of this forest are:

I.	*Abies pindrow*	*Cedrus deodara*
	Picea smiihiana	*Pinus wallichiana*
II.	*Acer* sp.	*Arundinaria* sp.
	Betula alnoides	*B. utilis*
	Corylus colurna	*Pyrus lanata*
	Quercus floribunda	*Q. semecarpifolia*
	Sorbus foliolosa	
III.	*Berberis* sp.	*Indigofera gerardiana*
	Rosa macrophylla	*Rosa sericea*
	Rubus niveus	*Smilax vaginata*
	Strobilanthes sp.	*Viburnum nervosum*
IV.	*Ainsliaea aptera*	*Fragaria vesca*
	Podophyllum hexandrum	*Spiraea*
V.	*Schizandra grandiflora*	*Vitis semicordata*

Cypress Forest

Champion, Seth and Negi (1989) have termed this forest type as the cypress forest . It is an open forest comprising of scattered trees occurring on steep rocky areas with individual trees attaining a height of about 20 mts. These forests occur between an elevation of

1800 and 2800 mts. The soil is shallow and prone to erosion. Heavy rainfall is received both during the monsoons and in late winter. These forests are well developed in the Kashmir valley, Chamba, Kulu, Shimla, Alaknanda valley and Almora areas. The main constituents of this forest type are:

I.	*Cedrus deodara*	*Cupressus torulosa*
II.	*Aesculus indica*	*Juglans regia*
	Pyrus pashia	
III.	*Abellia triflora*	*Berberis* sp.
	Cotoneaster bacillaris	*Prinsepia utilis*
	Rosa sp.	*Salix* sp.

Alder Forest

This forest type is an almost pure forest of alder occurring along stream and river banks upto an elevation of about 3000 mts. Champion, Seth and Negi (1989) have named this forest type as the alder forest. Well developed in Kashmir, Kulu, Parvati and Tons valleys. The main species constituting this forest type are:

I.	*Alnus nitida*	*Celtis* sp.
	Populus ciliata	*P. deltoides*
	Illmus villosa	
II.	*Crategus crenulata*	*Sarcococca* sp.
	Spirae sp.	
III.	*Berberis* sp.	*Plectranthus* sp.
	Prinsepia sp.	

Blue Pine Forest

This forest type is a more or less pure forest of blue pine *(Pinus wallichiana)* that occurs over an elevation of 2100 mts and upto 2500 mts. This type has been named as the riverine blue pine forest and the low level blue pine forest by Champion and Seth. Scattered individuals of other coniferous species are often mixed with blue pine. Moist, shady depressions may contain broad-leaved trees. The lower storey is suppressed and the forest floor is covered with a fairly thick layer of needles. Grass and herbaceous species come up during the summer and monsoon seasons.

The mercury drops to levels below the freezing point in winters. Summers are mild and warm. The average annual temperature in this tract ranges from 12°C to 20°C. Precipitation is received both from rain and snow. These forests experience rains during the monsoon season and in late winter.

The soils over which these forests occur vary from clayey loam to sandy loam. The soil is shallow. Very often, blue pine trees appear to be growing on almost bare rock with a negligible soil cover. Blue pine forests occur in the two main habitats—(1) moist temperate zone (over an elevation of 2100 mts), and (2) along rivers and streams (above an altitude of 2000 mts).

The forests occurring under these habitats have been classified Champion and Seth as a separate forest type viz., low level blue pine forests. These forests are well developed in the Doda, Chamba, Dalhousie, Karsog, Shimla, Chopal, Kinnaur, Rohru, Rajgarh, Yamuna valley, Pauri, Almora, Nainital and Pithoragarh areas. This forest type comprises of:

I. *Abies pindrow* — *Cedrus deodara*
Picea smithiana — *Pinus roxburghii*
Pinus wallichiana

II. *Aesculus indica* — *Juglans regia*
Quercus floribunda — *Q. leucotricophora*
Rhododendron arboreum

III. *Berberis* sp. — *Desmodium tiliaefolium*
Indigofera gerardiana — *Prinsepia utilis*
Rosa macrophylla — *Rubus nivenus*
Sarcococca saligna

IV. *Vitis* sp.

Dry Temperate Mixed Forest

This forest type is the dry-broad-leaved and coniferous forest This is how Champion and Seth have termed it. It is an open forest consisting of conifers and broad-leaved species occurring in the dry tracts of the higher-Himalaya. The area in which this forest occurs falls in the rain shadow of the main Himalayan range. Altitude range from 2000 to 2400 mts.

Rainfall is low and bulk of the precipitation is in the form of snow. Winters are very severe. These forests are well developed in Ladakh, Lahaul, Spiti, Kinnaur and Pithoragarh areas. Its main constituents are:

I. *Acer pentaponicium* — *Cedrus deodara*
Celtis australis — *Pinus gerardiana*
Quercus ilex

II. *Fraxinus* sp. — *Olea cuspidata*
Parrotia sp. — *Rhus succedanea*
Zanthoxylum alatum

III. *Abelia triflora* *Artemisia maritime*
Artemisia vulgaris *Berberis* sp.
Daphne oleoides *Lonicera angustifolia*
Rosa webbiana *Roylea calycina*
Sophora mollis

IV. *Agropyron* sp. *Agrostis alba*
Eragrostis nigra *Perotis indica*
Setaria viridis

Dry Temperate Coniferous Forest

According to Champion and Seth this forest type is the dry temperate coniferous forest.

Neoza Pine Forest: This is an almost pure forest of neoza pine (Pinus gerardiana) found in the dry zone of the higher and trans-Himalaya. The locality factors are not suited for tree growth. Rainfall is very low and winters are severe. The cold winds lash the area almost all through the year. The soil is shallow and prone to be blown away.

In Ladakh, Lahaul, Spiti, Kinnaur, Badrinath and Pithoragarh areas these forests are well developed. The forest type is comprised of the following species:

I. *Cedrus deodara* *Pinus gerardiana*

II. *Fraxinus xanthoxyloides*

III. *Artemisia maritima* *Daphne oleoides*
Ephedera gerardiana *Prunus* sp.

Dry Deodar Forest: This is a more or less pure forest of deodar found in the dry zone of the higher Himalaya. Occasional conifers also occur in between the pure patches of deodar. Rainfall is very low with bulk of the precipitation being received in the form of snow. Broad-leaved trees are confined to moist shady depressions.

Found well distributed in the dry zones of Ladakh, Lahaul, Spiti, Kinnaur, Badrinath and Pithoragarh between 2000 and 3200 mts. The main species are:

I. *Cedrus deodara* *Pinus gerardiana*

II. *Corylus colurna*

III. *Desmodium* sp. *Rubus niveus*

IV. *Abelia triflora* *Artemisia maritima*
Ribes grossularia *Rosa webbiana*
Lonicera hypoleuca *Microglossa* sp.

High Level Dry Blue Pine Forest

As per Champion and Seth, this forest type is the high level dry blue pine forest. The elevation at which this forest type is found varies from 3000 to 3600 mts. It is an almost pure forest of scattered blue pine trees found in the dry zone of the higher and trans-Himalaya of Ladakh, Lahaul, Spiti, Kinnaur, Badrinath and Pithoragarh. The main constituents of this forest type are:

I.	*Abies spectabilis*	*Pinus gerardiana*
	Pinus wallichiana	
II.	*Betuta utilis*	*Rhododendron* sp.
III.	*Caragana* sp.	*Ephedera* sp.
	Juniperus communis	*J. macropoda*
	J. wallichiana	*Rhododendron anthopogon*
	Salix sp.	

Dry Juniper Scrub

This forest type Champion and Seth have termed it as the west Himalayan dry juniper forest. It is an open, evergreen forest consisting of dwarfed and stunted individuals. Found in the dry zone of the higher and trans-Himalaya, between an elevation of 2700 and 4300 mts. Main species are:

I.	*Juniperus macropoda*	
II.	*Fraxinus* sp.	*Ribes grossularia*
	Rosa sericea	*Rosa webbiana*

Sub-alpine High Level Fir Forest

This forest is well developed in the Kashmir valley, Bhadrawah, Kulu, Tons valley, Gangotri, north Almora and Pithoragarh areas. It is found between an elevation of 2900 and 3000 mts in the higher Himalayan ranges.

Bulk of the precipitation is received in the form of snow that may lie on the ground for several days at a stretch. The average summer temperature ranges from 20°C to 22°C and during winters, the mercury drops to well below the freezing point. The main constituents of this forest type are:

I	*Abies spectabilis*	*Picea smithiana*
	Pinus wallichiana	
II.	*Primus padus*	*Taxus baccata*
III.	*Berberis* sp.	*Deutzia corymbosa*
	Juniperus wallichiana	*Rhododendron campanulatum*

	R. lepidotum	*Smilax vaginata Viburnum foetus*
	Strobilanthes sp.	
IV.	*Anemone obtusiloba*	*Osmunda claytoniana*
	Viola partinii	
V	*Clematis montana*	

Sub-apline Birch-Fir Forest

Trees are stunted in this with a low spreading crown. These forests are well developed in the upper reaches of the higher Himalayan ranges mostly above an elevation of 3000mts. Main species are:

I.	*Abies spectabilis*	
II.	*Betula utilis*	*Quercus semecarpifolia*
	Rhododendron campanulatum	*Sorbus foliolosa*
III.	*Cotoneaster acuminata*	*Lonicera* sp.
	Ribes glaciale	*Ribes rubrum*
	Rubus niveus	*Smilax vaginata*
IV.	*Anemone* sp.	*Geranium emodi*
	Lastrea barbata	

Birch-Rhododendron Scrub Forest

Birch-Rhododendron Scrub Forest is a low evergreen forest with stunted trees that may be slightly curved due to the pressure of snow that remains on the ground for a considerable time in winter. Champion and Seth have named them so the winter temperatures fall to much below the freezing point. A major part of the precipitation is received in the form of snow.

These forests are well developed in the upper reaches of die lower and main Himalayan ranges above an elevation of 3000 mts. It is comprised of the following species:

I.	*Betula utilis*	*Rhododendron* sp.
	Sorbus foliolosa	
II. & III.	*Berberis* sp.	*Lonicera parviflora*
	Polygonum sp.	*Rhododendron lepidotum*
	Viburnum nervosum	
IV.	*Coryalis stracheyii*	*Macrotomia benthami*
	Primula denticulata	*P. stuartii*

Deciduous Alpine Scrub

This is a very well developed forest. It is low, open, deciduous scrub forest with individual shrubs rarely attaining a height of over

1.5 mts. It is found all over the higher Himalaya above an elevation of 3350 mts. Summers are wild and warm. Winters are very cold and snow covers the ground for periods upto 5 months. The main species occurring in this scrub are:

I. & II.	*Betula utilis*	*Rhododendron* sp.
III.	*Berberis* sp.	*Lonicera* sp.
	Salix sp.	*Rosa* sp.
	Syringa emodi	
IV.	*Aconitum* sp.	*Trollis* sp.

Dwarf Rhododendron Scrub

All over Himalayas arctic condition are experienced during winter This scrub is occurring near the snowline all over the higher Himalaya. It is dominated by dwarf rhododendrons. The dwarf rhododendron scrub succeeds the sub-alpine forests towards lower elevation and it merges with the line of perpetual snow as one proceeds higher up. The soil is rich in humus. This scrub vegetation is well developed all along the snowline in the higher Himalayan ranges.

Main species are:

Lonicera obovata	*Rhododendron anthopogon*
R. campanulatum	*Sorbus foliolosa*

Dry Alpine Scrub

Schweinfurth has named this as the alpine steppe. It may further be subdivided into two sub-types.

Dry Scrub: This scrub vegetation occurs in the dry zones of the higher and trans-Himalaya which lie in the rain shadow area of the main Himalayan range. Rainfall is very low and snow accounts for bulk of the precipitation. It begins to snow in early October and the last snowfall of the season may occur as late as in May. Thus, a very short growing season is available. Soil is poor in humus and usually of shallow to moderate depth. Cold winds lash this tract almost all through the year.

This scrub thrives in shady depressions and along streams formed by snow-melt waters. The main species forming a part of this scrub are:

Arenaria sp.	*Artemisia maritima*
Artemisia sacorurm	*Caragana* sp.
Draba gracillima	*Eurotia ceratoides*
Juniperus communis	*J. wallichiana*

Kobressia duthei	*Myricaria* sp.
Potentialla fruticosa	*Primula* sp.
Saxifera imbricata	*Sedum crassipes*
Sedum crenulatum	

Dwarf Juniper Scrub: This is another scrub found in the dry zone of the trans-Himalaya. Rainfall is very low and extreme conditions of cold are experienced. Snow covers the mountain slopes for 5 or 6 months in a year. It is dominated by *Juniperus.*

Nepal

Forests in represent the transition zone between the forest types of the western and eastern Himalaya. These are endowed with forests that are rich, both in variety and extent. On the one hand, the eastern extension of a number of typical western Himalayan species is limited to Nepal, e.g., *Cedrus deodara* and on the other hand, many eastern Himalayan species are also found in Nepal. The major forest types of the Nepal Himalaya have been discussed in the following text. Due to paucity of space only a passing reference has been made to a number of forest types but this does not undermine either their significance or extent.

Sal Forest

(a) *Hill sal forest*—These forests are found on the Siwalik hills and on the southern slopes of the lower Himalaya upto an elevation of 1000 mts. Main species are:

I.	*Anogeissus latifolia*	*Bauhinia varigata*
	Semecarpus anacardium	*Shorea robusta*
II.	*Aporosa dioica*	*Kydia calycina*
	Mallotus sp.	*Symplocos racemosa*
III.	*Barleria cristata*	*Indigofera pulchella*
IV.	*Bauhinia vahlii*	*Spatholobus* sp.

(b) *Bhabar-terai sal forest*—This sal forest is found in the bhabar and terai tract along the Ganga plain. The forest is light and open. It is a more or less pure patch of sal. Rainfall in this tract is very heavy and bulk of the total annual precipitation is received from the SW monsoons. Summers are very hot and the mercury may soar to over 40°C. Its main constituents are:

I.	*Adina cordifolia*	*Amoora decandra*
	Anogeissus latifolia	*Dillenia pentagyna*
	Eugenia oojenensis	*Schleichera trijuga*

Shorea robusta — *Sterculia urens*
Terminalia bellerica — *T. chebula*
II. *Aporosa dioica* — *Careya arborea*
Croton oblongifolius — *Ehertia laevis*
Kydia calycina — *Litsea salicifolia*
III. *Antidesma diandrum* — *Ardisia humilis*
IV. *Bauhinia vahlii*

A. Tropical Evergreen Forest

These forests occur up to an elevation of about 1000 mts in the lower Himalaya. These are just narrow strips along water courses. Its main constituents are:

I. *Actinodaphne angustifolia* — *Castanopsis indica*
Cedrela toora — *Mangifera indica*
II. *Bischofia viscosa* — *Olea glandulifera*
III. *Morinda angustifolia* — *Murraya koengiikoengii*

B. Tropical Deciduous Riverine Forest

These forest remain devoid of leaves for about three months at a stretch. These are found along river and streams of the bhabar and dun tracts. These forests are similar to the khair and sisham forests of the western Himalaya. Summers are very hot while winter temperatures may drop down to 2°C. Most of the precipitation is received from the SW monsoons. Soil is sandy, gravelly, porous and poor in organic matter content. These forests are under heavy biotic pressure. Its main constituents are:

I. *Acacia catechu* — *Acacia lucida*
Adina cordifolia — *Albizzia procera*
Bombax ceiba — *Lannea grandis*
Sterculia urens — *Trewia nudiflora*
II. *Aporosa* sp. — *Bridelia retusa*
Cassia fistula — *Mallotus phillippensis*
III. *Acacia caesia* — *Adhatoda vasica*
Colebrookia oppositifolia — *Zizyphus jujuba*
IV. *Acacia concinna* — *Tinospora cordifolia*Sub-tropical Evergreen Forest

These forests are under intense biotic pressure. These are well developed between an elevation of 1000 and 1200 mts in the high rainfall zone of the lower Himalaya. The main constituents are:

I. *Acer oblongom* — *Albizzia procera*
Alnus nepalensis — *Cedrela toona*

II.	*Amoora decandra*	*Eurya acuminata*
	Schima wallichii	*Symplocos* sp.

Sub-tropical Lower Himalayan Forest

This forest is relatively well developed in Nepal. This is usually found on the lower Himalayan slopes up to an elevation of about 1500 mts. The main constituents are:

I.	*Acacia catechu*	*Adina cordifolia*
	Aegle marmelos	*Dalbergia sissoo*
	Flacourtia indica	*Kydia calycina*
	Lagerstroemia parviflora	*Lannea grandis*
	Sterculia urens	*Wendlandia* sp.
II.	*Hamiltonia* sp.	*Rhus parviflora*
III.	*Acacia megalandena*	*Mimosa rubicaulis*

Terminalia Forest

This forest type occurs in the transition zone of the tropical and sub-tropical forests of the lower Himalaya. The main species are:

Adina cordifolia	*Anogeissus* sp.
Cedrela toona	*Ehretia laevis*
Eugenia jambolana	*Lagerstroemia parviflora*
Terminalia bellerica	*T. tomentosa*

Khair-sissoo Forest

The khair-sissoo forest occurs along river courses and freshly laid alluvium in the bhabar, dun and lower Himalayan tracts. Its main constituents are:

Acacia catechu	*Colebrookea oppositifolia*
Dalbergia sissoo	*Zizyphus jujuba*

Schima-Castanopsis Forest

This is a degenerated forest occurring between an elevation of 1000 and 2000 mts. Its main constituents are:

Alnus nepalensis	*Bombax ceiba*
Carpinus viminea	*Castanopsis hystrix*
Castanopsis indica	*Castanopsis tribuloides*
Dodonea vulgaris	*Eurya acuminata*
Juglans regia	*Litsea oblonga*
Lyonia ovalifolia	*Myrica nagi*
Pyrus pashia	*Quercus glauca*

Schima wallichii
Terminalia sp.
Viburnum sp.

Sub-tropical Semi-evergreen Lower Himalayan Forest

This forest type is largely confined to the lower Himalayan slopes. It is found between an elevation of 1000 and 1600 mts. The main constituents are:

Albizzia procera
Ardisia floribunda
Cronus macrophylla
Ehretia wallichiana
Mallotus nepalensis
Mangifera indica
Phoebe lanceolata
Randia tettrasperma
Sarauja nepalensis
Tremna orientalis

Chir Pine Forest

Chir pine forests are very well developed in western Nepal. Broad-leaved forests may also occur in the moist shady depressions in between the chir pine forests. These are more or less pure forests of chir pine occurring between an elevation of 1000 and 2000 mts. Ground flora is virtually absent. The main species occurring in this forest are:

I. *Pinus roxburghii*

II. *Cedrela toona*
Engelhardtia spicata
Indigofera sp.
Quercus leucotricophora
Rhododendron arboreum
Terminalia bellerica
Woodfordia fruticosa

Oak Forest

Oak forests are very well developed in Nepal. These are of four types.

Ban Oak Forest: This forest is dominated by *Quercus incana* (Syn. *Q. leucotri-cophora*) and *Q. lauginosa.* They occur between an elevation of 1800 and 2800 mts. The canopy is closed and oak may occur as pure patches or in mixed associations. In the eastern parts of the country, *Quercus lauginosa* is more prominent. The soil is fairly deep and rich in humus. These forests are under an intense biotic pressure. The main species are:

I. *Quercus incana* (Syn. *Q. leucotricophora*)
Q. lauginosa

II. *Carpinus viminea*
Cornus capitata
Lyonia ovalifolia
Rhododendron arboreum

III.	*Berberis* sp.	*Cocculus* sp.
	Inula cappa	*Myrsine africana*
	Rubus sp.	*Sarcococca saligna*
IV.	*Clematis montana*	*Vitis himalayana*

Moru Oak Forest: These forests grow well under moist conditions where the soil is damp. This forest is dominated by moru oak (*Quercus dilatata*). It occurs between an elevation of 2800 and 3200 mts. It is comprised of:

I.	*Acer acuminatum*	*Alnus nepalensis*
	Quercus dilatata	*Q. leucotricophora*
	A. semecarpifolia	*Tsuga dumosa*
II.	*Lyonia ovalifolia*	*Rhododendron arboreum*
	Sorbus cuspidata	*Taxus baccata*
III.	*Daphne canabina*	*Lonicera webbiana*
	Rosa macrophylla	*Sarcococca saligna*
IV.	*Hedera nepalensis*	*Vitis* sp.

Kharsu Oak Forest: This forest occurs above an elevation of over 3200 mts and may extend directly upto the snowline. This is dominated by kharsu oak *(Quercus semecarpifolia)*. Occasional growth of bamboos comes up beneath the oaks. Kharsu oak may occur as pure patches or in mixed associations. Towards higher elevations, these forests are replaced by alpine/sub-alpine vegetation. Main species are:

I.	*Quercus dilatata*	*Quercus semecarpifolia*
II.	*Acer pectinatum*	*Dodecadenia* sp.
	Ilex dipyrena	*Prunus cornuta*
	Rhododendron arboreum	*Sorbus cuspidata*
III.	*Cotoneaster microphylla*	*Jasminum humile*
	Rosa sericea	*Viburnum grandiflorum*
IV.	*Clematis montana*	*Hedera nepalensis*

Buk Oak Forest: This forest occurs between elevation of 2500 and 3000 mts. This is restricted in occurrence to eastern Nepal, particularly in the upper catchments of the rivers Tamur and Arun. It is dominated by buk oak *(Quercus lamellosa)*. Main species are:

I.	*Quercus lamellosa*	*Q. semecarpifolia*
II.	*Acer* sp.	*Castanopsis* sp.
	Illex dipyrena	*Lyonia ovalifolia*
	Prunus nepalensis	*Quercus lineata*
III.	*Arundinaria* sp.	*Sikimmia arborescens*

Castanopsis Forest

Almost pure patches of this forest are found in the higher zone of eastern Nepal. It occurs between an elevation of 2000 and 2500 mts. The canopy is fairly closed. There is a dense undergrowth and the forest is more temperate than subtropical. Its main constituents are:

I.	*Castanopsis hystrix*	*C. tribuloides*
	Quercus lamellosa	*Q. leucotricophora*
II.	*Eurya acuminata*	*Ilex insignis*
	Litsea elongata	*Michelia* sp.
III.	*Berberis* sp.	*Cornus oblonga*
	Daphne canabina	*Viburnum coriaceum*
IV.	*Hedera nepalensis*	*Lonicera glabrata*

Moist Temperate Deciduous Forest

Chestnut, walnut and *Acer* dominate this forest. This type is found in the higher Himalaya of Nepal between an elevatiòn of 2000 and 3000 mts. A typical temperate climate prevails in this tract. Summers are mild and winters very cold. The mercury drops to below the freezing point. These forests are subject to heavy grazing which has led to the disappearance of the undergrowth. Snowfall occurs regularly in winter. The main species occurring in this forest are:

I.	*Acer caesium*	*Aesculus indica*
	Alnus nepalensis	*Betula alnoides*
	Juglans regia	*Picea smithiana*
	Pinus excelsa	*Quercus dilatata*
	Q. leucotricophora	*Q. semecarpifolia*
II.	*Ilex dipyrena*	*Morus serrata*
	Populus ciliata	*Prunus cornuta*
	Pyrus pashia	*Salix* sp.
III.	*Rosa* sp.	*Syringa emodi*
IV.	*Hedera nepalensis*	

Lower Wet Mixed Broad-leaved Forest

This forest occurs in moist areas between an elevation of 1800 and 3200 mts, usually on northern and western aspects. Its main constituents are:

I.	*Acer oblongum*	*A. thomsoni*
	Alnus nepalensis	*Betula alnoides*
	Castanopsis tribuloides	*Ehretia macrophylla*
	Liihocarpus spicata	*Quercus glauca*

II.	*Mallotus nepalensis*	*Prunus* sp.
	Rhododendron sp.	*Zizyphus recurva*
III.	*Cronus oblonga*	*Viburnum* sp.
IV.	*Hoya* sp.	*Jasminum* sp.

Upper Wet Mixed Broad-leaved Forest

In this forest, undergrowth is fairly dense. This is found between an elevation of 2800 and 3800 mts usually on north and west-facing slopes.The main species are:

I.	*Acer campbellii*	*Acer pectinatum*
	Alnus nepalensis	*Dodecadenia grandiflora*
	Ilex dipyrena	*Litsea sericea*
	Quercus lamellosa	*Q. semecarpifolia*
II.	*Cotoneaster acuminata*	*Piptanthus nepalensis*
	Ribes glaciale	*Viburnum* sp.
III.	*Clematis connata*	*Lonicera acuminata*

Rhododendron Forest

Rhododendron forests are occur at an elevation of over 2000 mts. The main species of *rhododendron* found in Nepal are:

R. anthopogon	*R. arboreum*
R. barbatum	*R. ciliatum*
R. dalhousiae	*R. fulgens*
R. hodgsonii	*R. lepidotum*
R. nivale	*R. pendulum*
R. setosum	*R. triflorum*
R. vaccinioides	*R. wallichii*

Betula-Abies spectabilis Forest

This forest may extend up to the line of perpetual snow. This found at elevations of over 3000 mts. The upper storey is almost entirely composed of birch. At lower elevations, this forest is associated with Kharsu oak. The undergrowth is shrubby. In the inner dry valleys, this forest gives way to an association of *Pinus excelsa, Betula utilis* and *Juniperus wallichiana.* Main species are:

I.	*Abies spectabilis*	*Betula utilis*
	Pinus excelsa	*Tsuga dumosa*
II.	*Abelia triflora*	*Acer caudatum*
	Berberis sp.	*Cotoneaster acuminata*
	Cotoneaster microphylla	*Juniperus recurva*

	J. wallichiana	*Lonicera spinosa*
	Lyonia villiosa	*Potentialla fruticosa*
	Rhododendron sp.	*Ribes glaciale*
	Syringa emodi	
III.	*Clematis montana*	

Tsuga Dumosa Forest

Pure stands of this forest occur on exposed ridges and drier localities whereas mixed broad-leaved associations are found in moist shady depressions. This forest occurs between an elevation of 2000 and 3500 mts. Its main constituents are:

I.	*Abies spectabilis*	*Betula utilis*
	Quercus semecarpifolia	*Tsuga dumosa*
II.	*Acer acuminatum*	*Ilex dipyrena*
	Prunus cornuta	*Rhododendron* sp.
	Sorbus cuspidata	
III.	*Cornus macrophylla*	*Daphne* sp.
	Jasminum humile	*Lonicera webbiana*
	Rosa macrophylla	*R. sericea*

Blue Pine Forest

Blue pine forests usually occur above an elevation of 2300 mts. Broad-leaved trees occur in shady depressions. They are well distributed all over Nepal. It colonizes abandoned fields, stream banks and gravel beds. Its main constituents are:

I.	*Abies pindrow*	*A. spectabilis*
	Betula utilis	*Cedrus deodara*
	Picea smithiana	*Pinus wallichiana*
II.	*Acer caesium*	*Aesculus indica*
	Alnus nepalensis	*Juglans regia*
	Quercus sp.	*Rhododendron* sp.
III.	*Cotoneaster macrophylla*	*Lyonia villosa*
	Rhus cotinus	*Ribes glaciale*

Spruce Forest

The spruce forests of Nepal occur between an elevation of 2500 and 3500 mts. are well-distributed in tracts that are to a large extent sheltered from the full force of the monsoons. TheseVery often spruce is mixed with other conifers though it dominates on north-facing slopes. Its main constituents are:

I. *Abies pindrow* *Cedrus deodara*
Picea smithiana *Pinus wallichiana*
II. *Acer caesium* *Betula utilis*
Juglans regia *Populus ciliata*
Prunus cornuta *Quercus lamellosa*
Q. semecarpifolia *Sorbus cuspidata*
III. *Cotoneaster acuminata* *Syringa emodi*

Fir Forest

Fir tends to colonize moist, shady depressions. The fir forests are found between an elevation of 2500 and 3200 mts. Very often, fir is intermixed with spruce and other conifers. The main species are:

I. *Abies pindrow* *Picea smithiana*
Pinus wallichiana
II. *Aesculus indica* *Betula utilis*
Juglans regia *Populus* sp.
III. *Indigofera* sp. *Lyonia ovalifolia*
IV. *Hedera nepalensis* *Vitis* sp.

Deodar Forest

This forest is dominated by deodar. It occurs between an elevation of 2000 and 3000 mts. Main species are:

I. *Cedrus deodara* *Picea smithiana*
Pinus wallichiana
II. *Cotoneaster macrophylla* *Rosa sericea*
III. *Clematis montana*

Cupressus Forest

The top canopy of this forest is fairly dense. This is found on limestone and/or dolomite topography between an elevation of 2300 and 3300 mts. These forests are very well developed in the valley of the river Suligad, a tributary of the river Bheri. The main species are:

I. *Cupressus torulosa*
II. *Abelia triflora* *Colquhounia coccinea*
Indigofera sp. *Rosa macrophylla*
Syringa emodi
III. *Clematis montana*

Juniperus Forest

These forests can be found at higher elevations all over Nepal. They develop usually over an elevation of 3000 mts. Individual trees are of a low height. This forest extends right upto the snowline. The main species are:

I. *Abies pindrow* — *Betula utilis*
Juniperus recurva — *J. wallichiana*
Quercus sp.

II. *Cotoneaster acuminata* — *C. microphylla*
Lonicera sp. — *Prunus cornuta*
Rhododendron sp. — *Rosa sericea*

III. *Myricaria* sp.

IV. *Clematis montana*

Alnus Forest

This forest is very well developed on moist, shady sites. This is occurring in the sub-alpine zone, usually above an elevation of 2700 mts and extending right upto the snowline. *Alnus* forests occur in pure form or in between temperate broad-leaved forests. The main species are:

Aesculus indica — *Alnus nepalensis*
Alnus nitida — *Betula alnoides*
Hippophae sp. — *Populus ciliata*
Principea utilis — *Quercus dilatata*
Q. semecarpifolia — *Rosa macrophylla*
Xanthoxylum sp.

Populus Forest

This forest occurs above an elevation of about 2700 mts and may extend upto the snowline. This is dominated by *Populus ciliata.* The *Populus* forest is found along streams and rivers. The main species are:

I. *Populus ciliata*

II. *Abelia triflora* — *Indigofera* sp.
Myricaria sp. — *Rosa macrophylla*
R. sericea — *Spirea sorbiflora*

III. *Clematis grata* — *Cynanchum* sp.
Jasminum sp.

Moist Alpine Scrub

These are heavily grazed scrubs. This scrub occurs in all moister parts of Nepal between the timber line and the line of permanent snow. It is best developed in the moist shady depressions above the tree or timber line. The winter is severe in this tract and a very short growing period is available. The plants attain best growth in July and August. Bulk of the precipitation is in the form of snow. Main species are:

Berberis sp.	*Juniperus recurva*
J. wallichiana	*Potentialla fruticosa*
Rhododendron anthopogon	*R. campanulatum*
R. fulgens	*R. lepidotum*
R. setosum	*R. wallichii*
Salix calyculata	*S. sikkimensis*

Hippophae Scrub

Hippophae tends to form pure thickets of about a meter in height. This is a sub-alpine scrub forest occurring above an elevation of over 3,000 mts and usually extending up to the snowline. The main species forming part of this scrub forest are:

I.	*Alnus nepalensis*	*Hippophae rhamnoides*
	H. salicifolia	*H. thibetana*
	Populus ciliata	
II.	*Berberis* sp.	*Ficus* sp.
	Indigofera sp.	*Lonicera myrtillus*
III.	*Clematis grata*	*Ribes glaciale*

Dry Alpine Scrub

This scrub forest is found at higher elevations in the drier valleys of northern Nepal. A short growing season is available and the plants develop dense roots. It is well developed in the following tracts—(a) alpine steppes, and (b) inner valleys of Langtang area. The main species are:

Artemisia sp.	*Berberis* sp.
Cargana sp.	*Clematis phlebantha*
Cotoneaster sp.	*Ephedera gerardiana*
Hippophae thibetana	*Juniperus recurva*
J. squamata	*J. wallichiana*
Lonicera sp.	*Myricaria wardii*
Plectranthus pharicus	*Potentialla fruticosa*
Primula sp.	*Rhododendron anthopogon*
R. lepidotum	*R. nivale*
Rosa sericea	*Sophora* sp.
Spiraea arcuta	*Syringa emodi*

Eastern Himalaya

The eastern Himalayan forests include the forests of Bhutan, Darjeeling hills, Sikkim and Arunachal Pradesh. Rainfall is very heavy and well distributed all through the year. They are rich both in flora and fauna. The major forest types found in the eastern Himalaya have been discussed in the following text.

Bhabar Sal Forest

These are extensive sal forests found in the bhabar tract of the eastern Himalaya. They are well-developed in the area to the north of Siliguri in the Darjeeling hills. These may further be subdivided into the following.

Lower Bhabar Sal Forest: This forest occurs in the lower bhabar tract of the eastern Himalaya, adjoining the Brahmaputra plains. It is dominated by Sal. The soil is alluvial, well drained and contains a large proportion of boulders. These forests are under an intense biotic pressure. Rainfall is very heavy. Bulk of it is received from the monsoons. The main species forming a part of this forest are:

I. *Albizzia odoratissima* — *Cassia fistula*
Dillenia sp. — *Lagerstroemia parviflora*
Salmalia malabarica — *Shorea robusta*
Terminalia bellerica

II. *Bridelia retusa* — *Careya arborea*
Emblica officinalis — *Glochidon acuminatum*
Garuga pinnata — *Grewia vestita*
Mallotus phillippensis — *Oroxylum indicum*
Premna integrifolia — *Wrightia tomentosa*

III. *Clerodendron viscosum* — *Coffea bengalensis*

IV. *Microstegium ciliatum* — *Saccharum* sp.

V. *Dalbergia stipulacea* — *Vitis sp.*

Upper Bhabar Sal Forest: This is a good quality sal forest. It is found in the upper bhabar tract of the eastern Himalaya. The soil consists of alluvium laid down by the rivers and streams draining the Himalayan foothills. The main constituents of this forest are:

I. *Amoora wallichii* — *Anthocephalus* sp.
Cedrela microcarpa — *Duabanga grandiflora*
Elaeocarpus aristatus — *Engelhardtia spicata*
Gmelina arborea — *Lagerstroemia parviflora*
Litsea monopetala — *Salmalia malabarica*
Shorea robusta

	Terminalia bellerica	*Terminalia tomentosa*
	Tetrameles nudiflora	*Turpinia pomifera*
II.	*Alangium chinense*	*Aporosa roxburghii*
	Artocarpus lakoocha	*Bauhinia purpurea*
	Callicarpa arborea	*Careya* sp.
	Emblica officinalis	*Garuga pinnata*
	Ilex godejam	*Mallotus roxburghiana*
	Oroxylon indicum	*Premna integrifolia*
	Syzygium cumini	*Vitex* sp.
III.	*Clerodendron viscosum*	*Coffea bengalensis*
	Leea crispa	*Morinda tinctoria*

Himalayan Sal Forest

These forests occur in the lower Himalayan foothills upto an elevation of about 1000 mts. These are dominated by Sal. Summers are fairly warm and the temperature may soar to about 40°C. The monsoon rains bring relief in mid-May. Winters are wet and cold. The soil is rich in organic matter. Main species are:

I.	*Cedrela microcarpa*	*Pinus roxburghii*
	Schima wallichii	*Shorea robusta*
	Terminalia sp.	
II.	*Aporosa roxburghii*	*Castanopsis indica*
	Phoebe lanceolata	

Terai Sal Forest

This forest is well developed in the terai tract of the eastern Himalaya. It occurs on dark alluvial soils, usually under damp conditions. Canes and ferns are abundant. Main species are:

I.	*Albizia procera*	*Amoora wallichii*
	Bridelia procera	*Cedrela toona*
	Dillenia pentagyna	*Eugenia* sp.
	Ilex godejam	*Lannea coromandelica*
	Schima wallichii	*Shorea robusta*
	Terminalia bellerica	
II.	*Bauhinia purpurea*	*Meliosma simplicifolia*
	Saurauja roxburghii	*Turpinia pomifera*
III.	*Leea indica*	*Morinda angustifolia*

Mesua Forest

This forest is dominated by *Mesua.* It is well developed in the lower hills of Darjeeling and Arunachal Pradesh. The soil is fairly deep, well drained and rich in humus. Bulk of the precipitation is received from the monsoons. The main species found in this forest are:

I.	*Ailanthus grandis*	*Altingia excelsa*
	Dysoxylum hamiltoni	*Echinocarpus* sp.
	Kayea assamica	*Mesua* sp.
	Quercus lamellosa	*Tetrameles* sp.
II.	*Beilschmiedia* sp.	*Gynocardia* sp.
	Sapium baccatum	*Vatica* sp.
III.	*Dendrocalamus hamiltonii*	
IV.	*Leea* sp. *Pandanus furcatus*	*Miliusa* sp.
V	*Strobilanthes* sp.	*Zingiber* sp.

Kayea Forest

Rainfall is very heavy and the mean annual temperature ranges from 18°C to 22°C. These forests are well developed over freshly laid down alluvium. This is a forest dominated by *Kayea*, found in the lower foothills of eastern Himalaya. The main species are:

Amoora wallichii	*Canarium* sp.
Echinocarpus sp.	*Kayea assamica*
Mesua sp.	*Michelia doltsopa*
Terminalia chebula	

Semi-Evergreen Forests

These forests have further been subdivided into the following:

Alluvial Plain Semi-evergreen Forest: These forests are found along the boundary of the eastern Himalaya and the Brahmaputra plains. Very well developed in high rainfall tracts of southern Bhutan, Darjeeling and Arunachal Pradesh. The canopy is closed and comprises of semi-evergreen trees intermixed with broad-leaved species. The undergrowth is dense. Very heavy rainfall is experienced. Bulk of the precipitation is received from the SW monsoons. The soils are alluvial, deep and rich in organic matter. The average maximum temperature ranges from 35°C to 38°C. In winter, the mercury may drop down to about 2°C. The main species are:

I.	*Castanopsis indica*	*C. tribuloides*
	Dysoxylum sp.	*Eugenia formosa*
	Litsea sp.	*Phoebe attenuata*
	Terminalia myriocarpa	
II.	*Amoora wallichii*	*Gynocardia odorata*
	Turpina pomifera	

Sub-montane Semi-evergreen Forest: This forest is found in the foothill tract of the lower Himalaya, usually between the dominant deciduous and evergreen forests. The canopy is closed, with evergreen species predominant in the upper storey. Rainfall may be upto 500 cms. The main species are:

I.	*Bauhinia purpurea*	*Castanopsis indica*
	Duabanga grandiflora	*Eugenia formosa*
	Gmelina arborea	*Michelia champaca*
	Schima wallichii	*Tetrameles nudiflora*
II.	*Garcinia stipulata*	*Gynocardia odorata*
	Meliosma simplicifolia	
III.	*Dendrocalamus hamiltonii*	

Secondary Semi-evergreen Forest: This is a secondary high forest consisting of mixed species similar to the climax type with a relatively more proportion of deciduous species. It is found in the lower hills of Arunachal Pradesh and Bhutan. The soil is loamy, well drained and fairly deep. Rainfall may be upto 300 cms. The main species are:

I.	*Anthocephalus chinensis*	*Artocarpus chaplasha*
	Castanopsis indica	*C. hystrix*
	Dipterocarpus pilosus	*Salmalia malabarica*
	Stereospermum personatum	*Tetrameles nudiflora*
	Terminalia myriocarpa	
II.	*Amoora wallichii*	*Macaranga* sp.
	Mesua ferra	*Premna latifolia*
	Vatica sp.	
III.	*Laportea* sp.	
IV.	*Combretum decandrum*	*Acacia prensans*

Swamp Forest

This is a swamp forest found along rivers and streams in the foothills of the eastern Himalaya. The site remains practically flooded for a major part of the year. Rainfall is very heavy and swampy vegetation has developed due to this. Some of the main species found in this forest are:

I.	*Bischofia javanica*	*Eugenia* sp.
	Ficus glomerata	*Mallotus albus*
	Ptereospermum sp.	*Syzygium cumini*
	Toona ciliata	*Trewia nudiflora*
II.	*Diospyros paraginia*	*Salix tetrasperma*
III.	*Acromychia pedunculata*	*Desmodium* sp.

IV. *Calamus tenuis*

Lower Mixed Deciduous Forest: These are mixed deciduous forests occurring on well-drained soils in the lower hills of the eastern Himalaya. These forests are heavily lopped for fuelwood and fodder. The mean annual rainfall may be upto 500 cms. The topography consists of moderate to steep sloping hills and deep river valleys. This has led to the degradation of the forest cover in the vicinity of human settlements. The main species are:

I.	*Duabanga* sp.	*Gmelina arborea*
	Shorea robusta	*Sterculia villosa*
	Terminalia tomentosa	*Tetrameles nudiflora*
II.	*Bauhinia purpurea*	*Callicarpa arborea*
	Litsea monopetala	*Premna integrifolia*

Sub-Tropical Forest: These forests are extensively developed in the lower hills of Darjeeling, Bhutan, Sikkim and Arunachal Pradesh up to an elevation of about 2000 mts. The upper canopy is made up of both evergreen and deciduous species though the former are dominant. The total annual rainfall may be up to 420 cms. The soil is well-drained, moderately deep and rich in humus. Slope conditions vary from moderate to very steep. The following associations have been reported by Negi (1985) within the sub-tropical forests of the eastern Himalaya:

— *Castanopsis-Schima* association

— *Engelhardtia-Castanopsis-Betula-Schima* association.

— *Schima-Phoebe-Castanopsis* association.

— *Phoebe-Engelhardtia* association.

The main species found in these forests are:

I.	*Betula cylindrostachys*	*Castanopsis* sp.
	Engelhardtia spicata	*Phoebe attenuata*
	Phoeba paniculata	*Quercus* sp.
	Schima wallichii	*Terminalia* sp.
II.	*Ficus cunia*	*Garcinia paniculata*
	Grewia vestita	*Meliosma simplicifolia*
	Nyssa javanicá	
III.	*Dendrocalamus sikkimensis*	
IV.	*Lastrea dissecta*	*Masesa chisia*
	Strobilanthes	
V.	*Impatiens* sp.	*Rauwolfia serpentina*
VI.	*Calamus flagellum*	*Mucuna macrocarpa*
	Thunbergia sp.	*Vitis* sp.

Oak Forest

In the eastern Himalaya chestnut is widely associated with oaks at higher elevations, whereas laurel is found intermixed with lower oak forests. Oak forests are very well developed in the eastern Himalaya. These forests are dominated by different species of oaks; found from an altitude of about 800 mts upto the timber line.

Lower Oak Forest: These forests occur in the high rainfall zone. The total annual rainfall is between 275 and 350 cms. These forests are found at lower elevations in the eastern Himalaya usually between 1800 and 2200 mts. The mean annual temperature varies from 18°C to 22°C whereas the lowest temperature may drop to below the freezing point. Bulk of the precipitation is from the SW monsoons. The slope varies from moderate to precipitous and topography is extremely rugged. This forest has also been referred to as *Lauraceous* forest by Negi (1985).

The main species constituting this forest are:

I. *Acer campbellii* — *Acer laevigatum*
Alcimandra sp. — *Belischmiedia* sp.
Castanopsis tribuloides — *Cinnamomum* sp.
Engelhardtia spicata — *Lithocarpus* sp.
Litsea sp. — *Machilus edulis*
Magnolia campbellii — *Mallotus nepalensis*
Michelia champaca — *Quercus fenestrata*
Schima wallichii — *Symplocos* sp.

II. *Eurya acuminata* — *Ilex* sp.

III. *Strolobianthes:* sp. — *Symplocos theaefolia*

Buk Oak Forest: This forest is dominated by buk oak *(Quercus lamellosa)*. It occurs between an elevation of 2000 and 2500 mts in different parts of the eastern Himalaya. The tract in which buk oak forests are found experience mean annual temperatures varying from 18°C to 22°C. Bulk of the precipitation is received from the SW monsoons. Snowfall also contributes to the total annual precipitation in the higher tracts. Winters are cold with the mercury dropping to below the freezing point. Rainfall is very high, usually ranging from 250 to 400 cms.

Soils are rich in humus, deep and well drained. Slopes range from moderate to precipitous. The main species constituting this forest are:

I. *Acer campbellii* — *Alcimandra cathcartii*
Castanopsis tribuloides — *Cinnamomum* sp.

	Lithocarpus spicatus	*Michelia cathcartii*
	M. doltsopa	*M. hylium*
	Prunus nepalensis	*Quercus lamellosa*
	Schima wallichii	*Slaonea* sp.
II.	*Eurya acuminata*	*Litsea* sp.
	Machilus sp.	*Mahonia* sp.
	Symplocos sp.	*Turpinia* sp.
III.	*Arundinaria* sp.	*Dendrocalamus* sp.
IV.	*Daphne cannabina*	*Rubus* sp.
	Strobilanthes sp.	

Upper Oak Forest: This is the high level oak forest of the eastern Himalaya occurring over an elevation of about 2500 mts. It is found in the very high precipitation zone with heavy rains from the SW monsoons and frequent snowfall in winter. Summers are mild and the mercury remains below the freezing point in winter. It rises to over 25°C in the hottest period.

Oak dominates the upper storey. The forest is fairly dense except in tracts lying near human settlements where there is a heavy biotic pressure. The terrain is extremely rugged. The main species forming a part of this forest are:

I.	*Acer campbellii*	*Quercus lamellosa*
	Q. pachyphylla	
II.	*Betula alnoides*	*Carpinus viminea*
	Machilus sp.	*Symplocos theaefolia*
III.	*Arundinaria maling*	*Dendrocalamus* sp.
IV.	*Daphne cannabina*	
V.	*Polygonum* sp.	

Upper Mixed Forests

These are mixed temperate forests found in the wet temperate zone of the eastern Himalaya. The upper mixed forests are usually dominated by evergreen species with associations of oak, rhododendron and hemlock. At higher elevations, hemlock gives way to silver fir and the transition to temperate coniferous forests is very gradual.

Relatively lower temperatures prevail in this tract as compared to those experienced in other forests of the temperate zone. The undergrowth is fairly dense and is comprised of bamboo, rhododendron and a number of evergreen shrubs. Snowfall is common during the winter months and it may cover the ground for several weeks at a stretch. Bulk of the rainfall is received from the SW monsoons. Rains bring about a further reduction in the temperature.

This forest occurs on moderate to very steep slopes and on extremely undulating and rugged terrain. The upper mixed forests are well developed on cooler northern aspects.

Based on composition, the following associations have been recognized by Champion and Seth (1968), Negi (1985 and 1989):

(a) *Tsuga-Abies* association—

I. *Abies densa* — *Tsuga dumosa*

II. *Acer campbellii* — *Acer pectinatum*
Betula utilis — *Brassiopsis alpina*
Quercus lineata — *Q. pachyphylla*
Symplocos sp. — *Taxus baccata*

III. *Arundinaria maling*

IV. *Daphne cannabina*

(b) *Abies-Rhododendron* association—

I. *Abies densa*

II. *Betula utilis* — *Rhododendron arboreum*
R. barbatum — *R. cinnamomum*
R. hodgsoni — *Taxus baccata*

III. *Thamnocalamus aristatus*

IV. *Berberis aristata* — *Daphne cannabina*
Rosa sericea — *Rubus niveus*

V. *Lekh dubo*

Fir Forest

This is an almost pure forest of fir found above an elevation of 2600 mts in most parts of the eastern Himalaya. The forest becomes mixed on warmer, southern aspects. Precipitation is received both from the SW monsoons and from winter rain/snow. The soil is of shallow to moderate depth, well-drained and rich in humus. The slopes on which fir thrives vary from steep to precipitous. There is heavy damage to the fir trees due to sliding snow. The main species forming a part of this forests are:

I. *Abies delavayi* — *A. densa*
Picea sp. — *Pinus* sp.

II. *Betula utilis* — *Litsea sericea*
Lyonia ovalifolia — *Rhododendron barbatum*
R. falconeri — *R. filgens*
R. hodgsoni — *R. maddeni*

III. *Thamnocalamus aristatus*
IV. *Rosa sericea* *Rubus* sp.

Blue Pine Forest

Blue pine forests are not very extensively developed in the eastern Himalaya. These forests are also found in the inner dry valleys where the influence of the SW monsoons is relatively less. They are found at altitudes of over 2500 mts. It occurs in pure stands or in association with silver fir. Scrub growth is more on exposed southern slopes.

Slopes vary from moderate to steep. The topsoil contains a thick layer of undecomposed vegetal matter consisting primarily of needles, twigs and branches. The soil is well drained. The main species found in the forest are:

I. *Abies densa* *Picea spinulosa*
Pinus wallichiana
II. *Betula utilis* *Quercus dilatata*
Q. lamellosa *Q. lineata*
Q. pachyphlla *Rhododendron falconeri*
R. hodgsoni
III. *Daphne cannabina* *Piptanthus nepalensis*
Rosa sericea *Rubus niveus*
IV. *Polygonum* sp. *Strobilanthes* sp.
Viburnum sp.

Dry Temperate Coniferous Forest

This is a mixed coniferous forest found in the dry temperate zone of the eastern Himalaya. It has a closed canopy with a mixed association of hemlock, spruce, blue pine, junipers and fir. These species occur either in pure patches or in mixed associations. Individual trees may soar upto a height of about 30 mts or even more. *Rhododendron* sp. forms the underwood. The ground flora is largely suppressed.

In some tracts of Sikkim, Bhutan and Arunachal Pradesh, coniferous forests are virtually untouched by man. The dry temperate coniferous forests are well distributed in the inner dry hills of Sikkim, Bhutan and Arunachal Pradesh, usually between an elevation of 2800 and 3400 mts. They are not found in the Darjeeling hills.

Very severe winters are experienced in the area in which these forests occur. The minimum temperature falls to below the freezing point. In summer, the mercury may rise to over 22°C. Snowfall occurs very frequently in winter and snow may lie on the ground for several weeks at a stretch. Severe snowstorms lash the area from December to February. Precipitation is both in the form of snow and rain. The average annual rainfall is usually less than 180 cms.

Not much is known about the soils on which these forests grow. The topsoil is covered by a thick layer of organic matter under various stages of decay. This comprises of needles, leaves and twigs.

The terrain on which this forest occurs is extremely rugged. Slope varies from moderate to precipitous. The main species forming a part of this forest are:

I.	*Abies delavayi*	*A. densa*
	Picea spinulosa	*Pinus wallichiana*
	Tsuga dumosa	
II.	*Betula utilis*	*Juniperus wallichiana*
	Rhododendron barbatum	*R. falconeri*
	R. hodgsoni	*R. maddeni*
III.	*Daphne cannabina*	*Piptanthus* sp.
	Rosa sericea	
IV.	*Polygonum* sp.	*Viburnum* sp.

Eastern Himalayan conifers have been reported to be absent from moister tracts, except hemlocks and firs. Extensive forests of conifers are well developed in the inner hills where the force of the monsoons is relatively weak. In many parts of the eastern Himalaya, it is difficult to differentiate between the wet temperate and dry temperate coniferous forests.

Larch Forest

This is an open forest dominated by *Larix griffithiana* and *Rhododendron.* The density is poor with individuals of low, stunted height. The ground flora is suppressed. Larch colonises high altitude glacial moraines.

These forests are usually found above an elevation of 3000 mts in Sikkim, Bhutan and Arunachal Pradesh. They are associated with the dry temperate coniferous forests discussed in the above text.

A large portion of the precipitation is received from winter snow that may lie on the ground for several weeks. Typical arctic conditions prevail in the tract in which this forest occurs. Winter temperatures remain below the freezing point. Summers are mild with maximum temperatures in the region of 2°C.

These forests usually occur on glacial moraines that are well-drained. The terrain is extremely rugged. The principal species forming a part of this forest are:

Larix griffithiana	*Picea spinulosa*
Rhododendron barbatum	*R. falconeri*
R. filgens	*R. hodgsoni*
Tsuga dumosa	

Dry Juniper-birch Forest

This is a fairly open forest of juniper and birch found in the inner dry hills of Sikkim, Bhutan and Arunachal Pradesh above an elevation of 3000 mts and extends up to the line of perpetual snow. Winter temperatures drop to far below the freezing point. Soils are well-drained and rich in humus. The trees are stunted and rarely attain a height of more than 3 mts. The ground flora is also suppressed. Climbers and epiphytes are few. Typical arctic conditions prevail in the tract in which this forest occurs. The main species found in the forest are:

Juniperus wallichiana	
Rhododendron barbatum	*R. falconeri*
R. hodgsoni	*Tsuga dumosa*

Sub-alpine Birch/Fir Forest

Fir, birch and rhododendron are the three main components of this forest. It is an open, irregular forest. It is found above an elevation of 3100 mts usually near the snowline in Sikkim, Bhutan and Arunachal Pradesh. It consists of a typically open growth of stunted, crooked trees or large shrubs intermixed with patches of conifers, which rarely attain a height of more than 15 mts except in sheltered depressions. The broad-leaved species are of a very low height. The undergrowth is dense. The forest floor is covered with grasses. Alpine pastures are intermixed with this forest.

A considerable part of the precipitation is in the form of snow. Arctic conditions prevail in the tract in which this forest occurs. The following are the main species found in this forest:

I.	*Abies densa*	*Juniperus wallichiana*
	Larix griffithiana	
II.	*Betula utilis*	*Pyrus aucuparia*
	Rhododendron falconeri	*R. hodgsoni*
	R. wightii	*Salix wallichiana*

III.	*Cassiopa fastigiata*	*Juniperus recurva*
	Polygonum sp.	*Potentillo fruticosa*
	Rhododendron sp.	
IV.	*Anemone obtusiloba*	*Lastrea barbata*
	Rosa sericea	*Rubus* sp.
	Strobilanthes sp.	*Viburnum* sp.

Alpine Scrub

In these Scrub forests, Tree and scrub growth is usually stunted. The forest is open. These scrub forests occur just below the snowline in all parts of the eastern Himalaya. Pressure of the snow leads to the bending of the stems at their base. Grasses, mosses and ferns cover the ground.

The trees have adapted themselves to withstand the pressure of the sliding snow. However, widespread damage is caused by avalanches near the snowline. A large part of the precipitation is received in the form of snow which falls from October to April or even during the rainy season. These forests are covered under a thick blanket of snow for a number of months in the winter season. The day temperature is quite warm in summer but it falls after sunset.

There is a thick, black layer of humus on the topsoil. The depth of the soil varies from few centimetres to 70 cms or even more. The soil is generally wet because of the melting snow.

The alpine scrub of the eastern Himalaya may be differentiated into the following two types on the basis of the conditions under which they occur:

(a) *Moist alpine scrub*—This scrub is found in the moister tracts. The main species are:

I.	*Quercus* sp.	*Rhododendron campanulatum*
	R. molle	*R. thomsoni*
	R. wightii	
II.	*Berberis* sp.	*Betula utilis*
	Pyrus sp.	*Rhododendron anthopogon*
	R. lepidotum	
III.	*Hypercium* sp.	*Mahonia* sp.
	Primula stuartii	
IV.	*Iris* sp.	
V.	*Clematis* sp.	

(b) *Dry alpine scrub*—Junipers are the main species in this forest. This scrub forest is found near snowline in the inner dry valleys. They are distributed as shown below:

Species	Altitudinal range (in mts)
Juniperus wallichiana	4400-5000
J. squamata	4200-4800
J. recurva	3500-4500

References

Aggarwal, S.C. (1959). Grasslands of Chakrata Forest Division, *Ind. For.*, 85(II).

Bor, N.L. (1960). The Grasses of Burma, Ceylon, India and Pakistan, Pergamon Press.

Champion, H.G. and Seth, S.K. (1968). A Revised Survey of the Forest Types of India, Govt. of India, New Delhi

Good, R. (1947). *The Geography of Flowering Plants,* Long. Green & Co., London.

Negi, S.S. (1985). *Himalayan Ecology* BSMPS, Dehradun.

Negi, S.S. (1989). *Forest Types of India,* Nepal and Bhutan, PEBA, Delhi.

Negi, S.S. (1993). *Himalayan Forests and Forestry,* IPC, New Delhi.

Osmaston, A.E. (1922). Notes on the Forest Communities of the Garhwal Himalaya, *Jour. Eco.*, 10(2).

Osmaston, A.E. (1927). A Forest Flora for Kumaon, Allahabad.

Puri, G.S. (1960). *Indian Forest Ecology*, Oxford Book Co., New Delhi.00000

2
The Geology of the Himalaya

The Himalayan range starts from Hindukush and through Kashmir and Nepal goes to Bhutan and Sikkim. But the largest mountain range in the world is strikingly poor in minerals of economic value, there being only three industries which can be said to be established on a commercial basis; these are the salt and the slate quarries in Kangra district and the sapphire and aquamarine mines of Kashmir. Active prospecting by the Mineral Survey of Kashmir, under Mr. C.S. Middlemis, has resulted in the discovery of many mineral deposits of potential value.

Salt: The salt quarries in Himachal are of local only important. They are situated at Guma and Drang in Mandi district. The output in 1932 being about 3,555 tons.

Slate: The Kangra slate quarries, which are at Kanyara, have been worked with considerable success for many years past.

The rock is sufficiently fissile for the production of slabs and roofing-slates. However, it is not true clay state.

Phyllitic slate, splitting into fairly thin glossy-surfaced laminae and belonging to the Silurian system or older, in found only at a few places in kashmir, one of them being around Banihal. It has already been extensively used with success for roofing many of the Banihal cart-road bungalows. A purer black slate from Mohri Dor in the Gulmarg hills is also known. Both these varieties, especially the latter, may have a large future of usefulness in Kashmir.

Sapphire: The beautiful azure blue sapphire of Sumjam in Padar, Zanskar, Kishtwar tahsil, was accidently discovered at an altitude of 15,000 feet among rocks some fifty years ago which have since been determined as felspathic pegmatite veins in actinolite-tremolite schist lenticles in the marble bands of the area. They are in Padar, Zanskar and Kishtwar tahsil. The actinolite-tremolite schist appears to have been a modification of the marble. Large quantities of excellent stones were found and they yielded considerable revenue to the Kashmir

Government and doubtless much profit to illicit traffickers in the stones as well as to those licensed to work the mines.

Subsequently, the actual source of the rock sapphires appeared to be exhausted, though the placer deposit continued to yield a diminishing output. Later on, several new veins of corundum, sapphire and pink corundum (ruby) were discovered in the above area and in its neighbourhood. The quantity available of these as estimated by recent work of the Kashmir Mineral Survey, is certainly very great. In colour, the sapphire is of a pale china-blue tint, but more generally it is a rich sky blue, which in the best stones becomes extremely vivid. Sapphire of more slaty blue tint is also found some time.

A reddish tint is also found, though somewhat rare. Where found it varies from pale pink to rosy red, and in a few cases to carmine with a slight blue tone in the *red.* The finding of true deep coloured rubies is probably only a matter of carefully working the veins and following them in depth.

The colour is irregularly and unevenly distributed in the sapphire crystals, being found in stripes and patches of different dimensions among the milky grey and colourless corundum.

Aquamarine: The semi-precious gem-stone, aquamarine, a variety of beryl, is found at Dasu on the Braldu River, in Baltistan in the Skardu tahsil of Kashmir.

The stones great limpidity and brilliance when cut and set suitably. They are of somewhat slight depth of colour. In pendant size and form they have a most attractive appearance. They are in considerable demand in Kashmir by both Europeans and Indians. In cut gem form they are sold at Rs. 3-12 per carat, and in uncut form, at Rs. 21-12 per tola (about 58 carats).

Some veins of this gem-stone have also been discovered in Padar *ilaka,* but they have not been exploited so far. They bear aquamarine and beryl varying in colour from a pale or, perhaps one should say, delicate sea-green tint, and in one case to blue approaching sapphire-blue.

Mr. Tipper found [*Records, Geological Survey of India,* Vol. LV, 13 (1923)] beryls of pleasing colour and some of almost gem quality at Sirwigh-o-gaz, a summer grazing-ground in western Chitral.

Abrasives (polishing powder): Geologically well-known Gangamopteris rock occurs near Khunamuh in Vihi district. When powdered to various degrees of fineness it makes a mild abrasive and effective polishing and scouring material for metals, marble, serpentine, cement floors, etc.

Antimony: Sulphide of antimony (stibnite) occurs in some quantity near the Shigri glacier in the valley of the Chandra river in Lahaul. The locality has long been known [F.R. Mallet : *Memoirs, Geological Survey of India,* Vol. V, 165 (1886)]. When attempts were made to work in these deposits there was not much success.

Arsenic: A small production of orpiment has been reported from Chitral for years [*Records, Geological Survey of India,* Vol. L1V, 17 (1922)], from six deposits in crystalline limestones. Realgar occurs as well and fluorite is found in both minerals. At another locality, Partial [*Records, Geological Survey of India,* Vol. LV, 14 (1923)], only realgar occurs, in scattered patches in calcareous shales of Cretaceous age. Specimens have also been obtained from the Rishipjerab valley in Hunza and the Shankalpa glacier in Kumaun [*Records, Geological Survey of India,* Vol. XXXV, 28 (1907)], but the amount available in either locality is unknown.

Barytes: At several places in Riasi tahsil of kashmir, Barytes is found penetrating the Great Limestone in the familiar form of narrow veins at several places. Its modern industrial uses for paint, lithopone, and in the ceramic and glass industries must await the general industrial development of the country and the provision of easy communications.

Bauxite, bauxitic clays and kaolin: Bauxite is an ore of aluminium, whereas the bauxitic clays are used for making refractories and the kaolin in the pottery industry. A very pure form of bauxite, forming a surface layer, averaging some 4 feet in thickness and passing downwards into bauxitic clay and kaolin or china clay, has been discovered at a large number of places in Jammu Province.

The bauxite is of the diaspore variety, having one molecule of water only, and contains between 70 and 80 per cent alumina and 1 to 5 per cent silica. Kaolin, known locally as "makol," occurs in the neighbourhood of the bauxite and tiles and pottery articles are made from it. The coal of Jammu occurs in close connection with the bauxite, stratigraphically at an horizon 60 feet above it, and could be used for calcining the bauxite. The quantity of first grade bauxite has been estimated to be about 1,810,000 tons, that of the second grade being roughly about 10,000,000 tons, easily available at the surface.

Bentonite: Bentonite, a clay with several useful industrial properties, forms a continuous bed 2 feet thick in the gently dipping Siwalik conglomerates, extending for 28 miles, at least, in the neighbourhood of Bhimber, Jammu Province, Kashmir.

Borax: Borax is found in Ladakh, there it is obtained as an efflorescence from the surface of the alluvium of the Puga valley.

The superficial coating is scraped up and boiled with water in coppers; the resulting brine is then cooled in small pits, when the borax crystallises out. The production. Almost the whole supply of borax brought into India being imported from Central and Western Tibet. at Puga is quite insignificant.

Chromium: Pure olivine-chromite rock (dunite) has been discovered in the higher hills of Kashmir near Dras, Bembat and Tashgam, where it is present in enormous quantities, forming large mountain masses. It is practically impossible to consider this bulky ore for industrial purposes at present. Without any road communications other than a bridle path, and with a high pass of 11,300 feet (the Zoji La) between it and the Valley of Kashmir.

It may be of some importance to remark that there is a possibility of finding platinum if proper exploration is carried on. It has not so far been discovered by the Kashmir Mineral Survey, in the peridotites, pyroxenites and dunites of the above areas or further north-west in Gilgit Wazarat. These are the rocks in which platinum is generally found.

Coal: The chief occurrences of coal in the Himalaya are among the Gondwana rocks of the Darjeeling Terai and Assam Duars and in the Tertiary beds of Jammu and Kashmir. The Gondwana coal is usually too crushed to be of commercial value and such attempts as have hitherto been made to work it have not met with success. Coal of excellent quality (semi-anthracite) occurs in the province of Jammu, Kashmir, consisting of a number of seams 2 to 20 feet thick in the Subathu series.

Its continuity over a distance of 36 miles has been proved, though concealed here and there under debris or under the overlying rocks. The quantity may be reckoned to be over 100,000,000 tons easily available within a reasonable depth. Samples from the various deposits yield 60 to 82 per cent of fixed carbon.

Extensive and thick beds of lignite have been discovered in the Karewa (Pliocene) deposits of the Kashmir Valley by the Mineral Survey Department of Kashmir. So far, the Nichahom (Handwara) and Shaliganga areas have been mapped and proved, and the estimated quantity available in these areas is 128,000,000 tons, but the presence of lignite in other parts of the valley is also known and a much greater quantity of this fuel is confidently expected. It is not a high class fuel, but it has its other uses for the manufacture of gas, oil and tar, etc. Lignite is also found underlying the Nummulitic limestone of Thakiala, in an outcrop over 18 miles in length. It occurs in lenticular seams, up to 3 feet in thickness, on two horizons, of fair quality. The extreme crushing of the coal, and the high inclination of the seams do not permit its successful commercial exploitation militate against its successful exploitation.

Copper: Copper-ore, chiefly in the form of the sulphide, chalcopyrite, is common in the schistose beds of the Daling series in Darjeeling district (*supra*, p. 296) and in Sikkim [*Records, Geological Survey of India,* Vol. XLII, 75 (1912)] and in the similar rocks of the Himalayan zone in the Lesser Himalaya of Kumaun. As a rule the lodes are patchy and irregular and no successful attempt has yet been made to exploit them on a large scale.

The Mineral Survey Department has discovered the presence of copper ore in the copper bed of Gainta and Sukhwal Gali, also in the Rad nala, Riasi tahsil, at Kangan, Sindh Valley, Kashmir, as well as at various places in Kishtwar tahsil. These deposits have not been examined in any great detail, though, some of them have been mapped on a large scale. Not being in the form of regular beds they require careful examination, and it is quite likely that some of them may become useful deposits of copper when properly developed.

Fuller's earth: Fuller's earth forms a 7-foot bed near Budil, Rajouri tahsil of Jammu Province, in a slate formation of the older rocks of the area. A large quantity of it is easily available at the surface, but its unfavourable situation, far away from the plains, among the lower hills at the foot of the main Pir Panjal ranges, may stand in the way of its being put to any use in the near future.

Gold: Gold is found in small quantities in the gravels of almost All the chief rivers of the Himalaya have small quantities of gold in their gravel. [V. Ball: *Manual of the Geology of India,* Part 3 (1881)] and its recovery provides occupation for the local inhabitants during the winter, when agricultural work is at a standstill. In the Indus and its tributaries, and in the Satluj, washing by means of primitive cradles is carried on to a considerable extent, but the results are at present too insignificant to raise this intermittent occupation to the status of a regular industry.

In the Eastern Himalaya, the gravels of the Brahmaputra and neighbouring rivers have long been known to be auriferous [J.M. Maclaren: *Records, Geological Survey of India,* Vol. XXXI, 205 (1904)], but so far no serious attempt has been made to exploit them on modern principles.

The output of the Tibetan fields, is quite unknown a circumstance to which the many stories of their fabulous wealth are no doubt to be attributed.

In Tibet, the goldfields of Rudok and Thok Jalung have been worked from very early antiquity and Herodotus reference to the gold-digging ants, with the many ingenious commentaries to which it gave rise, is no doubt familiar to everyone. [For literature on the subject see *Manual of the Geology of India,* Part 3, Art. *Gold* (1881)].

Gold was also found in Afghanistan, but what was formerly the most productive mine in the country, that of Kandahar, has long been closed owing to the miners having lost the vein [C.L. Griesbach: *Memoirs, Geological Survey of India,* Vol. XVIII, Part 1, 56 (1881)].

Graphite, gypsum, ochres: Enormous quantities of these minerals occur grouped together along a line of country fifteen miles long, to the north of the Jhelum valley cart-road near Braripura, in the Uri tahsil of Kashmir.

Ochres need only a little preparation for making good oil paints. Ochres of Rata Sar are fairly rich in colouring matter, About 160,000 tons are known at the surface in this locality ; they are also known at Jhuggi and Nur Khwah in Uri tahsil. The graphite of the above locality is of the amorphous variety; it is distributed through a 400-foot thickness of phyllites and contains only 25 to 30 per cent carbon.

Flake graphite is also found in the Kashmir State in the neighbourhood of the sapphire mines, Padar, Kishtwar. It is distributed as flakes in a number of bands varying in thickness from 6 feet to as much as 30 to 40 feet, they have a great extension along the strike. The quantity available of both varieties is certainly very great.

Gypsum: The gypsum is a pure alabaster-like product of the alteration of a pyritiferous limestone. Hundreds of millions of tons, forming mountain sides, lie exposed for easy quarrying. Gypsum also occurs in thick beds, as the product of the alteration of limestone, in lower Spiti, at a short distance above the junction of the Spiti and Satluj rivers. Although the quantity available is very large and the quality high, the locality is too far from markets and too inaccessible to offer any prospects of remunerative exploitation of the deposits [H. H. Hayden: *Memoirs, Geological Survey of India,* Vol. XXXVI, Part 1, 101 (1904)].

Iron: The lower hills in Kumaun have iron one in some quantity. [T. H. Hughes : *Records, Geological Survey of India,* Vol. VII, 15 (1874)]. Numerous attempts have been made to establish a smelting industry on a commercial basis. All attempts failed however, presumably owing fo the cost of transport of ore and fuel. There is doubt if any smelting units can kick start in the region.

Iron was also once worked at several places in Jammu and Kashmir; the excellent suspension bridge at Ramban over the Chenab River was built of iron smelted from the ores of Chakar, Matah or Salal in Riasi tahsil of Jammu Province (where innumerable pits are still noticeable honeycombing the country), during the rule of late Maharaja Ranbir Singh. These deposits have not yet received the serious attention of the Mineral Survey of Kashmir, but a 15-feet thick bed of pure haematite has been located by the Mineral Survey at Khandli in Rajouri, forming lenticular masses of sometimes great extension in the Nummulitic series, whose continuation towards the north-west has also been proved. This ore contains 60 per cent of iron. If it is worked on a commercial scale, it is a very rich proportion.

Lead, silver: Buniar in Uri tahsil of Kashmir contain huge deposits of galena. There galena deposits have been explored at various times in a desultory way and without much success. Recent work there by the Mineral Survey of Kashmir has indicated the probability that these galena veins form the north-western continuation of the Ramsu and Khaleni occurrences recently discovered, along the line of strike of the containing rocks. The galena from these localities has been found, to contain 0.1 per cent silver. Old workings of galena are also known in Nigote sub-division of Riasi tahsil. In the past when work was done on them, much are was taken out.

Recent work by the Mineral Survey has shown the occurrence of galena at various other places in the Great Limestone formation of Riasi tahsil, along the line of strike of the Nigote deposit.

During his survey of Chitral, Mr. G. H. Tipper found numerous occurrences of galena, zinc-blende, copper and iron pyrites, tetrahedrite and jamesonite in the quartzitic portions of the Sarikol shales, and galena associated with azurite, occurs at Chapari.

Manganese: Manganese ore has been located recently at a place 1 mile west of Lidrer nala, Padar, Kishtwar, where it is found impregnating a quartz vein 200 feet long and 4 feet thick. No analysis has so far been made.

Marble and serpentine: Deposits of marble have been found at different places in Kashmir. A layer of it, white to grey in colour, near Braripura, is available for ornamental building purposes in very large quantities. Other excellent marbles and serpentines are found distributed in the higher hilly areas. These, except the translucent apple-green serpentine ("Zehr Mohura", the poison detector) from Shigar, are too far away from civilisation to be of economic value.

The "Zehr Mohura" is carved into small cups and other articles and has a pleasing appearance.

Mercury: Cinnabar has been detected in concentrates from auriferous sands from the Chitral river [*Records, Geological Survey of India,* Vol. LIV, 26 (1922)].

Nickel: Ramsu, Buniar and Khaleni, and neighbourhood of the Sapphire Mines, Padar, are home to huge quantities of nickel are. Nickel has also been found in the copper-bearing horizon of Riasi tahsil, all in Kashmir. The surface samples in certain cases gave a good percentage of nickel (in one case 1.68 per cent), but no opportunity has been found so far to examine these occurrences in any great detail.

Petroleum: There are hopes that liquid fuel in the form of petroleum, may be hidden in one or more suitable geological structures, such as the Nar-Budhan dome and the Ramnagar "terrace" already discovered. The development of the Khaur Oilfield near Rawalpindi by the Attock Oil Company, and the recent discovery of a bituminous horizon with thin veins of asphalt at various places in the Jammu Province of Kashmir, hold this out. Others may be brought to light by future survey work in rocks of the same age and composition as those existing at Khaur. But this is a matter about which there can be no certainty until deep drilling is undertaken.

Crude oil and many other useful by-products can also be obtained from lignite by its distillation, as the following yield per ton of Kashmir lignite shows:

Liquor	55.83 gallons.
Sulphate of ammonia	10.85 lbs.
Oil	5.43 gallons.
Spirit from gas scrubber	1.00 gallons.
Gas	(about) 4,250 c.ft.

Talc (steatite): A. pure, compact, translucent talc of the palest shade of yellowish green occurs in the Great Limestone at several places in the Riasi tahsil of Jammu Province in Kashmir. Others of a slate-grey colour are also found. The several exposures have been surveyed, and thick veins located and mapped, but their underground continuation cannot be determined without development work. There is enough visible for anyone interested in the trade to start work upon.

Zinc: There are veins and lentiels of Zinc blends in the Great Limestone near Darabi, Riasi tahsil, Kashmir. The ore lenticles vary in dimensions from a few cubic feet to as much as 576 cubic feet, and the veins vary in length from a few inches to as much as 150 feet and in width from a few inches to 10 feet. A specimen of pure ore gave on analysis 67.52 per cent zinc. Cadmium to the extent of 0.174 per cent has also been reported to be present in it. Zinc-bearing calcite veins also occur at various other places in the Great Limestone on the line of strike of the Darabi occurrence. A few thousand tons could be collected from the surface. On account of its lenticular nature only actual mining can prove the depth of the ore.

LIST OF PAPERS ON THE ECONOMIC GEOLOGY OF KASHMIR MOSTLY BY C.S. MIDDLEMISS

1. Note on the Aquamarine mines of Daso on the Braldu R., Shigar Valley, Baltistan. (Published in *Records, Geological Survey of India,* Vol. XLIX, Part 3, 1918, with plates 6 to 10)
2. Possible occurrence of Petroleum in Jammu Province : Preliminary note on the Nar-Budhan dome of Kotli tahsil in the Punch Valley. (Published in *Records, Geological Survey of India,* Vol. XLIX, Part 4, 1919, with plates 13 to 16)
3. Lignitic Coalfields in the Karewa formation of the Kashmir Valley. (Published in *Records, Geological Survey of India,* Vol. LV, Part 3, 1923, with plates 28 to 30)
4. Abrasives : Note on the polishing material of Risin Spur, Khunamuh, near Srinagar. (Printed by order of the Kashmir Government, with plates 1 and 2)
5. The Graphite deposits of Braripura, Uri tahsil, Kashmir. (Printed by order of the Kashmir Government, with plates 1 to 5.)
6. Ochre deposits of Nur Khwah, Rata Sar and Jhuggi in the Jhelum Valley, Uri tahsil, Kashmir. (Printed by order of the Kashmir Government, with, plates 1 to 6)
7. The Gypsum deposits of the Lachhipura, Bagna, Islamabad, Limbar and Katha nalas, Uri tahsil, Kashmir. (Printed by order of the Kashmir Government.)
8. Bauxite deposits of Jammu Province. (Printed by order of the Kashmir Government, with plates 1 to 17)
9. A Resurvey of Jammu Coalfields : The Kalakot, Metka and Mahogala fields, with notes on the Chakar, Chinkah and newly discovered Dhansal-Sawal-kot fields. (Printed by order of the Kashmir Government, with plates 1 to 25)

10. **Ore deposits of Lead, Copper, Zinc, Iron and other metals in Jammu and Kashmir State. (Published by order of the Kashmir Government, with plates 1 to 16)**
11. **Non-Metallic Minerals of Jammu and Kashmir. (Printed by order of the Kashmir Government, with plates 1 to 7)**
12. **Precious and semi-precious gemstones of Jammu and Kashmir. (Published by order of the Kashmir Government, with plates 1 to 7)**

3

Ethnobotany of Eastern Himalaya

Section I
Introduction

Biological Ecology and Human Ecology

Ramon Margalef[1], an expert in biological ecology, defines ecology as, "the study of systems at a level in which individuals or whole organisms may be considered elements of interaction, either among themselves or with a loosely organized environmental matrix. Systems at this level are named ecosystems, and ecology of course is the biology of ecosystems". Does the ecology of humans fit this definition? It does. Human individuals interact among themselves, and the interaction patterns are described as systems. People also interact with environmental matrices, which are again considered to be systems or parts or conglomeration of systems.

These human ecosystems have biological properties. According to John W. Bennet[2], they possess regularities that might form the basis of theoretical constructions. Bennet further amplifies the statement, describing man as an animal who moves on earth through its spaces and properties, consuming what he needs to survive, dealing with other biological species, largely unaware of the complicated relationship among the phenomena that he disturbs or changes—or that may disturb or change him.

All this can be included in Margalef's definition quoted above. One such related subject of biological ecology of human ecosystems is the study of ethnobotany. Human ecological research remains incomplete without details of ethnobotany of a given area, including the inputs of traditional plants ecological knowledge of its long time inhabitants.

Paradigms of Ethnobotany and Ethnobotanical Research

The term ethnobotany was coined by the University of Pennsylvania botanist John Harshberger (1896) E. Wade Davis[3] elaborates that ethnobotany as a practice goes back in Western and Eastern traditions to prehistoric times.

The scope of a field of inquiry is reflected in the questions essential for ethnobotanical research. Specific questions asked by ethnobotanists include the following (Lanis B. Alcorn, 1995)[4]:

(a) What plants are available?
(b) Why are they available?
(c) What plants are recognised as resources?
(d) What social, political, biological, economic and ecological factors cause particular plants to be perceived as resources?
(e) How does the use of certain set of resources influence the use/availability of others?
(f) How is ethnobotanical knowledge distributed among the human population?
(g) What do people think about plants?
(h) How do they differentiate and classify elements of their natural environment?
(i) From what resource zones are plant products harvested ?
(j) How are they used?
(k) What are the economic and financial benefits derived from plants?
(l) How are the populations of resources maintained?
(m) What effect does their management have upon the structure of local vegetation?
(n) What effect does their management have upon the structure and functioning of local institutions?
(o) What factors influence resource management decisions, and thereby affect local plant populations?
(p) How have human activities and their consequences influenced the evolution of local plant populations?
(q) For what purposes are resources needed?
(r) To what stressors are human populations adapting?
(s) Are human choices of particular resources adaptive?
(t) If so, how are they adaptive?
(u) How are human adaptive strategies affected by change?
(v) What changes are presently occuring, and what changes have occurred in the past?

If one looks at the questions raised, modern ethnobotany is concerned with the "totality of the place of plants in a culture" (Ford, 1878)[5]. It is the study of plant-human inter-relationships embedded in dynamic ecosystems of natural and social components. The above questions formed the basis during the field work proceedings of present research work for this thesis.

The object of ethnobotanical inquiry is actually a sort of "text" (Ricoeur, 1971)[6], the meaning of which is derived partially from the natural, social and cultural contexts in which that text is played out. An ethnobotanical text evolves around human community's use and management of vegetation. In this chapter have been listed the results of the studies conducted on ethnobotanical resources and their non-timber uses in areas of Yuksom. In this chapter have been listed the results of the studies conducted.

Ethnobotany of Traditional Agroecosystems and Conservation of Wild Species

If was the farmer who always decided what he needed for his family's need. Accordingly he managed the traditional system of agriculture usually containing many different patches, gardens or fields of various ages containing different combinations of cultivated and wild plants. The wild vegetation diversity created by traditional systems apparently functions to protect the agroecosystem from pest outbreaks (Speight 1983; Alteieri 1984[7]. Indigenous maintenance of wild resources is, in effect, indigenous "conservation" of wild species. Traditional farming systems often create fallows and other corridors or patches of natural vegetation that act as resource zones, biodiversity conservation units and gene banks for the regeneration of natureal communities (Lynch and Alcorn, 1991)[8]. The study of resource conservation is an area of ethnobotanical inquiry that reaches into the heart of ethnobotanical text and contributes to reaching the applied goals of the ethnobotanical endeavour. By identifying ecologically adaptive aspects of resource management, ethnobotanists contribute to the development of resource-conservative, sustained-yield agroecosystems (Hart 1980, Wilson and Kang 1981)[9].

The Human Ecology Connection

Ethnobotany plays a major role in facilitating the study of human ecology. Modern ethnobotanical data are often used as analogues for interpreting past plant-human interrelationships (Dimbley 1978)[10]. By providing data about the plants of the ecosystem, ethnobotanists do contribute to more sophisticated analyses of human ecological relations. (Boster 1984)[11]. As applied human ecologists, economic and social anthropologists have been granted an expanded role in rural development projects (Barlett 1980;[12] That brings a wider scope to the study and research into ethnobotanical aspects being conducted by International Potato Centre 1984)[13].

Ethnobotany of Medicinal Plants

Aboriginal knowledge of the physical properties of plants and the accompanying familiarity with those components of the vegetal environment that permit indegenous peoples to use various plants for their presumed medicinal value is one of the subdivisions of modern ethnobotany in the study of applied human ecology. This subdivision is now known as ethnopharmacology (Schultes and Reis 1995)[14].

In the dawn of human kind, the art of curing was essentially magical (Narenjo 1984)[15]. Few plants were used and those employed were usually psychoactive ones, now known as magic or psychedelic plants. Later, empirical medicine arose, using many plants for the treatment of various affliations. Scientific medicine arose much later. The 17th century, in particular opened the doors to true scientific understanding of medicine. Although the art of curing was refined, plants continued to occupy a pre-eminent position. Until 1930, around 90 per cent of the official medicines were of plant origin (Swain 1972)[16]. As previously analysed by many authors (Fransworth and Bingel 1977; Von Reis Altschul 1973; Balendran 1985; Duke 1985)[17-20], there are many powerful reasons for doing broad ethnobotanical ethnopharmacological and also clinical therapeutic research. Among these reasons the following could be cited (Klayman 1985)[21]

(a) To rescue knowledge in imminent danger of being lost.
(b) The utility of plants in current therapy.
(c) To find new molecular models in plants.
(d) The usefulness of plants in the development of physiopathology.
(e) The wide use of plants in folk medicine.
(f) To obtain intermediate chemicals.

A case study of medicinal plants, including ethnic group-wise case study, and plants in Yuksom and Dzongri areas is included in this chapter.

Applied Ethnobotany in Home Gardens

Compound farms, homestead and mixed gardens) are usually the small plots of land surrounding the house. We can call them home gardens. They are found in traditional communities all over the world, and are one of the more intensively cultivated parts of an overall farm. Home gardens are important agroecosystems and are a source of subsistence and cash resources. They are characterised by a mixture of annual or perennial species grown in association. (Godbole, 1998)[22]. Home gardens commonly exhibit a layered vertical structure of trees, shrubs and ground cover plants which recreate some of the features of nutrient recycling, soil protections and effective use of space below and above the soil surface. They also act as a repository and testing site for uncommon species and varieties of plants (Padoch and Jong 1991)[23] and can be used to spread farmwork output and income more evenly throughout the year (Ninej 1984)[24].

This chapter includes a study on Home Gardens as available near the confluence of Rathong Chu and Rangit Chu in the areas of Tashiding and Western slopes of Ravangla.

Sale of Wild Plants/Plant Products

Plants/plant products are the main stay of rural folk. In mountain regions in local folk markets they are largely dependent on them for their existence. The local markets are full of wild vegetables, fruits and medicinal plants. They make a variety of fish traps, hats, agricultural implements, containers and other household articles and sell them in these markets.

In smaller places these markets are held on a fixed day. In many large towns these markets are permanent. Interestingly most of these markets are run by women. The buyers are often from neighbouring localities (Saklani and Jain 1994)[25]. A case study of markets traditionally held at Ravangla forms a part of this chapter. These markets in small towns are by the day are held on.

Eating Habits: Traditional Fermented and Non Fermented Foods

In the Sikkim Himalayan regions including the Upper Rangit Basin, there exists a unique dietary culture of different ethnic groups of people. They use traditional fermented and non-fermented foods and beverages to provide basic components of diet with diverse characteristics of nutrition, flavour, palatability and texture. A survey conducted randomly in the Upper Rangit Valley representing the ethnic communities of the Nepalis, the Bhutia and the Lepcha was carried out. This chapter contains the findings of this study.

Data Presentation of Sikkim Ethnobotanical Resources

In some cases whole plants are also used. Various parts of plants, such as seeds, flowers, bark, fruits, rhizomes and tubers are also used for different purposes. An inventory of such plants, and their uses according to different parts of the plants for the state of Sikkim is presented at the end of the chapter. The research for this inventory has been carried out from available literature. Local government and non-government organisations collaborated in the field work.

Section II
Home Gardens in Upper Rangit Basin

Introduction

Brownrigg (1985)[26] defines the term home gardens as, "A supplementary food production system by and for the members of a group of people with rights to the land, who eat meals together regularly." Home gardens can be defined as the land surrounding a house on which a mixture of annual and perennial plants are grown, together with or without animals, and largely managed by the household members for their own use or commercial purposes. Fernandes and Nair (1986)[27] state that the term Home Garden can mean anything from growing vegetables behind houses to complex multistoried systems. They defined the term as "Land use practices involving deliberate management of multipurpose trees and shrubs in intimate association with annual and perennial agricultural crops and, invariably livestock's, within the compound of individual houses, the whole crop-tree-animal unit being intensively managed by family labour."

The cropping pattern of home gardens changes with altitude. The size and shape of the gardens is dictated by gradient, contours and terrace availability. The prevalent climatic condition ranges from subtropical to alpine with major area under temperate climate in the Upper Rangit Basin of Sikkim. One Single spur rising Westwards from Rathong chu upto the watershed on Singalila Ridge experiences climatic conditions from tropical to subtropical to temperate and finally to alpine at the summits of the ridge. As such ecological situations vary greatly at very short distances which limits the adaptation of crop species and their varieties within a narrow range. These are an ancient and widespread agroforestry system in Eastern Himalayas including Sikkim.

This has the advantage of growing many kinds of fruits, seasonal and off-seasonal vegetables and other commercial crops in the hills at different altitude and in different seasons (Subba, 1984)[28].

Home Garden Structure

Although the variation of height within any one stratum has led to some arguments as to the distinctness of the various strata recognised by various still the vertical stratification of vegetation within Home Gardens has long been recognised as a characteristic feature authors, Barrau (1961)[29], Michon (1983)[30], Altieri and Farrell (1984)[31], Fernandes et al (1984)[32], Okafor and Fernandes (1987)[33], Oduol and Aluma (1990)[34], Millat-e-Mustafa (1996)[35] give schematic presentations of vertical structures from various geographical regions and observe that the canopies of most Home Gardens consist of strata between two and six.

General summary of strata as found in the Home Gardens in Tashiding and in the areas immediately adjacent on the East and West of Rathong chu and Rangit chu just north of their confluence is as under:

< 1 m	Vegetables, tubers and roots including cardamom broomgrass and flowers.
1-3 m	Food plants e.g. lemon, banana, papaya and broom grass.
3-5 m	Oranges and Saplings of fruit/timber trees all growing taller.
5-7 m	Bamboo, timber/fruit trees, some growing taller.
7-9 m	Mango trees, timber trees, fodder trees and bamboo.
> 9 m	Timber trees (Oak and Chestnut) and bamboo.

It is stressed that the above strata are dynamic and there is a constant recruitment from one stratum to another.

Floristic Diversity in Home Gardens of Study Area

The definition of diversity neatly encapsulates the concept of diversity in Home Gardens, since there is a great variety of interactions taking place vertically, horizontally and temporally within one garden often of less than one hectare. Diversity is defined as, "Many different species and their intensity of interactions occuring in a small space at one time". (Harmer 1991)[36].

Vegetables Diversity. The vegetable cultivation extends from river beds at the confluence to elevations upto 2000 m above sea level at Tashiding and on either side of the confluence. Following vegetables are grown:

(a) **Kharif Vegetables.** Brinjal, chilli, capsicum, french beans, cow pea, bhindi, cucumber, pumpkin, bottle gourd, sponge gourd, ridge gourd, snake gourd, bitter gourd, sweet gourd etc.

(b) **Rabi Vegetables.** Cabbage, cauliflower, broccoli, garden pea, french beans, radish, carrot, turnip, palak, amaranthus, methi leafy mustard, lettuce, celery, coriander, leafy onion, garlic, leak, potato, colocasia, elephant's yam, etc.

(c) **Off-season Vegetables.** Cabbage, cauliflower, broccoli, brussel sprouts, radish, carrot, tomato, green pea, french beans, palak, leafy mustard, chayote, cucumber, amaranthus, leafy onion, summer potato, capsicum, aspargus, bamboo shoots, fern shoots, stinging neetles, mushroom etc.

Fruits Diversity. Mango, banana, peach, plum, orange, strawberry, jackfruit, papaya etc. Apples are grown in the upper slopes of Yuksom.

Feed and Fodder Diversity in Home Gardens. The farmers mostly feed animals with fodder tree leaves and fodder grasses, in addition to agricultural crop residues and fodder crop concentrates. Tarnutzer and Batting (1994)[37] found that 87 per cent of the farmers were growing grasses on bunds in agricultural fields, steep slopes etc.

Fodder Grasses. Bush type fodder grasses, average per farm and percentage of farmers involved are given in Table 3.1 below:

Table 3.1
Bush Type Fodder Grasses

Grass Species	*Bushes per farmer (Average)*	*Farmers Involved (%)*
Amlisha	527	62
Napier	33	31
Guatam mala	2	9
Bamboo	74	17
Narkat	3	1

Paljor (1998)[38]

Fodder Trees. All the farmers on the spurs extending Westwards and Southwestwards from Ravangla and Ralong respectively are having fodder trees with a range of 72-99 per Home Garden. The different types of fodder species grown in and around Home Gardens are presented in Table 3.2 below:

Table 3.2
Fodder Trees in Home Gardens and Farms

Species	*Local Name*	*Species*	*Local Name*
Major Fooder Trees		*Minor Fodder Trees*	
Artocarpus lakoocha	Barar	Brassaiopis mitis	Chuletro
Ficus roxburghi	Nevaro	Bauhinia purpurea	Taki
Ficus cunia	Raj-khenew	Castanopsis tribuloides	Katus
Ficus calarata	Lutey-Khenew	Celtis tetrandra	Khari
Ficus nemoralis	Dudilo	Evodia fraxinifolia	Khanakola
Ficus Saemoarpa	Bar	Ficus hookeri	Chbra
Saussuria nepaulensis	Gogun	Litsaea polyantha	Kutmero

Factors Affecting Diversity

There are many factors which affect the diversity. These came to light during the course of this study. The factors are corroborated by the literature available from earlier research by eminent ethnobotanists. Mergan (1987)[39] cites personal choice of the farmers, but more often external forces come into play. Soemarwoto (1987)[40] has listed a concise catalogue of factors:

(a) Better financial position leading to fewer food crops and more ornamentals.

(b) Scarcity of labour prompting farmers to grow more labour saving perennials.

(c) Proximity of markets, influencing farmers to include cash crops to their gardens.

(d) Population pressures, which decreases the size of land holdings, subsequently although cropping intensity increases.

(e) Prices of commodities usually cause the sacrifice of species diversity.

Individual farmers over the generations have acquired have certain skills empierically. These management skills are constantly emphasized. Most farmers possess traditional ecological knowledge, such that they are often able to choose the correct 'niche' for each plant, depending on the gradient of light and altitude. This seems to correspond to the ecological niche in the natural forest.

There are wide range of uses from gardens such as:

(a) Multipurpose tree crops provide shade for cardamom plantations and for sitting under.

(b) Parameter plantations act as living fences, fodder and mulch, bee forage, fuelwood, fruit, timber and poles.

(c) Other components provide for home consumption and also for sale.

(d) Certain varieties are used for arts and crafts, fibres for ropes, mats and even ornamentation.

(e) Diversity of plants reduces soil erosion. There are two categories of vegetation in relation to soil erosion. These act as barriers against erosion by rain. The ground litter acts as surface cover against splash and surface erosion due to winds.

(f) Home gardens with biotic diversity are a valuable genetic resource. They are a valuable gene pool for breeding and improvement programmes since selection processes, both natural and human, have occurred over the years and generations.

(g) Diversity acts as a safeguard against pests and disease. (FAO 1989)[41]

Animal Diversity

In addition to the variety of nutrition derived from food crops, diets are further augmented by animal products. Brownrigg's literature review (1985)[42] indicated that all types of Home Gardens support domesticated animals. Same is true for the Upper Rangit Valley study area. Poultry, pigs, cows, goats, sheep and buffalo are supported by most gardens in the area. It was however felt during the field visits, that far less attention is paid to animals than to plant species.

Labour Requirements for Home Garden Management

Larger Home Gardens of the size up to one hectare demand half hour to two hours of daily labour in the study area. The smaller gardens demand up to one hour of daily labour. 35-45 days of family labour per year are utilised at the initial establishment of Home Gardens. Subsequently approximately 30 days of the year are utilised towards tending of the gardens. There seems to be a clear sharing of tasks between women and men for the management of the Home Gardens. The initial heavy labour is done by men. Later women spend about 10 per cent of their working time on the gardens, while men work for 4-5 per cent of their working hours. Rich farmers from erstwhile Kazi families employ hired labour.

Interviews and Questionnaire Methodology

There were guided interviews conducted for checking different management issues for which farmer's opinion was wanted. The interviews were guided to cover the key topics on the checklist, while leaving room to pursue relevant subjects brought up by the farmers themselves. The semi-structured questionnaire is mentioned below:

Question 1. "What planting materials do you use for your Home Garden Plants?"

What did a farmer known about regeneration procedures with different Home Garden plants. This question was asked to elicit his knowledge. The relative advantages and disadvantages of various type of planting material for different species were ascertained through further questions.

Question 2. "What are the sources of different planting materials?"

This was to establish the relative contribution of different sources of planting materials.

Question 3. "Do you follow any criteria to select mother trees to collect planting materials?"

When this question was asked, farmer try to recall what he knew about the introduction of improved varieties of species in the Home Gardens. If the farmer said '*yes*' then details of the criteria for mother tree selection and the types of species for which mother trees are selected were sought with more questions.

Question 4. "What sizes of seedling are available to plant and which one do you prefer and why?"

This was to explore farmers silvicultural knowledge about different sizes of seedlings.

Question 5. "Do you adopt any spacing at the time of planting?"

This question was to gather information on horizontal arrangements of species in the Home Gardens. When the answer was 'yes' further questions were asked to ascertain the planting, spacing and the reasons for the same.

Question 6. "Do you carryout weeding, lopping, pruning, thinning, coppicing, pollarding in your Home Garden?"

Pruning determines how the farmers regulate sunlight in the Home Garden. Weeding and thinning determine the horizontal structure of the Home Gardens. Division of labour between men and women in these contexts was also discussed and answers sought.

Question 7. "Do you water and manure your Home Garden plants?"

This question was posed to produce an idea of the effort given to managing the Home Garden. When the reply was '*yes*' the frequency, quantity and calendar of watering and manuring, and the name of the species to which these were applied was determined with further questioning.

Socio-economic and Ecological Aspects of Home Gardens

Socio-economic aspects and community dynamics were closely observed. These were found to be important factors for maintaining the traditional systems. The interaction dynamics were mainly qualitative. The social, cultural, economic and management aspects are given at Figure 3.1.

Figure 3.1

Social Economic Aspects of Home Garden

Social	*Economic*	*Cultural*	*Management*
social functions	Productivity	Attitudinal Change	specific practices
Role of Women	Utilisation	Cultural ethos	Calendar of activities
Social Relationships	Provisions for adverse conditions	Social trends	Decision-making
		Social functions	Working pattern

The aspects of human ecology of the Home Gardens form an array and an internet of inter-relationships. Figure 3.2 amplifies the interactions.

Figure 3.2

Ecological Aspects of Home Gardens

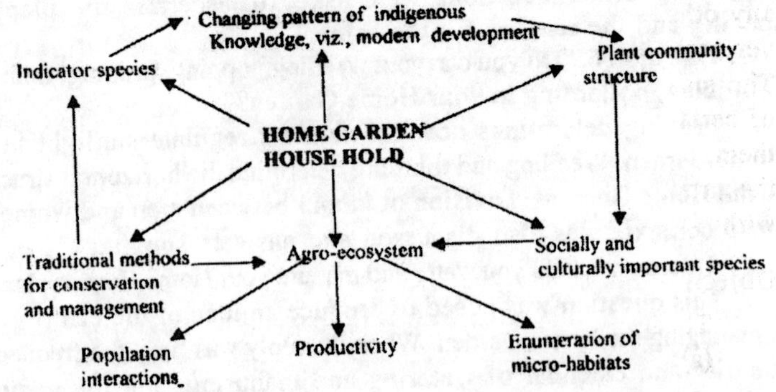

Conclusion

The home gardens in Sikkim have been used throughout and contenously : But this note been taken much notice of Sikkim Home Gardens are traditional resource management technologies, that have recently been hailed as highly productive and largely sustainable agroecosystems. The Home Garden is but one of a very large array of agroecosystems that traditional communities maintain.

Many of the species that are grown in Home Gardens are also found in agricultural fields and on the fallow lands adjacent to the households. Many are collected from nearby forestlands. Thus, Home Gardens of the Sikkim indegenous communities deserve to be examined in far greater detail. The study of Home Gardens could be used as a tool when methodologies for the application of traditional knowledge in conservation and community development are required to put in place.

Section III
Local Folk Market: A Survey of Modes of Transactions of Forest Produce Relating to Ethnobotany

Introduction

A local folk market survey exercise was undertaken there for the purposes of assessing availability of plant and animal products in and comparing it with the markets of Namchi and Gangtok. The local weekly market in Ravangla function on each wednesday.

Diversity in use of plant and animal resources is best reflected in local markets.

Wild food plants, medicinal plants, edible animal products and any other products of biological origin were found to be having a very specific regional value in day-to-day life of local community. The market survey included qualitative analysis and quantification of certain items, such as number of vendors, the products sold by them, commodities and prices. These were helpful in understanding the natural resource use patterns and availability of natural resources within the region.

Objectives

The main objectives of local market survey were:

(a) To assess the local use of resources.

(b) To determine natural resource use patterns for specific commodities.

(c) To understand the dependence of Ravangla locals and population of nearby rural folks on the surrounding resource areas.

(d) To evaluate the sustainability of the natural resources the factors responsible for it.

Methodology

A simple methodology was devised. It was used for this local market survey. It mainly involved participatory observations of the vendors and buyers alongwith use of semi-structured and structured interviews. These were composed with the surveys of the Home Gardens to check the origin of various commodities in the market.

Observations

Commodities Diversity

(a) The farmers were selling a variety of plants, animals and other products of biological origin. See Table 3.3 and 3.4 for some important wild plants available at Ravangla and their comparison of price range with the market price at Gangtok and Namchi. The prices at Ravangla are minimum, perhaps due to minimal labour costs in carting the products. Namchi is cheaper than Gangtok for the same reasons. The market at Gyalshing is quoted to be the cheapest in this regard.

(b) These products were either harvested from the Home Gardens or gathered from the wild.

(c) There was a clear division of Items available from the Sikkim hill/mountain regions and from the West Bengal plains, had a clear distinction.

(d) Most commodities were being sold raw, i.e., fruits, vegetables meat and fish. Dehydrated fish were available in plenty. Fermented bamboo shoots and Rhus seeds were however sold processed.

Vendors

(a) Permanent vendors occupy the main shelters erected in the market.

Table 3.3
Some Important Wild Plants Available in the Weekly Market at Ravangla in South Sikkim

Plant Species	*Local Name*	*Time of*	*No. of retailers*	*Ravangla Market Price (Rs)*
Bassia butyracea	Chiuri	May	5	3 per kg
Agaricus sp.	Chayo	Jun-Sep	2	15-25 per kg
Castanopsis tribuloides	Katus	Oct-Dec	2	30 per kg
Cinnamonum sp.	Sinkauli	Whole Year	4	30 per kg
Dendrocalamus hamiltonii	Tambu	Jun-Oct	2	12 per kg
Dioscorea sp.	Bantarul	Jan-Mar	5	5 per kg
Diplanzium sp.	Ningro	Mar-Aug	20	5 per kg
Elaeocarpus Sikkimensis	Bhadrase	Apr-Jun	1	10-15 per kg
Elaeagnus Latifolia	Malido	Feb-Mar	2	8 per kg
Emblica officinalis	Amala	Oct-Jan	3	5 per kg
Ficus benjamina	Kabra	Feb-Mar	2	8-10 per kg
Heracleum Wallichii	Chimfing	Aug-Nov	3	8 per unit
Junglans regia	Okhar	Sep-Nov	4	20 per kg
Machilus edulis	Pumsi	Jan-Feb	1	5 per unit
Rhus Succedanea	Timbur	Aug-Sep	2	3 per 50 gms
Rumex nepalensis	Halhale	Whole Year	2	10 per kg
Spondias axillaris	Labsi	Oct	2	5 per kg
Swerlia chirata	Chirauto	Jun-Dec	2	15-20 per kg
Tamarindus indica	Titri	Mar-May	3	4 per kg
Terminalia belerica	Barra	Whole Year	2	15-20 per kg
T Chebula	Harra	Feb-Mar	7	20 per kg
Urtica dioica	Sisnoo	Dec-Mar	7	2 per unit
Viscum album	Harchur	Whole Year	4	5-10 per kg

(b) Temporary vendors are allowed to occupy specific space allotted by the Sub-Division office at Ravangla.

(c) The number of temporary vendors far exceeds the permanent vendors.

(d) There were two types of vendors : temporary and permanent. The permanent vendors are generally Bhutias, while most temporary vendors are Nepalese of different castes, and Tibetans form the Tibetan Refugee Settlement named

Table 3.4
Some Important Wild Plants Available in the Weekly Market at Namchi and Gangtok in Sikkim

Plant species	*Local Name*	*Time availability*	*Namchi*		*Gangtok*	
			No. of Retailers	*Market price (Rs)*	*No. of Retailers*	*Market price (Rs)*
Agaricus sp.	Chayo	Jun-Sep	6	10-20*	8	15-25*
Bassia butyrace	Chiuri	May	6	3-5*	5	5-8*
Castanopsis tribuloides	Katus	Nov-Dec	7	40*	4	40-60*
Cinnamonum sp	Sinkauli	Whole year	10	30*	11	40*
Dendrocalamus hamiltonii	Tambu	Jun-Oct	4	12*	6	15*
Dioscorea sp.	Bantarul	Jan-Mar	5	12*	6	10*
Diplanzium sp.	Ningro	Mar-Aug	10	10-15*	13	15-20*
Elaeocarpus Sikkimensis	Bhadrase	Apr-Jun	3	10-20*	3	15-20*
Elaeagnus Latifolia	Malido	Feb-Mar	–	–	6	10*
Emblica officinalis	Amala	Oct-Jan	3	4*	–	-
Ficus benjamina	Kabra	Feb-Mar	5	8-10	2	15-20*
Heracleum Wallichii	Chimfing	Aug-Nov	4	10+	3	80+
Junglans regia	Okhar	Sep-Nov	8	20=	14	50=
Machilus edulis	Pumsi	Jan-Feb	8	15*	12	20-25*
Rhus Succedanea	Timbur	Aug-Sep	3	2-3++	5	3-5++
Rumex nepalensis	Halhale	Whole Year	4	10*	6	2++
Spondias axillari	Labsi	Oct	7	4*	10	5*
Swerlia chirata	Chirauto	Jun-Dec	4	15-20*	3	20-30*
Tamarindus indica	Titri	Mar-May	8	5*	10	8*
Terminalia belerica	Barra	Whole Year	3	20*	2	–
T Chebula	Harra	Feb-Mar	5	20=	5	25-30=
Urtica dioica	Sisnoo	Dec-Mar	7	5++	6	3++
Viscum album	Harchur	Whole Year	6	5-10*	4	15*

*per kg, oer 100 units+ per 50g++ per 100 g (Adopted from G.B. Pant Institute (46 Annual Report 1996-97).

Kunphenling on the southern outskirts of Ravangla. Marwaris who occupy permanent shops in main market do not open stalls in the weekly Wednesday market. Bengali and Bihari tradesmen who frequent other weekly markets in Sikkim also display utility items such as readymade clothing items, shoes and other household goods brought from wholesale market in Siliguri. Imported items (some of them locally made imitations) are also on display in some stalls.

(e) The market functions in the main bazaar square. The square functions as volleyball and basketball playfield on non-market days. The Indian Republic Day and Independence Day functions are also celebrated in the market square. This is also the focal point of all election rallies. As such, there no permanent structures available for the market.

Buyers

(a) Buyers include persons from all walks of life and from all ethnic groups. Government servants including soldiers from local military camp also frequent the market.

(b) The local villagers demand priority is household goods, clothing and other items brought from the plains of West Bengal.

(c) Ravangla locals mainly buy vegetables, meat, poultry and other ethnic commodities on display.

(d) Some individuals of both sexes frequenting the market freely indulge in consumption of 'chhang' and 'rakshi' locally processed fermented alcoholic drinks) and other Sikkim manufactured foreign liquor such as beer, rum, whisky and brandy. Beer is the most preferred drink with the local ethnics and the Tibetans of Kunphenling Settlement. Violence due to alcohol consumption is conspicuously absent.

Role of Women in the Local Markets

(a) It was observed that 80-85 per cent of vendors were women.

(b) Women vendors reported that men were engaged in collection of commodities from the wild.

(c) Women looked after management, cultivation, harvesting and processing of products. Men help in bringing the products from their village to the Ravangla market.

(d) In a way, Women are also beneficaries. A result of trading, they do achieve a certain control over the household economy, but it is usually restricted to using the money gained from marketing for buying necessary commodities such as clothes, toiletries, bamboo baskets etc.

Rhythms of the Market. It is very interesting to note the rhythms of the market, i.e., the changes that occur at regular intervals.

Rhythms of Ravangla Market (Most Vendors Are Women)

(a) During the first two hours there is a rush for sale of items such as perishable vegetables and freshly slaughtered meat. Marketing activities are at a peak during these two hours.

(b) After this initial sale range of commodities such as dried fish, spices, poultry meat, fermented bamboo shoots and chhang etc become available.

(c) The household goods stalls have a more or less regular sale during the entire day.

(d) The vendors in the market begin to thin out by 3 p.m. during winter months, and by 4 p.m. during summer months. By 5 p.m., barring hangers on, the market is virtually empty.

Statutory Framework

The first attempt for managing the bazaar activities under a statutory framework was in the form of Sikkim Bazaar Committees Act, 1969 and Gangtok Municipal Corporation Act, 1975. Both of these Acts were repealed by the Sikkim (Repeal and Miscellaneous Provision) Act, 1985. Under this Act, the functions, powers and duties of the Bazaar Committee and Gangtok Municipal Corporation were transferred to and vested in the State Government in the Housing and Urban Development Department (Mahandra Lama, 1994)[43].

Strategy for Development

The role of the informal sectors has to be recognised as a potential for employment generation. A state like Sikkim which has an agrarian base and ample natural resources for development, would have to encourage the local market systems for its products and employment generation, mainly for the following reasons:

(a) The markets act as a first contact point for local residents, petty traders and small farmers.

(b) They provide place for distribution of local produce and exchanging rural surplus.

(c) They provide an opportunity to petty traders and small farmers for earning their livelihood.
(d) They provide place for buying daily necessities as well as farm supplied foods and implements, at less expensive prices, especially to the small farmers.
(e) They play a vital role in well being of small farmers, petty and mobile traders.
(f) They are the best mechanism of serving a dispersed population, mostly agrarian in nature with limited demand.
(g) The means of transportation still being difficult, and many commodities being of perishable nature, dispersed market places, not involving big investment for development, are the best alternatives.

Conclusion

In semi-urban townships of Sikkim weekly markets have there own utility. They focus on local demands. Such local market surveys could be used to identify local resource needs. Such studies would also help to assess the role of existing agroecosystems in natural resource use and management.

Quantitative studies carried out during such market surveys will help to evaluate the sustainability of resource use. Such studies can also identify commercial opportunities in resource utilisation, and may also be used to develop enterprise potential for economic and environmental sustainability. Local markets and transactions within them throw light on cultural aspects of natural resource use patterns.

Suggestions/Recommendations

There are many wild vegetables, fruits and even animals. They are much in demand. They need to be domesticated. That way their availability will increase. This will afford following advantages:

(a) Domestication will help to reduce the pressure on existing forests and ensure a continuous supply.
(b) Some vegetables and fruits have a high demand but cannot be marketed because of non-availability of proper post-harvest technology and storage facilities. Specific research is needed to develop post-harvest technology and storage facilities.
(c) The market is unorganised. Domestication, improved post-harvest techniques and organised markets will help to achieve proper and sustainable resource use.

Simple village folk do not understand statutory. These laws need to be simplified for their benefit. The banking and loan procedures should be made simple, and the by-laws be made clearly understood to the rural vendors.

Section IV
Dietary Culture of Local Ethnic Communities of the Study Area

Introduction

General

Availability of food, vegetables, fruits depend on many ecological factors. These factors ought to be available in the culture of the land. These factors include climatic conditions, vegetal zones, local faunal and floral diversity, agroecosystems, socio-religious factors and the application of traditional ecological knowledge.

The term 'culture' includes symbolic, social and economic factors, which in interaction with sensory tastes and preferences shape food patterns and influence the selection of foods. The collective eating habits of a cultural group forms a 'cultural cuisine'. The term cultural cuisine is used to describe, "The culturally elaborated and transmitted body of food related practices of any given culture." This includes (Messer, 1989)[44]:

(a) The selection of a set of basic (staple or secondary) foods.
(b) The frequent use of characteristic set of flavourings.
(c) The characteristic processing (e.g., chopping and cooking) of such foods.
(d) The adoption of a variety of rules dealing with acceptable foods and combinations, the social context of eating and the symbolic use of foods.

People eat discontinuously; that is, food is structured into breakfast, lunch, dinner and supper in a 24 hour cycle. The cycle differs for each culture or ethnic group, and also for gender and age groups. Within cuisines, people select foods to conform particular styles of eating, as well as cultural concepts of what items are edible and preferred, and how they should be prepared and served.

Dietary Structure in Sikkim

The inhabitants of the Upper Himalayan region, including those of the upper Rangit Basin (above 2500 m) have common dietary

Table 3.5
Indigenous Fermented Foods of the Sikkim Himalaya

Fermented Food	*Substrate*	*Nature of Use*
Common fermented foods		
Kinema	Soybean	Cooked soybeans showing stickyness with Typical flavour; side dish
Gundruk	Leafy vegetable	Dried, sour-acidic taste; soup, pickle
Sinki	Radish root	-do-
Selroti	Rice/wheat flour	Pretzel-like, deep fried; confectionary bread (doughnut)
Dahi	Milk	Thick-gel; savory (yoghurt)
Mohi	Milk	Butter-milk; non-alcoholic drink
Chhurpi	Milk	Soft-mass is used for curry, pickle. Hard mass is consumed as masticatory
Sukako masu	Mutton/beef/pork/ Yak	Smoked meat; curry
Common fermented beverages		
Marchaa	Rice, wild herbs, Spices	Solid, dry, while cake-like starter culture to ferment beverages
Kodo jaanr	Finger millet	Mildly alcoholic, slightly acidic-sweet beverage.
Bhaate jaanr	Rice	-do-
Makai jaanr	Maize	-do-
Raksi	Starchy substrate	Distilled alcoholic drink
Lesser-known fermented foods		
Masauyra	Black gram	Ball-like hollow; spicy condiment
Mesu	Bamboo shoot	Sour-acidic flavour; pickle.
Khalpi	Cucumber	-do-
Somar	Milk	Soft-mass paste, brownish colour with Strong flavour; condiment

habits as the Tibetans. Balance of the inhabitants, which form over 95 per cent of the total population use traditional fermented and non-fermented foods and beverages to provide basic components of diet with diverse characteristics of nutrition, flavour, palatability and texture. For many centuries, the people of this region prepare and consume varieties of traditional fermented and non-fermented food products (Tamang et al 1988; Tamang 1998)[45-46]. This is a unique dictary culture.

The cereal-based fermented food products are mostly consumed as alcoholic beverages. The *Bhat-dal-tarkari-achar* (rice-legume-soup-curry-pickle) constitute the daily food supply in the meal. Rice is the staple food.

Fermented Foods

General

Fermented foods are defined as the products that have been subjected to action of selected microorganisms in the substrates changing texture, aroma and flavour, and are acceptable for human consumption (Kwon 1994, Steinkraus 1994, Campbell-Platt 1994)[47-49].

More than seventeen varieties of indigenous fermented foods are traditionally prepared and consumed by the people at households level for long centuries in Sikkim (Table 3.5). The people of the Sikkim Himalaya developed traditional food processing technology for preparing fermented foods from locally available substrates largely governed by the ethnic preference, the agro climatic conditions, socio-cultural ethos and religion. People might not be knowing what was going on during fermentation in terms of scientific knowledge, but they certainly knew what they had to do to get desired products. This is how indigenous fermented foods emerged as the basic components of diet and reflect a dietary-culture of the various ethnical groups of people in the Sikkim Himalaya (Tamang 1995b)[50]. These inexpensive culturally acceptable traditional foods supplement enhanced nutritional qualities, palatability, imparting appealing flavour and increased shelf-life. Some of the common fermented foods have been cited here. Figure 3.3 depicts distillation apparatus, and drinking vessels for consumption of *'raksi'*.

Kinema

Kinema curry is delicious local cuisine eaten along with boiled rice in main meals (Tamang 1996)[51]. Kinema is an indigenous fermented soybean food, which serves as a sustainable supply of low-cost source of high protein food in the local diet.

Synonym of kinema in local language

Kinemba (Limbu)
Hokuma (Rai)
(Bhutia) Bari
Satlyangser (Lepcha)

Similar products like kinema

Hawaijar (Manipur in North-East India)
Bekang-um (Mizoram in North-East India)
Troombai (Meghalaya)
Akhoni (Nagaland)
Itohiko-natto (Japan)
Tooa-nao (Northern Thailand)
Chungkook-jang (Korea) (Tamang 1998)[52]

Gundruk and Sinki

Gundruk and Sinki are consumed as soup and pickle in main meals. They are very popular fermented vegetable products traditionally prepared during winter when perishable vegetables are plenty. The quality attributes to gundruk and sinki basically depends upon the typical flavour and acidic taste.

Synonyms of gundruk

Gunduru (Newar)
Mashit (Rai)
Kandruk (Limbu)

Synonyms of Sinki

Sinke (Newar)
Samchetwa (Rai)
Thektubalawak (Limbu)

Socio-economy of gundruk and sinki

Some rural people are economically dependent upon these products. They sell gundruk and sinki usually during winter in the local markets. Cost of gundruk is Rs 60 to Rs 70 per kg, and sinki is Rs 50 to Rs 60 per kg. The technique of gundruk and sinki production has been limited to household level and transferred from mother to daughter.

Similar products

Kimchi (Korea)
Sauerkraut (Germany)
Sunki (Japan)

Mesu

Mesu is similar to *naw-mai-dong,* fermented bamboo-shoot of Thailand. It is a traditional fermented bamboo-shoot pickle with sour acidic flavour confined to limited places. The word mesu is directly derived from the Limbu dialect meaning "me" the young bamboo-shoot, "su" soury taste.

Fresh mesu has a shelf-life of only about a week, its pickle can be stored for a year or more (Tamang and Sarkar 1996)[53]. In the traditional method of mesu preparation, young edible shoots of bamboo are defoliated, chopped, pressed tightly into a hollow bamboo stem, covered tightly with leaves of bamboo and left to ferment at ambient temperature for 7-15 days.

Some rural women sell mesu at local markets. The cost of 2.50 g of fresh mesu is about Rs 5.00 which is sold in the green bamboo stem.

Marchaa

Marchaa is not a food. It is a mixed inocula used as a starter culture for preparation of various indigenous fermented mild alcoholic sweet-acidic food beverages such as *kodo* jaanr, bhaate jaanr, makai jaanr, etc. Marchaa is dried round to flattended, creamy white solid ball like starter. Size of marchaa varies from 1.9 to 11.8 cm in diameter with the weight ranging from 2.3 to 21.3 g (Tamang et. al., 1996)[54].

Synonym of marchaa

Khesung (Limbu)
Bopkha/Khabed (Rai)

Phab (Bhutia)
Buth/Thanbum (Lepcha)

Similar products

Bakhar (Noth-west India)
Ragi (Indonesia)
Nuruk (Korea)
Bubod (The Philippines)
Loogpang (Thailand)
Chiu-yueh (China)

Marchaa makers are confined to the Limbu caste and some Rai caste and the Lepcha of these regions. The trade is protected as a hereditary right of these castes. Price of marchaa depends on the size.

Ethno-Implication

Worshipping Gods and Goddesses with alcoholic beverages such as jaanr and raksi is deep-rooted ritual of the various ethnical groups of people in the Sikkim Himalaya. During marriage, traditional fermented beverage is obligatory to solemnize the ceremony for non-Brahmin Nepali Bhutia and Lepcha. On the other hand, to solemnise marriage, fermented dairy product is essence to Brahmin Nepali to whom drinking alcohol is a religious taboo. Indigenous fermented foods whether alcoholic or non-alcoholic, not only provide nutrients to local diet but influence customs of the people in these regions.

Non-fermented Foods

Introduction

Non-fermented foods make the bulk of the diet of the Sikkimmese population. According to Yonjan and Tamang (1998)[55] 90.2 per cent of the diet consists of non-fermented foods, while balance 9.8 per cent consists of foods which are fermented.

Traditional Non-Fermented Foods

The traditional non-fermented foods are tabulated below (Tamang, J.P. and Tamang, N. 1998)[56].

Table 3.6
Traditional Non-fermented Foods of the Sikkim Himalaya

Product	*Ingredient*	*Nature and use*
Foods common to the Nepali		
Dheroh	Maize/millet	Cooked maize/millet; staple food
Phulaurah	Buckwheat	Deep-fried, snack
Khalo dal	Black gram	Thick dal, staple
Sidra	Dry small fish	Roasted dry fish, achar
Kwathi	Legumes	Cooked sprouted legumes; curry
Kodo ko roti	Finger millet	Baked millet flour; staple food
Phapar ko roti	Buckwheat	Baked buckwheat flour; staple food
Chambray	Rice	Soaked, fried and cooked rice; staple
Rayo sag	Brasicca spp (Leaf)	Fried vegetable; cooked leafy vegetable
Ban tarul	Dioscorea hamiltonii	Boiled/roasted
Shimrayo	Cardamine hirsuta	Boiled/roasted
Ghario Sishnu	Urtica dioica: nettle	Boiled and cooked; soup
Patle Sishnu	Laportee terminalis	Boiled and cooked; soup
Bhangrey Sishnu	Girardinia diversifolia	Boiled and cooked; soup
Sauney Ningro	Diplazium polypodiodes	Fried vegetable, mix with meat/ chhurpi
Kali Ningro	Diplazium spp.Fern	Fried vegetable, mix with meat/ chhurpi
Tama	Young bamboo shoot	Boiled; curry
Kalungey Cheu	Agaricus sivaticus	Curry
Kanney Cheu	Pleurotus sajor-caju	Curry
Chhwelaa	Buff meat	Boiled, cooked meat curry
Lhakha mari	Wheat flour	Deep fried, sweet confectionery
Siltimbur	Listea cubeba	Pickle
Chinday	Pentapanax leschnaultii	Pickle
Lapsi	Choerospondis axillaris	Pickle
Dalle khorsani	Green/red chilli	Pickle
Thotne	Aconogonum molle	Pickle
Koirala	Bauhinia vareigata	Pickle
Chinping	Heracleum nepalenese	Pickle

Product	*Ingredient*	*Nature and use*
Kukurdaine	Smilax sp	Pickle
Kabra	Ficus infecdoria	Pickle
Silam		Pickle
Vatamas ko achar	Soybean	Pickle
Philinge		Pickle
Foods Common to the Bhutia		
Momo	Wheat flour/meat/vegetable	Steamed dumpling; staple food
Thukpa/Gyathuk	Wheat noodle	Boiled, mixed with minced meat; staple
Shya phaley	Wheat flour, meat	Stuffed, fried mixed with meat
Chempo	Pork/beef	Liver cooked in sauce
Phituk	Rice/barley flour	Porridge with meat/chhurpi; staple
Phing	Vermicelli	Cooked with mushrooms, meat; soup
Khuri	Milet/buckwheat flour	Roll with meat and vegetable; snack
Phaktoo	Macroni	Macroni, cooked with meat; soup
Nya phachung	Fish	Fish baked in bamboo, side dish
Zhero	Wheat	Deep fried; Snack
Khapjay	Wheat	Deep fired; snack
Quasi	Wheat flour	Deep-fried, cookies; snack
Tsampa	Rice/Barley	Roasted and ground
Yonten	Fried churpi	Fried in butter. Looks like staple momo
Foods Common to the Lepcha		
Kasalok	Sweet potato/yam	Cooked roots; staple
Sorongbee tulak	Rice and nettle	Cooked as porridge; staple
Cho-nyok	Rice, butter, vegetable	Cooked as porridge; staple

A Case Study of Dzongri and Tsoka Dietary Structure in High Altitude Settlements

Dzongri and Tsoka and the higher reaches of Singalila Ridge consist almost entirely of subsistance agriculturists and pastoralists. Dzongri and Tsoka have long been part of the Tibetan cultural world. The eating habits of the inhabitants also are quite akin to Tibetans.

Dzongri and Tsoka food habits as listed by the villagers are as under:

(a) **Tukpa** (*thug. pa*) (soup/stew containing water, vegetable oil, onion, salt, dried cheese, dried peas, wheat flour and optionally meat and in summer, fresh vegetables).

(b) **Tukpa namtuk** (*thus.pa.nam.thug*) (soup/stew containing water, tsampa (l.c) and salt).

(c) **Tukpa Pahtuk** (*thug.pa.phag.thug*) (soup/stew as tukpa, using butter in place of vegetable oil).

(d) **Tagyi** (*ta.qyi*) (flat unleavened bread made with wheat flour and water).

(e) **Tagyi taltak** (*ta.gyi.pral.dag*) (spherical unleavened bread, made with wheat flour and water).

(f) **Tagi skyurchuk** (*to.gyi.sKyur.chug*) (muffin-shaped slightly leavened bread, made of wheat flour and chang (q.v).

(g) **Paba** (*Phag.phag*) (solid doughy balls, consisting of a mixture of part-roasted wheat and barley flour, water, salt and ground dried peas).

(h) **Skiu** (*sKyu*) (small dumplings of wheat flour and water, boiled in a meat and spice broth).

(j) **Cha** (*ja*) (butter tea, made with boiling water, tea leaves, salt and butter, frequently consumed with *tsampa*.

(k) **Tsampa** (*tsam.pa*) (ground roasted barley grains, occasionally with ground roasted dried pea).

(1) **Kolakh** (*ka.lag M*solid doughy balls, consisting of a mixture of tsampa (q.v) and cha (q.v) or tsiri (q.v).

(m) **Chang** (*chang*) (a mild 'beer', made by fermentation of barley grains).

(n) **Tsiri** (*tsi.ri*)(*watered* down chang (q.v)).

(o) **Das** (*bras*) (rice).

(p) **Dasil** (*bras.sil*) frice. with melted butter and sugar). *a.lu* (patatoes) *nyung.ma* (turnip) *gobi* (cabbage).

(q) **Saraktuman** (*sa.rag.tur.man*) (carrot) *la. bug* (radish) *lo.ma* (radish leaves) *sran.ma* (peas)

(r) **Momo** (*mog.mog*) (dough ball (wheat flour), filled with a mixture of meat, onion, spices and salt, and steamed).

(s) **Oma** (*ao.ma*) (milk),

(t) **Tara** (ta.ra) (buttermilk)

(u) **Labo** (*la.* fto) (fresh cheese)

(v) **Churpi** (*chur.pe*) (dried cheese)
yos (roasted whole barley grains)
tsa.mig (mixture of chili seeds, salt fresh chopped onion

and radish leaves, and buttermilk; usually eaten with paba)
pha. ting (Apricots)
ka.ra (sugar)
mar (butter, from milk of drimo (female yak)
or dzomo (female yak cow hybrid)
jo (yogurt)
tsong (onion)
pemar (soild doughy balls, made as kolakh (q.v) with the addition óf cheese and sugar and butter)
tso. chu (thickened broth, made by addi salt, spices, water and a little meat to small amount of paba (q.v)).
Chub.tsos (small dumplings of wheat flour and water, boiled in a broth with spices and salt).

Conclusion

The food intake of the populace also largely depends upon the economic conditions of individuals . Availability of food in the environment and the relative cost, both in money and time of acquiring and then processing are different for different classes of people. The overall dietary concept however remains common. This section of the chapter on ethnobotany of the Upper Rangit Basin inhabitants has reviewed the factors and structures of their dietary habits.

Section VI
Non-Timber Forest Products in Yuksom: A Survey

General Description of Yuksom

The lowest altitude of Yuksom at the Rathang Chu is about 700 m which goes upto 3000 m in the forest situated above Yuksom. It is bound on its NW & SW by Rathang Chu. The habitation is mostly on the spurs and gentle slopes. There is one village called Ramjithang which in Lepcha means the deposit of landslide. The area is steep to precipitous except the spurs and the main Yuksom, Khyontey and Norbugang. Most of the natural forests up to 1800 m are converted into settlements. Easier slopes wherever available are under cultivation, and steeper, rocky areas covered with either secondary growth or bamboos.

Areas where paddy used to be grown once are replaced with cardamom under *Alnus(alder)* trees of about 25 years in age conversion. This was done on account of poor paddy production, On the south-west side above the road to Pelling from Yuksom, there has been large scale landslide caused by construction of approach road to the Rathong Dam site. *Castanopsis,* Oaks, Laurel, Maple, Rhododendron with thick under growth of Maling bamboo, *Rebus, Daphne, Symplocos, Eurya, Viburnum* ferns, are found in plenty in forests around Dubdi Monastery and above 1800 m. etc.

Historical Importance. From Yuksom if one walks for 15 minutes he will be in Norbugang where one can see a Royal sear in stone masonry where the crowning ceremony of the first Chogyal, Dharma Raja of Sikkim took place under guidance of Lhotsum Chhenbo, a Tibetan priest from Tibet. It has also the distinction of having the oldest monastery, Dubdi. Therefore, Yuksom is regarded as the first capital of Sikkim.

Folk Belief. The Famrang Fall on the entry from Tashiding and view of Kanchendzonga while entering from Pelling side are attractive sites for outsiders as well as the locals. The snowclad Pandim mountains on its North looks like the shining crown on its head. There are two holy lakes, Kathok within Yuksom and another Khecheopalri some distance away from Yuksom which sanctifies the whole region. There is belief of the people that the Khechopalri was once in Yuksom itself as the female consort of Kathok but on account of neglect and pollution by the people it shifted to its present position. The depression with opening is still there on South West of Yuksom Bazaar indicating the old site of its existence. How far this belief is true is not easy to ascertain. It remains a folklore. However, one can say, Yuksom is endowed with rich natural beauties.

Besides these, rich forests surround the upper boundary, which goes right up to alpine region. These have been the source of clean water in the various rivers and streams that flow through Yuksom. Under the cool shades of these forests and in the folds of these Himalayan mountain there are a large number of plants in Yuksom are important medicines, which are used by local people even to cure serious diseases, sprains, cuts and fractures etc. Rich treasure of forest products other than timber are available that are so important to sustain the life system. They consist of bamboos, broomstick grass, fruit trees, buds, leaves, flowers, valuable medicinal plants, mushrooms, ferns, natural decoratives, etc.

The language specialists deserve special thanks by giving the names of different species in their own languages. The names of each languages specialist is given against the following languages: Limbu (Lm) Sri Man Bahadur Subba of Topsing, Sri H.B. Khamdak, Limbu teacher of Yuksom High School, Sri Sanchabir Subba of

Khyongtey village. Bhutia (SkBh): Sri Sonam Wangdi of Yuksom. Lepcha (Lp): Sri Sonam Tshering Lepcha of Yuksom and Sri Motey Lepcha of Khyongtey village. Gurung (Gn): Megraj Gurung, President Simmik Gurung (Tamu) Youth Association. Sherpa (Sh) Phurbu Sherpa. Shri SD Lama (IFS) provided most researched data as presented in this section of this chapter.

Sikkim Biodiversity and Ecotourism receives support from the collaborating institutions and communities, donations and grants obtained from the United States Agency for International Development including support from the Biodiversity Conservation Network (a programme of the Biodiversity Support Programme, a consortium of World Wildlife Fund, the nature conservancy and the World Resources Institute), and the Bureau of Humanitarian Response. This project is a collaboration of the Mountain Institute (USA), G.B. Pant Institute of Himalayan Environment and Development. The Travel Agents Association of Sikkim and the Green Circle.

Non-Timber Forest Products Uses

Till the recent past, transportation and communication was a matter of concern for Sikkim. People depended for their requirement of food, fuel, fibre, fruits and medicines on these products called Non Timber Forest Products (NTFP). Bamboos and canes were used commonly by local people for construction of bridges across various hill streams as the only means of communication. The section aims at bringing out the various non-timber forest products, identify them with the help of local people in their own languages and its underlying importance as essential commodities of our life system, so that awareness is created for their propagation and preservation. A total of 72 NTFPs of Yuksom are described under the following headings:

1. **Bamboos.** There are more than 10 varieties of bamboo in Yuksom. Here only 8 varieties of economic importance are given. Most of the bamboos are cultivated except Niglo, Gopey and Maling. The Pareng bamboo though cultivated, is also found in village forest and government forest. Some carrier items made of out of bamboo stripes are shown at Figure 3.4.
2. **Amliso (Broom Grass).** Market forces have come in the way of cultivation of this variety. Though Government had also supported its extension through social forestry scheme and people also had necessary will to plant this grass as cash crop for its broomstick, but its slide in price from 1997's harvest of January-February has seriously affected the interest of the growers.

However, the value of this grass as cattle fodder and soil stabiliser should not be lost sight of.

3. **Fruits, Berries etc.** Trees in forest as well as on own land offer a variety of fruits not only to human beings as nutritional diet but they are good source of food for wild life as well as birds. Some of them happen to be good medicines also. Some 23 fruits bearing trees are described in this report.
4. **Buds-Young Shoots and Leaves.** There are a number of trees in forest whose young shoots, leaves and flowers are eaten as vegetable or made into pickle. Some of them also are sources of medicine. Six plants are described under this section.
5. **Medicinal Plants.** A host of plants available in Yuksom and around are used by local practitioners (Bijuwa or Baidya) of herbal medicines, But there are medicinal plants who herebal efficacy is not known. However, the idea of giving detailed use of these plants under Ayurved or Unani is to create awareness about these valuable species. The details of medicinal plants are enumerated in another section of this chapter.
6. **Decoratives.** Natural forests are source of varieties of natural attractive materials in the form of decoratives. Roots of plants, dry flower, capsules, dry, mushrooms cones of conifers, leaves of fern, fern shoots, seeds of 'totala' all go to form decoratives of all designs and imaginations. In Yuksom nothing is done in this field.
7. **Mushrooms.** 11 varieties of mushrooms are available in Yuksom in Yuksom. Except one, all are found on natural dead wood during rains. Local people collect and eat them. Only eight varieties are described under this chapter.
8. ***Diplazium* (Ningro).** Good quantity of Diplazium (Ningo) comes to market during rains. Many directly collect and take the young shoots of fern as good vegetable. Three varieties of Ningros are described here. They form important vegetables for the local people.
9. **Yams.** Forest have a number of dioscoreas which provide food to people through their yams. Only one variety, i.e., *Dioscorea* (Ban Tarul) is collected from forest. The other dioscorea that is *D. bulbifera* (Ghar Tarul) is cultivated in lower zones upto 1000m. The first one only is described.
10. **Fibres.** Argeli (*Edgeworthia*) and Lokhtey (*Daphne*) are two plants widely used by locals for making fibre materials. These plants especially Argeli grows abundantly in and around Yuksom.

Description, Habitat and NTFP Uses

Bamboos

(*a*) Dendrocalamus sikkimensis– Bhalu Bans, Dhiri Bans, Dhungra Bans (Np), Patek pu (Lp), Hang bha (Lm), dhungsing (Bh), Patep (Sp), Ngugma (Tb), Rein Rama (Gu).

Description: Very large and handsome bamboo growing in the lower hill valley upto 1800 m. Density tufted, evergreen culms erect 25-30 m high. Internodes 35-50 cm, diameter 15-20 cm.

Habitat: It is available in Yuksom upto 1800 m.

Uses: The Sherpas call it Tolang. It is also split and used for making walls, partition of houses and shades, floors and fencing of garden. Pictures drawn on small pieces can form good decorative pieces. Local artisan could be trained on this art, which may become good source of income through sale to tourists. The local people use it for carrying water, churning milk to make butter milching bucket, etc.

(*b*) Dendrocalamus hamiltonii– Tama or Choya bans (Np), Yekyot-pao (Lp), Dheybha (Lm), Chhasing (Bh) Rie (Gu).

Description: It is the most common tufted forest bamboo. The culms have thick walls when old. The lower parts are glaubose. The culms grow upto 24 m high with 10-18 cm diameter, intermodes are 30-50 cm.

Habitat: The bamboo is found naturally occurring in village forest it is also cultivated in the village up to 1730 m in Khoyngtey above Yuksom bazaar.

Uses: Matured culms are used for construction of houses for structural purpose and as fencing material. Bigger culms are used as water-conduit, water carrying vessels called Dhiri. Its bigger internodes are made into beer jug called Tongba. Young shoots are extensively collected in July-August and eaten as vegetable or made into pickles. Semi-fermented tama is sold in the market as "meso." It can be preserved and used in off season to add flavour and taste to curry. Very good bending cane is extracted from outer layer of this bamboo which is locally called choya, hence, the name choya bans. This also forms good raw material for paper pulp. The leaves form good fodder for cattle. Also these bamboos can be made into decorative pieces.

(*c*) Dendrocalamus hookeri– Chilley Bans (Np), Pata (Lp), Rein Pochoarey (Gn).

Description: Tufted culms 18 to 20 m, internodes 45 to 50 cm, diameter 7.5-12 cm. Stem bright green smooth, young ones covered with brown hairy sheaths gradually narrowed from a broad based to a truncate at top.

Habitat: This bamboo is cultivated quite extensively in Yuksom for use in various constructional purposes upto 1750 m.

Uses: Used in wall and roof structures, fencing support ot squash etc. The shoot is bitter hence not eaten. However, some villagers boil and throw the water and eat the shoot as vegetable, like that of *D.hamiltonii.*

(*d*) Arundinaria hookeriana– Pareng (Np), Pagjiok po (Lp), Parangma (Lm), Paran (SK, Bh) Chyoba rien (Gn).

Description : Medium sized tufted bamboos with glaucous stem, Culms 4 to 10 m, internodes 20-30 cm, diameter 20-40 mm.

Habitat: Between 1200m to 2100m in village forest as well as reserved forest in Yuksom.

Uses: It is used for making mats, roofing materials for houses shades, baskets of various sizes, winnowing tray, etc. Roofs are also built with short splits of this bamboo. The shoots from the villagers own field are taken as vegetable.

(*e*) Arundinaria intermedia– Niglo (Np), Parmiok (Lp), Thing mey (Lm), Barming (Sk, Bh), Thing ningma (Sh), Reen chetowa (Gu).

Description: Small thin bamboo. Height 2.5-3.5 m internode 12-25 mm.

Habitat: They are found on dry slopes of village forest between 1200 m to 2100 m.

Uses: It is used for making mats, baskets, house tieing by its cane etc.

(*f*) Arundinaria racemosa– Malingo (Np), Mikla (Lm), Phiung (Sk, Bh), Ningma (Sh), Phylum, Pervok (Lp), Rien chayba (Gn).

Description: It is the most common bamboo of the forest of Yuksom, grows gregariously,single stemmed, 3-10 m high with internodes 30-35 cm. Its diameter is 15-40 mm.

Habitat: 1850 m upward upto 2750 m in forest of Yuksom.

Uses: It is extensively used for making roofing mats, basket fencing, walking stick and flute. The splitted pieces are used in reinforcement of wall. Villagers are seen collecting this bamboo in two bundles of 30 each with 3.0 m length for above purpose from forest.

(*g*) Bamhoosa nutans– Mala bans, Mahlu (Np), Multapha (Lm), Thuysing (Sk,Bh) Leemalu po (Lp), Malarien (Gn),

Description: Large, graceful bamboo, stem solitary grows upto a height of 6-20 m internode 30-60 cm, 5-12 cm diameter, wall thick, 300-1550 m.

Habitat: It is cultivated extensively below the road to Pelling from Yuksom, at an altitude of 1300mm.

Uses: Buddhists use this bamboo as prayer flagstaffs. This bamboo has hardwood this is used for structural purposes such as poles, support for shuttering in building construction. Many split this bamboo and use it as reinforcement in cement or earth plastered house in the villages. Also used for making basket.

(*h*) *Cephalostachium capitatum,* Gopey bans (Np), Yuem (Lm), Pangrim (Sk,Bh), Peyong (Lp), Rein Kayey (Gn).

Description: It is gregarious, densely branching, more or less scandent, culms 3, 5-10 m, yellow internodes 60-90 long, 25-40 mm diameter. Leaves pale green ovate-lanceolate blade 15-20 cm.

Habitat: In Sikkim its starts occurrence at 600 and goes up to 2400 m. Plants are found scattered in steep slopes in village forest in lower zone and in Reserved Forest at higher reaches

Uses: The leaves are excellent fodder. Culms are used by Lepchas for making bows and arrows. The internode also makes good flutes. The locals use the bamboo for making straw for drinking local beer (Chhang).

Bamboo Flowering: Almost all the species of bamboo flower gregariously followed by its death. The profuse seeds that fall after flowering regenerates in the entire area provided it is not damaged by fire. Different bamboos flower at various intenvals vaying between 12 years to 25 years.

Broom Grass

(*a*) Thysanolacna maxima– Amliso (Np), Setlu (Lrn), Passeam (Sk,Bh) Passeor (Lp), Chakusey (Sh), Burdhun (Gn).

Description: A very large glabrous grass growing upto 1-4 m high, diameter of the stem upto 12 mm. Leaves broad flat 60-40 cm by 5-10 cm coriaceous, tapering to a tine point. it has typical dented mark across the leaf blade at 2/3rd Its length. The panicles are 0.4-12 m long from the broomstick.

Habitat: Grows in the sub-tropical Himalayas from plains io 2000 m altitude. It is extensively planted in the hills in waste land and as inter-crop in agroforestry system and also on edges of terraces.

In lower villages the amliso is cutivated for the last 4-5 years in small areas and on edges of terraces with government incentives.

Uses : The leaves serve as very good fodder for the cattle especially during the lean period. The stick are used as fuelwood after drying. The inflorescence produces the soft broom for cleaning the floors.

The following table gives the per hectare production of broom stick, green fodder and drystick as per study conducted in Karmat village at 600 m altitude in of Darjeeling District (Lama 1998)[51].

Age (year)	*Dry Broom (kg)*	*App value (Rs)*	*Green fodder (Kgs)*	*App value (Rs)*	*Dry stick (Kg)*	*App value (Rs)*	*Per ha value (Rs)*	*Fodder for cattle*
1.5	676	6780	7040	3520	313	313	10593	141
2.5	1099	10990	12400	6200	708	708	17898	248
3.5	1553	15530	11800	5900	605	605	22035	236
4.5	882	8820	9640	4820	388	388	14028	193
5.5	595	5950	7240	3620	215	215	9785	145

From the above table it transpires that with every year the crop production starts failing from 3.5 years onwards. This calls for application of fertilizer and replacement of old clumps by new vigorous seedlings.

Fruit Bearing Trees

(*a*) Castanopsis hystrix, Patle Katus (Np), Chestnut (Eng), Seybheuengma (Lm), Sumsi (Sk, Bh), Kushukung (Lp), Kasing (Gn) Kasyopot (Sh).

Description: Generally medium sized tree rarely large size, young shoots pubescent, leaves thinly coriaceous entire sometime serrate near the apex long acuminate. Blade 10- 20 cm. Flowers March-April, Fruits October-December.

Habitat: Occurs quite gregariously in upper hill forest of Yuksom between 1800 m to 2450 m altitude.

Uses: The dry leaves are collected for making bedding of cattle and form very good compost. The seads from this tree occur at an interval of 3-4 years. They are collected by villagers either for sale or for consumption.

(*b*) Castanopsis tribuloids, Musre Katus (Np), Khechingsey (Lm), Sokey kap (Sk, Bh), Kushu nok (Lp), Seshy (Sh).

Description: This is a middle sized rarely large tree. Stem rough, irregular, bark grayish. Leaves thinly coriaceaous, entire sometime serrate near the apex, lanceolate, long acuminate. Blade 10-20 cm upper side glabrous, underside pale or reddish sometimes pubescent. Spikes are upto 25 cm long spikes upto 10 mm long, usually on short ridges, often stellate on branches. Nuts 1-3 glabrous when mature, cotyledons ruminated flowers in March-April Fruits in October-December.

Habitat: It is found gregariously growing near the Forest Rest House in Yuksom and around and below Dubdi Monastery.

Uses: Same as C. *hystrix*

(*c*) Quercus pachyphylla, Sungurey Katus (Np), Mikthumba (Lm), Den (Sk, Bh), Songpang-kung, Sarob-kung, Sri-Kung (Lp), Oak (Eng).

Description: Large sized trees with spreading crown. Leaves entire, acuminate, glabrous above with minute stellate hairs. Leaves 12 to 20 cm long. Flower in June-July. Fruits in November in clusters with thick cover, covering nuts more than half it portion.

Habitat: Grows between 1830 to 3000 m along with patley Katus, Buk, Maple and laurel and in upper zone with rhododendron.

Uses: Bears enjoy the acorns for which they break branches and make temporary abode at the top. The bark and acorns are used as astringents in Sikkim. Similar use is made from the bark and acorns of *Quercus semicarpifolia* another oak that occurs in the hills between 1830 to 2450 m its leaves are broader and silvery underneath with prominent lateral nerves. The nuts are found and dried and made into flour out of which bread used to be made in the past as per version of old people.

(*d*) Junglans regia, Okhar (Np), Khese (Lm), Taga (Sk,Bh), Kalkung, Kowal (Lp), Kotachi, Kolpot (Sh), Kado (Tarn).

Description: Large deciduous aromatic tree, young shoots tomentose. Bark grey deeply fissured vertically. Blaze red brown. Leaves imparipinnate, leaflets 5-13 sub-sessile, opposite or nearly so, usually entire, serrate in seeding stage. Flowers March-April, fruits Sep-Nov with hard shells.

Habitat: Middle hill forest between 1000 m to 2000 m mostly in depression also cultivate in private land and cardamom field in Yoksom.

Uses: (i) Bark—used as an anthelminitic and detergent.

(ii) Leaves—Astringent and tonic. Its decoction is specific in strumous sores. Also anthelmentic bark and leaves are used in herpes, eczema, scrofula and syphilis. externally the infusion is used as an application for skin eruptions, ulcers, etc.

(iii) In Yuksom fruits are sold in the market. Vinegar of pickled young fruits make effective gargle for sore throats. The oil from kernel is applied externally to cure troublesome skin diseases of leprous type. Kernels are also used by some to cure heart burn, colic and dysentery.

(*e*) Machilus odoratissima, Lalikaulo (Np) Sapsing (Lm), Phamlex (Sk, Bh), Rohunkung (Lp), Olglya, Kansindu (Gn).

Description: Medium sized tree. Bark rough brown, thin, blaze reddish while inside, Leaves glabrous, dark green shining above, pale beneath, lanceolate-ovate or slightly ovate. Midrib very prominent on the under surface, aromatic scented. Flowers March-May, sepals glabrous, fruits October-December.

Habitat: Hill forests of Sikkim between 1500 m to 2150 m altitude in association with oak, maple, magnolia, etc.

Uses: Leaves are good fodder for cattle, but it should not be allowed to be lopped as this will hamper the growth of the tree. Mature fruits are collected from ground and the outer pulp eaten like that of *Machilus edulis.*

(*f*) Machilus edulis, Lapche Kawla (Np), Phumsey (Lm), Pamshi (Sk, Bh), Phumkung (Lp).

Description: Large sized tree. Bark brown with prominent lenticels, bole cylindrical. Leaves glabrous above tomentose beneath Blade 12-30 cm. Young leaves densely pubescent. Main veins prominent beneath. Flowers May, fruit January-March, size upto 3.5 cm diameter. Fruiting at 3-4 years interval.

Habitat: Middle to upper hills 1220 m to 2400 m. Also cultivated in Yuksom.

Uses: Fruits are cured for some days in earthen pits and the pulp eaten after kneading. Leaves are good fodder for cattle. They are also sold in the market.

(*g*) Quercus lineata, Phalant (Np), Srising (Sk,Bh), Sri Kung (Lp).

Description: Large sized trees. Bark grey brown with rough spots. Leaves ovatelanceolate serrulate on the upper half glaucous beneath. Capsule shallow 25 mm diameter surrounded by thin lamellae. Flower April-May, fruits September-October.

Habitat: Upper hill forest of Sikkim 1850-2700 mm. Also in forest of Yuksom.

Uses: Acorns good food for bears.

(*h*) Prunus nepalensis, Arupate (Np), Khamkin (Sk, Bh), Tukporuynok (Lp).

Description: Bark dark brown with horizontal lenticels. Leaves with acute or rounded base. Serrate margin, acuminate young leaves pinkish to light green appearing in February-March, fruits May-June.

Habitat: Yuksom forest above 1800 m.

Uses: The fruits are edible. The outer thin pulp turns black when ripe. Birds also devour the fruits

(*j*) Cinnamomum impressinervium, Sis (Np), Slothkung (Lp).

Description: Medium sized tree. Bark brown, blaze scented. Leaves opposite, triplinerved, shining above pale beneath small, veins deeply impressed on the upper side. Aromatic small when crushed in July, fruits in December.

Habitat: From middle to upper hill growing in second storey. Occurring between 1220 m-1830 m in Yuksom forest.

Uses: The ripe fruits attracts birds like maina, parakeet, grey pigeon, green pigeon etc. to the hills during winter, Fruits mature in December. They are collected from ground and the outer bark rubbed and washed. The seeds are fried and eaten.

(*k*) Spondias axillaris, Lapsi (Np), Silotkung (Lp), Phindruksa (Lm), Lingsu (Sk, Bh), Phalaan (Gn).

Description: A tall evergreen tree. Bark brown or reddish peeling off in long flakes. Leaflets 6-8 pairs, opposite, or nearly so, ovate lanceolate, acuminate, in old trees entire in young trees, serrate 7-12 cm long, petiole 6 mm long. Flowers in April, fruit ripens in December. Drupes around 25-30 mm long yellow when ripe.

Habitat: In Yuksom it grows between 800-1400 m.

Uses: Raw fruits can be made into pickles. The ripe ones can be eaten. Out of pulp 'Titora' a dry pickle is also made. The fruits are sold in the market in Yuksom.

(*l*) Elaeocarpus lanceaefaius, Bhadrase (Np), Pego lechey (Lm), Khasyamkeon (Sk, Bh), Zeerkung, Sakyu kung (Lp).

Description: Large sized tree with dark brown bark. Leaves lanceolate, thinly coriaceous narrowed into a short petiole. Secondary nerves 6-12 pairs joined by intramarginal veins. Old leaves red. Flower spikes pendent. Flower April-May, fruit September, ellipsoid 30mm long.

Habitat: Yuksom forest above 1830 m to 2450 m

Uses: The fruits are edible. The stones are often collected from the ground left by deer after regurgitation or after the outer mesocarp is rotten. The kernels are extracted by breaking these stones and eaten.

(*m*) *Bassi butyracea.* Chewri (Np), Imsekwa (Lm), Neorchung (Sk, Bh), Yelkung (Lp), Chuna Phala (Gn).

Description: Large sized evergreen tree. Bark light grey, blaze pink and white, streaky with a few drops of milky juice. Leaves clustered near ends of branches. Coriaceous, ovate or ovate-oblong. Blade 15 to 30 cm petiole 25-38 mm. Flowers December-January fruits May-June fleshy.

Habitat: Lower hills of Yuksom on rocky and dry slopes ascending upto 1200 m. One tree was observed at 1775 m in Yuksom lopped for fodder.

Uses: The seeds yield white vegetable butter. This butter is eaten by villagers as vegetable oil. This is also sold in the market. Fruits are eaten. The leaves offer good fodder for cattle during lean period. This is a good species to rehabilitate drier, rocky hill slopes.

(*n*) Litsaca citrata, Siltimur (Np), Warekpa (Lm), Nanghri (Sk, Bh), Tanghercher kung, Samkung (Lp), Dom (sh).

Description: Small tree of plains and hills, bark smooth, whitish brown, green on the large branches. Leaves membranous 10-18 cm long, lenceolate, fresh bright green above, dull glaucous beneath. The whole plant has delightful fragrance of oranges. Flowers December-February, Fruits March-May.

Habitat: Occurs in sub-Himalayan tract from plains to hills upto 2700 m. Common in Yuksom.

Uses: The fresh fruits are made into pickles. The local people use the dread fruit (dried) for nausea and giddiness. The old people have seen wine distilled out of its fruits and used in gastritis. In the past as per local people, oil was also extracted for cooking.

(*o*) Evodia fraxinifolia, Khanakpa (Np), Khunu (Sk, Bh), Kunu (Lp).

Description: A moderate sized strongly aromatic tree. Bark smooth light grey with horizontal lenticels. Leaves glabrous, leaflets 3-6 pair 10-22 cm long, oblong-lanceolate, acuminate, sometime slightly crenulate, base often oblique. Flowers May-June. Fruits October-December. Inflorescence stout. Young shoot, leaf rachis and fruits are red.

Habitat: In Yuksom it is found between 1200 m to 2100 m.

Uses: The used as medicine for dysentery. These are also used in making pickles.

(*p*) Zanthoxylum acanthopodium, Timur (Np), Midhing (Lm), Timbur (Sk,Bh), Nangryupot (Lp), Yarma (Sh).

Description: An erect shrub 1.2 to 3.0 m high with stem upto 7.5 cm diameter. Young glabrous or shortly pubscent. Stem and branches armed with conical prickles. Bark greenish ashy, smooth, with numerous pale circular raised lenticels. Blase greenish. The whole plant is very aromatic. Leaves imparipinnate, 11-25 cm long rachis with faliaceous green wing upto 5mm broad. Rachis and midrib usually armed with straight prickles. Leaflet 5-13, sub equal 3.8 to 7.5 cm long oblong, lanceolate or the basal pair often ovate acute, serrate with a bland at the base of each tooth. Main lateral nerves distinct 10-20 pairs. Flowers in June and fruits September-Novermber.

Habitat: Outer Himalaya upto 2250 m in Yuksom forest.

Uses: The fruit removes pain tumors and abdominal troubles. Useful in eyes and ear disease, headache, heaviness, leucoderma, asthma, trouble of spleen, difficult micturation (Ayurveda). The seeds are sharp with a good taste and smell, tonic, astringent to the bowels and useful in diarrhoea, carminative, good in brain diseases and insanity, useful in stomatitis, strengthen the liver, purify the blood, remove foul smell from the mouth (Yunani). Local people use small quantity for pickles. They also use it to kill leeches in the forest during rains. It is sweetish, bitter, hot, tasty and digestible, appetiser and anthelmentic.

(*q*) Symplocos theifolia, Kharane (Np), Mutsang (Lm), Sembau Kung (Lp).

Description: A middle sized tree bark brown blaze white. Leaves glabrous, blade 7 to 15 cm. Petiole 10 mm. Nerves prominent above. Flowers October-March, fruits November-April.

Habitat: Upper hills from 1800-3000 m grows gregariously as a secondary crop. In natural forest it is scarcely found.

Uses: The profuse seeds offer good food for the birds and sloth bear. In the past, oil used to be extracted for cooking as per the people of this area.

(*r*) Garcinia cowa, Roxb Kaphal (Np).

Description: An evergreen medium sized dioecious tree. Drooping branches. Leaves broadly to elliptically lanceolate at both ends acuminate 10 to 12 cm long. Nerves faint very oblique 6-10 pairs. Flower yellow or reddish yellow. Flowering time December. Fruit May-June, size of a cherry, mesocarp reddish yellow.

Habitat: Lower and Middle hill forest found on way to Tshong. In flower during December at 1725 m.

Uses: The gum-resin to this fruit is used medically. It is also edible. Many local people are unaware of this species.

(*s*) Pyrus pashia, Syn pyrus variolosa, Mehel (Np), Thumbausey (Lm), Lupey (Sk, Bh), Leekung (Lp).

Description: A middle sized tree, young parts woolly (Barren branches spinescent). Leaves ovate or ovate-lanceolate, acuminate, crenulate, glabrous turning red when old. Flower March-April, fruit August-September. Fruit nearly globose when ripe 20 to 30 mm dia, crowned with base calyx.

Habitat: in Sikkim 800 m to 2400 m. Abundant around Yuksom.

Uses: Pickles are made from this fruits. These are also used for medicinal purposes. The fruits are crushed, juice extracted under pressure and boiled to get an extract, locally called 'chook' which can be preserved for years and used as medicine for dysentery.

(*t*) Rhus semialata, Bhakimlo (Np), Essebha (Lm), Tyoga sing (Sk, Bh), Tanghir Kung (Lp), Ritchi (Sh), Khyuba phala (Gn).

Description: A middle sized deciduous tree. Bark grey with numerous reddish brown lenticels. Blaze with white sticky milky juice. Banches, petioles, underside of the leaves and inflorescence clothed with short soft brownish grey pubescence. Leaves pinnate leaflet 4-6 pairs, opposite dentate, lateral sessile. Flower pale yellow green. Flowers in June-October, fruit October-December.

Habitat: Outer Himalayan Ranges grows between 900 to 1850 m very common on old cultivation and often occurring near forest boundaries quite common in Yuksom.

Uses: The seeds are crushed and 'chook' is made out of this to be used as medicine to cure dysentery by local people.

(*u*) Citrullus colocenthes, Indrenni (Np).

Description: Large deciduous climber. The stem is about 40mm dia. Distinct node is formed at every point from where the old branches have fallen. Distinctly striate stem. Branchlets zigzag with alternate leaf. Leaf deeply palmately lobed. Top lobe in the form of minarette. Base cordate. Size 10-18 cm long by 7-15. Fruit ripens in Nov-Dec globose 7.5 to 10 cm dia bright red in colour making itself prominent wherever it occurs.

Habitat: It is abundantly available in Yuksom. One climber was found near the Forest Rest House in Yuksom. One Gurung family has also cultivated Indernni in his field for fruit.

Uses: The red fruit when ripe becomes very soft. The inner pulp is yellow in which black seeds of the shape of pumpkin seed but double its thickness are found. These seeds are washed in water.

Then these are rubbed with ash so that the bitter taste of the pulp is not left in seed. The seeds are then fried in pan or karai and eaten. It is oily and very tasteful. It is also said to be of medicinal value. There is no record if this has been investigated for medicinal value.

(*v*) Pyrularia edulis, Amphi (Np), Toktor kung (Lp).

Description: Small or middle sized tree. Bark thin greenish grey. Leaf buds with white silky scales. Leaves elongate elliptic. Blade 12 to 18 cm with acute base. Glabrous Flowers March-May, Fruit July-October.

Habitat: This tree can grow between 600-1800 mm. One tree is on way to Dubdi Monastery from Yuksom at 1750 m.

Uses: The fruit is pear shaped. The globose inner stone has wax in its kernel, which burns like candle. Old people of Yuksom had the experience of using this for lighting purpose in their house in the past. It tastes like guava.

(*w*) Rubus ellipticus, Aselu (Np), Tumse (Lm), Chilum (Sk, Bh), Khaseemjeeo (Lp), Nangyan (Sh), Paula (Gn).

Description: A large shrub with long trailing angular branches. The branches and petioles are covered with dense brown bristles without glands. Stout hooked prickles on branches petioles and midrib. Leaflets three sometimes only one, almost coriaceous, broadly elliptic or ovate, obtuse or shortly acuminate, densely clothed beneath with soft grey pubescence. Flowers white in Feb-March, fruit in April-May yellow.

Habitat: In wasteland open forest from 1000-2200 m in Yuksom.

Uses: The fruits are edible. Can be made into jam. Birds also feed on. These fruits.

(*x*) Rubus niveusb, Kalo Ghyampey Asilo (Np), Patangwa (Lm), Rungkong Jeeo (Lp), Theba Panla (Gn).

Description: A straggling thorny shrub with purplish stem. Silky mostly grey pubescence on branchlets, leaves and inflorescence small conical prickles on branches and petioles. Leaflets 1 or 2 pairs, membranenous deeply incised-serrate often slightly lobed generally ovate acuminate. Petal pink. Flower May-July, fruit June-October. Oblong red edible.

Habitat: Available in waste land and openings of forest in Yuksom.

Uses: Berries are edible.

Buds, Young Shoots and Leaves

(*a*) Heptapleurum impressum, Chinde (Np), Sang (Lm), Jaysing (Sk, Bh), Sang Jam Kung (Lp), Khaareydhum (Gn).

Description: Large tree. Leaves digitable. Leaflets lanceolate entire, those on young trees often distantly serrate, upper side shining, the nerves impressed, underside softly stellate-tomentose. Blade 15-25 cm. Common petiole is 12-40 cm. Flower May-Aug. Fruits September-December.

Habitat: In Yuksom 1800 to 3000 m. A lopped tree was observed on way to Dubdi at 1750 m.

Uses: Leaves are also lopped for fooder. Young shoots make good vegetable and pickles.

(*b*) Bauhinia vareigata, Koirala (Np), Chirabey (Lm), Rhar Kung (Lp), Reysing (Sk, Bh) Kroidhum (Gn).

Description: A deciduous middle sized tree. Bark grey with numerous grey lenticels. Blaze pink and white streaks. Leaves as long as broad 11-15 nerved. Flower February-April, white except for a purple patch on the standard petal., when tree is leafless.

Habitat: In drier lower hills upto a height of 600 m in Yuksom.

Uses: Young leaves and flowers-buds are quite in demand locally for their culinary values. These are used for local packing of goods.

(*c*) Ficus infectoria, Kabra (Np).

Description: A large widely spreading deciduous fast growing tree with long young shoots that appears in February-March. The young shoots are covered with equally long membranous stipule. It is sometimes ephiphytic. Bark light grey and shiny. Leaves thinly coriaceous, glabrous, shining ovate-oblong shortly acuminate, margin undulate base acute, blade 7.5 to 15 cm petiole 2.5-7.5 cm long.

Habitat: It is mostly cultivated in and around Yuksom.

Uses: The shoots are made into pickle. It is also lightly boiled and dried and preserved to be added as souring agent to curry. The leaves form a very good fodder for cattle especially during lean period. Leaves are also lopped for fooder.

(*d*) Laportia terminalts, Patle sisnu (Np), Sasungey (Lm), Sochya (Sk, Bh), Kunlobee (Lp), Sanyuma (Sh), Pocho Bhoarey (Gn).

Description: A shrub upto 60 cm high armed with stinging hairs specially on leaves and young shoots.

Habitat: Very common in Yuksom.

Uses: Preferred for blood pressure patients. This is collected almost the whole year in Yuksom for vegetable. The young leaves and shoots that come up in March-April are boiled and eaten as dal.

(*e*) Girardinia Palmata Bhangre Sisnu (Np), Hyagma (Lm), Dongey Sochya (Sk,Bh), Kaztobee (Lp), Lengochema (Sh), Pocho renga (Gn).

Description: A tall coarse herb armed with long stout stinging hairs, leaves large broad cordate variously lobed, often palmately coarsely toothed. Stipules large. Flowers in July in higher altitude and August in lower altitude.

Habitat: Grows densely in open areas and in moist places, as undergrowth. Occurs between 1000 to 2500 m in Yuksom.

Uses: Preferred for blood pressure patient. The bark gives good fibre for making ropes, twine etc, and for coarse cloth like gunny for making bags. The leaves and shoots are also boiled and fed to cattle and pigs. The young shoots and flowers are boiled and prepared as soups.

(*f*) Urtica spy, Gharia Sisnu (Np), Pangyokpa (Lm), Milleryappa (Sk,Bh), Kaiyang (Lp), Sekcheme (Sh), Dhir pocho (Gn).

Description: Dense shrubs, monoecius or dioecious pubescent, stinging hairs copious. Leaves ovate-cordate oblong or lanceolate serrate usually free.

Habitat: From 1000 m to 2500 m. Comes densely in open areas. Some villagers have cultivated in their field.

Uses: The roots are ground and mixed with quartz stone dust, Harchur (*Viscum articulatum*) and root of chipley (*Pouzolsia sp*) and plastered to cure fractured bones. Leaves also boiled and fed to pigs. The lower and young shoots are boiled and eaten by high blood pressure patients.

Decorative

(*a*) Dry mushroom, Sukha Chew (Np).

In natural forest, brace like formation of various shape, sizes and colour in dry condition are found either on dry branches or dead wood as natural show pieces or are painted and produced as attractive decoratives. They belong to poolyporacea or thyloporaceac group of fungi. These are not collected in Yuksom.

(*b*) Anaphalis triplinervis, Bhukiphul (Np), Khawa Rang (Lm), Reep (Lp). Description : Stem rather stout often flexuous leafy and leaves beneath densely clothed with while wool. Leaves 7.5 to 20 cm ovate or elloptic oblong acute amplexicaul 3-5 nerved cobwebby above. Head in 12 mm to 20 mm dia in open or close corymb.

Habitat: These are found in open places in Yuksom.

Uses: The flowers are collected, dried and used as pillow stuff in villages. The dried flowers are used as decoratives in natural condition, which last for about 2 years without deterioration. This is, however, not collected by locals.

(*c*) Anaphalis contoria, Buki Phul (Np).

Description: Stem 15 to 60 cm stout or slender branches prostrate or ascending leafy. Leaves both surface cottony 12 to 24 mm very crowded. Narrowly linear or oblong and nerved. Head 5 mm dia. Subglobose in dense simple or lobed, contracted corymbose clusters. White or yellowish.

Habitat: Available in the open areas of forest and outside in Yuksom.

Uses: Flowers in dried condition are collected and used as pillow stuffs.

(*d*) Pollinia mollis (Erianthus), Memkesh (Np), Yang (Sk, Bh), Parphek (Lp).

Description: Stem 30-90 cm slender, tufted leafy chiefly at the base. Leaves narrowly lanceolate, sheath glabrous or ciliate. Spikes, 3-10, 2.5 to 5 cm long crowded, flexuous, joints and pedicels slender beautifully silvery silky with very long hairs. Spikelets pale glume thin villous hairs much longer than itself lower half dark brown upper pale. Hooker described it as almost intermediate between pollinia and Erianthus.

Habitat: Temperate Himalaya - Sikkim 1550 m to 2450 m. In Yuksom these are seen on rocky road cuttings, exposed rocks.

Uses: The spikes in small bundle made beautifully bouquet of dry flowers that last for more than a year as decorative. But people here do not collect.

(*e*) Moss, Jhau (Np), Tamsung /Yangbew (Lm), Mamah (Sk, Bh), Amal-Sungphon (Lp), Jhyambo (Gn).

Description: These are found attached on trees and on rocks in the forest of Yuksom.

Uses: Moss is used mostly in nursery as moisture absorbent. Also used as decorative.

(*f*) Lycopodium clavatum, Nagbelli (Np), Ghisingdermu (Lp), Sisingderma (Sk, Bh).

Description: A trailing creeper growing in open areas on ground or rocks spreading with roots at every node. Stem green covered with dense thick spiny leaves all over except on the under surface. Spikes on the tips of each branchlets. On maturity the spikes burst the powder like spores.

Habitat: Growing on open areas between 1850 m to 2750 m.

Uses: The entire plant is collected for use as decoratives. The spores can be used for various purposes including powder, (*g*) Kalamay Uneu, Fern Washeing (Lm), Chya Kim (Sk, Bh), Zeethung Krok/Purmulasong (Lp).

Description: These ferns grow in dense clumps with spreading branches and have 1-1.5 m long woody stems.

Habitat: It grows in the hills from 1650 m-2450 m in more or less open areas. A clump is seen near Dubdi Monastery.

Uses: The stem can be used as sticks in making 'Stools (Muras)'. The young shoots are collected in huge quantity from Darjeeling hills as decoratives. Here, this fern is not much in use. In the past writing pens were out made of stem.

Mushrooms

Mushrooms form delicacies in food of local people these are also a good source of nutrition. There are 106 varieties of edible mushrooms in India. Out of them about 11 edible varieties were seen in Yuksom. The following varieties are described here:

(*a*) Agaricus silvaticus, Kalungey Cheu (Np), Peepath (Lm), Sangey Jhyamu (Sk, Bh).

Description: With the onset of monsoon in May this particular mushroom starts appearing on ground in scattered groups. The pileus usually 3.5 to 10 cm dia convex when young becomes flat when old. Upper surface whitish or brown. The stipe (stem) is 3-12 cm long 1-1.8 cm dia. The villagers of Dosthang informed of having single variety known as ekley Kalungey which is 20-25 cm diameter and 35-50 mm dia stipe and 20-30 cm high.

Habitat: It is found in Yuksom upto 1300 m altitude.

Uses: Local people call it poor man's meat because of its taste. This is available for about two months in May and June. The ekley variety is said to appear in September and October. One such mushroom is enough for a family of 6-7 members.

(*b*) Pleurotus Sajor Caju, Kanney Cheu (Np), Nak Thuk (Lm), Kayley (Sk), Tumung Dorby (Lp), Shyamu (Sh).

Description: Sporophores are found growing in dead trees either fallen or standing Specially on Dudhilo, Nebharo, Gobre, Saur and Khanankpa, Pileus kidney shaped. Some are round with short stalk white or grey 2.5 to 10 cm dia.

Habitat: In natural forest 1500 m to 2450 m on dead wood. They are said to sprout after lightening during August–September.

Uses: It is one of the most tasty mushrooms. In the past one could find about 5 kg in one harvest.

(*c*) Chipley Cheu (Np), Warreng Lemba (Lm), Ghetka Shyamu (Sk,Bh), Phukip Dur (Lp).

Description: The top surface is glistening reddish with brown and with white margin. Since the mushroom is slippery, hence the name. They grow gregariously on rotten stumps or logs during rains. These mushrooms have their pileus 2 cm to 3 cm dia 2.5 to 3 cm stalk.

Habitat: Available in the forest of Yuksom from 1500 to 2450 m altitude.

Uses: These are mostly collected as vegetable from rotten trees like sour and rani champ.

(*d*) Jhari Cheu (Np).

Description: Their colur is greyish white with pileus having 20 mm maximum dia. With the monsoon this particular species of mushroom occur in abundance on humus in forest.

Habitat: These occur in the hills above 1800 to 2000 m in the natural forest of Yuksom.

Uses: Collected as vegetable.

(*e*) Pleurotus ostratus, Syn Pleurtus *salignus* Chamrey (Np), Muya Lappa (Lm), Khomtu Shyamu (Sk, Bh), Kombu Dur (Lp).

Description: Whitish large tough when old Pelius 8-20 cm or more broad spathulate to kidney shaped. White grey or sometime yellowish. Surface smooth, margin incurved. Stipe 1-3 cm accentric or lateral 0.5 to 2 cm thick. Sporophores growing on dead trunk of Tarsing or its branches.

Habitat: Found in forest of Yuksom.

Uses: Tasteful when cooked though tough to chew.

(*f*) Polyporous umbellatus, Per Exfr, Syn, Boletus kumbellatus Pers, Grifola ramosissima Scop Ex. Murr, Polypilus Pers Exfr, Thankrey (Np), Thukchuk, Shyamu (Sk, Bh).

Description: Pileus whitish to smoky brown small round fleshy surface fibrillose or smooth stipe, white several stipe of the adjacent pilea united at the base to form a large clump. Sporophores growing at the base of tree specially phalant (Q. lineata), stipitate 7-20 cm in dia compound formed by a main stipe with numerous small branches each bearing a single centrally attached pileus arising from a sclerotiod base.

Habitat: High altitude mushroom found rarely above 2500 m in the forest of Yuksom.

Uses: This is also collected as vegetable.

(*g*) Hieun Cheu (Np), Nang Nakthuk (Lm), Khau Shyamu Sonangdur (Lp).

Description: Villagers are said to collect upto 50 kg in one season. This is good for day to day consumption. This mushroom brown in colour grows profusely on dead woods of Asare, kaulo and other dead wood and also on ground after snowfall.

Habitat: Above 2500 m altitude after snowfall.

Uses: Very popular vegetable for people in Yuksom.

(*h*) Katusey Cheu (Np), Singdambey (Lm), Sgey Jhamu (Sk, Bh), Kusue Dhur (Lp).

Description: This mushroom is found on dead and rotten *Castanopsis* tree for which the name is after this tree.

Uses: This mushroom is quite tasteful it is collected during rains for vegetables.

Diplazium (Fern Shoot, Ningro)

(*a*) Diplazium polypodiodes Mett, Sauney Ningro (Np).

Description: The axis errect, stout densely clothed at the crown with long brown, fibrilous scales, 25 mm long, stipes densely tufted, stout green 30cm or more long, fronds 90-120 cm and wide, bipinnate with 8-9 primary pinnase on each side below the simple one. The upper surface looking coarse and pale green. The lower ones generally distant.

Habitat: Most common fern in almost all moist and shady places and banks of jhoras in Yuksom.

Uses: The young shoots are covered with fibrilous brown hair and they are popular vegetables during July-August (Saun). That is why it is called Saun Ningro.

(*b*) Pahakhuttev (Np).

Description: Caudex is short, leaves 0.5-1.0 m long, fronds 0.3-2.5 cm long, rachis 1-6 mm. Primary pinnae sub opposite to alternate upto 13 pairs, lower ones 7-18 cm. Upper ones tapering 20-25 mm. Baby plants develop like small knurled bulbs on the rachis in December. On maturity it drops on the ground and forms independent plant, normally 3 or 4 such plantlets are developed from one mother plant.

Habitat: It is found in shady and moist areas above 1750 m in Yuksom.

Uses: This is a favourite vegetable of the people of Yuksom. The shoots are brought in large quantity in the market during August-September.

(*c*) Kali Ningro (Np).

Description: Caudex is dark brown about 7.5 cm dia and 15 cm long with fibrous and long roots. The leaves look like that of Sauney but is light green in colour and soft in texture. The position of the secondary pinnae is alternate of sub-opposite as against opposite of Sauney.

Habitat: These are at altitude above 1750 m in jhoras and depressions.

Uses: The young shoots which are dark green in colour have long white streak on the side. The shoot is bit slippery.

Yams

(*a*) Dioscorea hamiltonii, D.hookerii, Ban Tarul (Np).

Description: A climber with angled glabrous stem, twining to the right. Leaves opposite on thicker stem often alternating towards the end. Bulbils abundant. Tubers long and deeply penetrating into the ground. Flesh white and edible.

Habitat: Available in the private forest along the road to Tshong village.

Uses: It is most esteemed among wild yams but it is difficult to dig. However, pits are dug upto 1.2 m deep to extract the tuber.

Fibre

(*a*) Edgeworthia gardneri, Kagate or Argeli (Np), Dhenok (Lp).

Description: A large shrub. Branches long scrambling. Leaves glaucous lanceolate 10-18 cm 2.5-4 cm. Flowers in December-May in dense heads. Fruits June-September.

Habitat: Local people use its bark for making paper and ropes for carrying loads and also for tying cattle, etc.

(*b*) Daphne cannabina, Kagatey or Lokhtey (Np), Dhenok (Lp).

Description: It grows upto 4m height. Bark and shoot, rough scaly. Branches horizontal and drooping, dense. Leaves dark shining green, veins invisible on upper surface. Lower surface pale green. Flower in Dec-Feb white with pink tinge, fruits July, red in colour. Habitat: It is available in Yuksom above 1850 m upto 2500 m.

Uses: Its bark also is used locally for ropes only. This, however, has potential as raw material for paper along with Edgeworthia.

Suggestions

(a) This is of great economic importance to people. The cultivation prospects are also good. Villagers ought to to be involved also for its propagation specially those for medicinal plants that are getting rare and extinct.

(b) Collection and sale should be encouraged for cultivated items and those allowed from wild on sustainable basis only.

(c) Research needs to be conducted to study the various uses of NTFP not covered so far in other areas.

(d) NTFP like 'tama' (Shoot of bamboo) mushroom, ningro (Diplazium), Sisnu (nettles) and pickle could be served in local hotels as delicacies to popularise these products. Items like pickle can be sold also with local brand which can become a source of income for the local people.

(e) Community involved management and monitoring of NTFP could be one approach followed at organisational levels as. NTFPs are resources to sustain local needs of life and it can also act as source of economic benefit to the local community. It has great potential but its sustainable harvest strategy has to be developed.

References

1. Margalef, Ramon; *Perspectives in Ecological Theory*, University of Chicago Press, Chicago, USA, 1968, p. 4.
2. Bennett, John. W. *The Ecological Transition*, A. Wheaton & Co. Exeter, Great Britain, 1976 p. 25.
3. Davis, E. Wade; from *Ethnobotany : Evolution of a Discipline* , by Schultes and Reis(ed), Diosconrides Press, Oregon, USA,1995 p. 40.
4. Alcorn, Janis. B.; from *Ethnobotany : Evolution of a Discipline* , by Schultes and Reis (ed), Dioscorides Press, Oregon, USA, 1995 p. 23.
5. Ford, R.I.; *Ethnobotany: Historical Diversity and Synthesis*, Anthropological papers, No. 67, Michigan Museum of Anthropology, 1978 pp. 33-49.
6. Ricour, P.: *The Model of the Text : Social Research* 5, University of Chicago Press, Chicago, 1971 p. 529.
7. Speight, MR; The Potential of Ecosystem Management, in '*Agriculture, Ecosystems and Environment*, 10, 1983 pp. 183-199.
8. Lynch, O., and Alcorn J.B. *Empowering Local Forest Managers*, World Resources Institute, Washington, DC, 1991.
9. Wilson, G.F., and B.T. Kang; Developing stable and productive biological cropping. In *Biological Husbandry*, (Ed). B. Stonehouse. Boston: Butterworths (1981).

10. Dimbleby, G.W.; *Plants and Archaeology*, Atlantic Highlands, Humanities Press, New Jersey, USA, 1978.

11. Boster, J.S.; *Ethnobotany in Neotropics*, Vol.1., Bronx, NY: New York, 1984 p. 34.

12. Barlett, P.F., ed. *Agricultural Decision Making: Anthropological Contributions to Rural Development*, Academic Press: New York, 1980.

13. International Potato Centre, *Breaking New Ground: Anthropology in Agricultural Research*, Lima, Peru, 1984.

14. Schultes, R.E., and S von Reis, ed. *Ethnobotany: Evolution of a Discipline*, Dioscorides Press, Portland, Oregon, USA, 1995.

15. Naranjo, P., *Medicinal Plants in Ecuador*, Ecuat de Medicina, Quito, Ecuador, 1984.

16. Swain, T. *ed. Plants in the Development of Modern Medicine*, Cambridge, MA: Harvard University Press, 1972.

17. Farnsworth, N., and A. Bingel. *New Natural Products and Plant Drugs*, Springervelag Press, New York.

18. Von Reis and Altschul, S., *Drugs and Foods from Little Known Plants*, Cambridge, MA: Harvard University Press, 1973.

19. Balandran, M.F., *Natural Plant Chemicals: Sources of Industrial and Medicinal.*

20. Duke, J., *Medicinal Plants,Science* Magazine 229: 1038; USA, 1985.

21. Klayman, D.L., *Qinghaousu: An Antimalarial Drug from China*, Science Magazine 228: 1049; USA, 1995.

22. Godbole, A. Ajay Rastogi and Peishengji, *Applied Ethnobotany in Natural Resource*

23. Padoch, C. and Jong, W.de, *The Home Gardens of Santa Rosa*, Economic Botany, 42 (2) : 166-175, 1991.

24. Ninej, V.K., *House Hold Gardens*, International Potato Centre, Lima, Peru, 1984.

25. Saklani, A. and S.K. Jain, *Crosscultural Ethnobotany of NE India*, Deep Publishers, New Delhi, 1994.

26. Brownrigg, L., *Home Gardening in International Development*, The League for International Food Education, Washington, D.C, 1985.

27. Fernandes, E.C.M. and P.K.R. Nair, An Evaluation of the structure and Function of Tropical Home Gardens, *Agricultural Systems*, 21: 279-310, 1986.

28. Subba, J.R., *Agriculture in the Hills of Sikkim*, Sikkim Science Society, Gangtok, 1984.

29. Barran, J., Subsistence Agriculture in Polynesia and Micronesia, *Bishop Museum Bulletin* No. 223, 1961.

30. Michon, G., *Village-forest Gardens in West Java*, International Centre for Research in Agroforestry, Nairobi, Kenya, 1983.

31. Altieri, M.A. and J.Farrell, Traditional Farming systems of South-Central Chile, *Agroforestry Systems, 2:3-18*, Nairobi, Kenya, 1984.

32. Fernandes, E.C.M.; A. Oktingati and J. Maghembe, The Chhaga Home Gardens, *Agroforestry Systems 2: 73-86*, Nairobi, Kenya, 1984.

33. Okafor, J.C., and E.C.M. Fernandes, The Compound Farms in SE Nigeria, *Agroforestry Systems, 5:153-168*, Nairobi, Kenya, 1987.

34. Oduol, P.A. and J.R.W. Aluma, The Banana-Coffee Robusta : Traditional Forestry System in Uganda, *Agroforestry Systems*, 11: 213-216, Nairobi, Kenya, 1990.

35. Millat-e-Mustafa, *The Ecology and Management of Traditional Home Gardens of Bangladesh*, Ph.D. Thesis. University of Wales, Bangor, UK, 1996.

36. Harmer, K., *The Potential of Mixed Orchards in Britain*, Undergraduate Thesis, University of Wales, Bangor, UK, 1991.

37. *Ibid.*

38. Paljor, S., Feed and Fodder Resources of Sikkim, in, *Sikkim : Perspectives for Planning and Development*, by S.C. Rai, R.C. Sundriyal and Eklabya Sharma, (eds), Sikkim Science Society, Tadong, Gangtok, 1998.

39. Mergen, F., Research opportunities to Improve the Production of Home Gardens, *Agroforestry Systems*, 5:57-67, Nairobi, Kenya, 1987.

40. Soemarwoto, O., Home Gardens: A Traditional Agroforestry System with a Promising Future. In, *Agroforestry : A Decade of Development*, by Steepler, H.A and P.K.R.Nair, (eds), International Centre for Research in Agroforestry, Nairobi, Kenya, 1987.

41. FAO, *Household Food Security and Forestry (An Analysis of Socio-economic Issues)*, FAO, Rome, 1989.

42. Brownrigg, L., *Home Gardening in International Development : What the Literature Shows* ; The League for International Food Education, Washington, D.C, USA, 1985.

43. Lama, Mahendra, P., (ed) *Sikkim : Society, Polity, Economy, Environment*, Indus Publishing Company, New Delhi, 1994.

44. Messer, Ellen, Methods for Studying Determinants of Food Intake, In *Research Methods in Nutritional Anthropology*, by, Gretel. H. Pelto; Pertti. J. Pelto and Ellen Messer; The United Nations University, Tokyo, 1989.

45. Tamang, J.P., P.K. Sarkar, and Hesseltine, C.W., Traditional Fermented Foods and Beverages of Darjeeling and Sikkim— a review, in *J. Science of Food and Agriculture* 44: 375-385, 1988.

46. Tamang, J.P., Indigenous Fermented foods of Sikkim Himalaya : Socio-Economical prospective. In *Sikkim-perspectives for Planning and Development* (Eds: S.C. Rai, R.C. Sundriyal and E. Sharma), pp. 513-522, Sikkim Science Society, Gangtok, 1998.

47. Kwon, T.W., The Role of Fermentation Technology for the World Food supply. In: *Lactic Acid Fermentation of Non-Dairy Food and Beverages,* (eds) G.H. Loe, J. Adler- Nissen and G. Barwald, pp. 1-7. Ham Lim Won Publication, Seoul, Korea, 1994.

48. Steinkraus, K.H., Nutritional Significance of Fermented Foods. *Food Research International* 27: 259-267, 1994.

49. Camphell-Platt, G., Fermented Foods - A World perspective. *Food Research International* 27: 253-257, 1994.

50. Tamang, J.P., Role of Micro-organisms in Traditional Food Fermentation Technology in the Himalayan Regions. *Proceeding Abstract of the Tenth International Conference on Global Impacts of Applied Microbiology and Biotechnology;* Elsinor, Denmark. p. 61, 1995 b.

51. Tamang, J.P., Fermented Soybean Products in India. In : *Proceeding in the Second International Soybean Processing and Utilization Conference,* Bangkok (ed) A. Bucharan, p. 189-194. IFRPD, Kasetsart University, Thailand, 1996.

52. Tamang, J.P., *Studies in the Microflora of Some Traditional Fermented Foods of Darjeeling Hills and Sikkim,* Ph.D. Thesis, NBU, India, p. 224, 1993.

53. Tamang, J.P., Kinema— A non-salted Fermented Soybean Food of Darjeeling Hills and Sikkim. Proceeding abstract of Third Asian Symposium on Non-Salted Soybean Fermentation, Akita, Japan, 14, 1994.

54. Tamang, J.P., *Study of Traditional Fermented Foods Production in Darjeeling Hills and Sikkim, with Emphasis on Kinema.* Post Doctorate Dissertation, United Nations University, Tokyo, Japan, 1995.

55. Karki, T., Okada, S., Baba, T., Itoh, H., and Kozaki, H., Studies on the Microflora of Nepalese pickles Gundruk. *Nippon Shokuhin Kogyo Gakkaishi,* 30: 357-367, 1983.

56. Tamang, J.P. and Sarkar, P.K., Sinki : A Traditional Lactic Acid fermented Radish tap root product. *J General and Applied Microbiology, 39 : 395-408,* 1993.

57. Hoffman, Albert, Medicinal Chemistry's Debt to Ethnobotany. In, *Ethnobotany: Evolution of a Discipline,* (eds.) R.E. Schultes and S. Reis, Dioscorides Press, USA, 1995.

4
Medicinal Plants

The use of plants in healing and treating diseases has been evolved from the time of man's earliest social and cultural groupings. The ancient Indian literatures such as 'Atharveda', 'Sushrut Samhita' and 'Charak Samhita' are rich with such information.

The direct relationship of people with plants is termed as ethnobotany, which includes the study of species used as food, fibre, dyes, tannins, resins medicines, and traditional magico-religion. Although, Harshberger first used the term ethnobotany in 1895, its scope in Indian context was elaborated and organised much later by Jannaki Ammal in 1956 and Faulks in 1958.

Ayurveda mainly depends on tridosa (three humours) concept that is cough, pitta and vat. According to this system, the life is believed to be the constituents of five elements such as ether (akash), wind (vayu), water (ap), earth (prithwi), and fire (agni). The age-old medical system prevailing in whole of northern India is known as Ayurveda, which is embedded in distinct cultural premises and symbols. This medical system cannot be fully understood outside the stream of history. The practitioners of this medical system are known as Vaidya, who are traditional healers of this medical system.

Ayurveda consists of beliefs and practices connected by an underlying logic and underpinned by a coherent network of assumptions about pathophysiology, therapeutics and so forth. Prior to the dominance of allopathic medicine in Europe, similar logic, ideas and practices commonly dominated medicine in the west. The old people in Bhyundar valley do still have reasonable knowledge on many medicinal plants. Earlier, almost in every village of Garhwal region there was a Vaidya who had the sole responsibility of curing the illnesses. Apart from Vaidya, both sexes of the society know the healing power of many medicinal plants around them.

Unfortunately, all societies are permeable to exogenous influences and so is the technicality in any system, whether industrial or medical.

Similarly, over the years Ayurveda has been consistently misinterpreted due to invasion of different cultures and traditions. However, the success and failures are built into the systems of medicine that determine its longevity. Ayurveda possesses a highly abstract Meta theoretical framework for explaining diseases, and is grounded in well-recognized procedure of validation and experimentation. Since the invasion of modern health care facilities, the traditional system of therapy and the use of medicinal resources such as plants have drastically declined and now are restricted to rural and tribal communities.

Due to the precariousness of agricultural practices and low agricultural yields, these people have distributed their subsistence activities across the variety of marginal resources such as agriculture, pastoralism, handicrafts, collection and trade of medicinal plants. However, these traditional practices for sustenance are easily pierced by outside forces through tourism, mountaineering, and presence of defence personnel. In the Himalayan mountains, due to the difficult and inaccessible terrain, the rural people are usually away from developmental activities and depend on a wide range of biological resources for various purposes. With the increasing population and decreasing forest to man ratio, there is an obvious conflict between resource management and the local communities. Among the depleting resources of this region wild medicinal herbs are of utmost conservation significance. Traditionally, local people have been using medicinal herbs for their own consumption. However, the invasion of market economy put an extra pressure in the form of over exploitation of medicinal herbs that led to rapid decline of their wild populations.

The small farmers and unemployed youths also like to earn more money to meet their aspirations, most of them do not have resources and vision to cope up with the changed scenario. The traditional values, ethnobotanical knowledge and respect for the nature and natural resources are being neglected in many areas. Associated with this heritage is the cultural diversity of the Himalayan valleys, which need to be protected from degradation. I thank ICIMOD (International Centre for Integrated Mountain Development, Nepal) for providing me financial assistance for gathering information on the indigenous uses of medicinal plants found in Bhyundar valley. Ethnobotanical information was collected by using semi-structured and unstructured questionnaires as well as direct observations in the field. Information was collected on trees, shrubs, herbs and their parts used for medicinal purposes. Local herbal practitioners were taken in confidence and field visits were made with them to gather information on the identity and occurrence of medicinal plants and mode of their utilization. Each household was surveyed for information on quantity of extraction of these medicinal plants from wild.

The verification of data was done by repeated interviews with more than one informant. To study the effects of various anthropogenic pressures on the population of medicinal plants, the entire Bhyundar valley and its environs was stratified into three broad pressure zones viz., (a) the Valley of Flowers being a protected area was considered as a controlled site, (b) the buffer of park which is under the severe pressure due to tourism and livestock grazing was taken as a high pressure zone, and (c) Khiron valley which is grazed mostly by sheep and goats, was taken as a moderately disturbed (grazed) area. In addition to intensive search across the various pressure zones and trails, 25 randomly placed quadrats of 50 × 50 cm were laid in each landscape unit, which formed one sampling stand. A total of 20 sampling stands were laid in each pressure zone.

The data obtained from these strata were compared to assess the conservation status and population of medicinal herbs. The inhabitants of Bhyundar and Khiron valleys have been using traditionally a total of 121 species of medicinal plants. Of these herbs were maximum (95 herbs), followed by shrubs (13), trees (7) and ferns (6). Of the total 54 rare and endangered species of the Valley of Flowers and its environs, 31 species were used for medicinal purposes, of which 5 species are listed in the Red Data Book of Indian Plants. Out of 31 rare medicinal plants, 23 species have been categorized for rarity according to new IUCN Red List Criteria in Conservation and Management Assessment Plan (CAMP) meeting held in Lucknow, of which 12 are critically endangered, 4 are endangered and 7 are categorised as vulnerable.

The National Park contained the highest number of medicinal plants (51), followed by the buffer zone (45) and Khiron valley (37). Out of 121 species of medicinal plants, 65 were occurred in the sampling plots. The densities (individuals m^{-2} ±SD) of medicinal herbs in the Valley of Flowers were highest for *Potentilla atrosanguinea* (32.20 ± 12.32) and *Geranium wallichianum* (28.56 ± 10.42), in the buffer of the Valley of Flowers for *Prunella vulgaris* (25.20 ± 20.40) and *Urtica dioica* (23.55 ± 14.21) and in the Khiron valley for *Iris kumaonensis* (41.30 ± 38.91) and *Prunella vulgaris* (18.93 ± 15.61; Table 4.1).

Various anthropogenic pressures, such as grazing, burning, over collection of medicinal plants and deforestation. Some of the rare medicinal herbs (e.g., *Picrorhiza kurrooa, Fritillaria roylei* and *Cyananthus integer)* found in the park have not seen in the Khiron valley and buffer zone of the park are extinct now have left their mark. In the high altitudes of the Himalaya underground parts (roots, tubers and rhizomes) of medicinal herbs were used in highest cases (45%), followed by leaves (26%). Most of the alpine plants reproduce vegetatively by tubers, rhizomes, and roots and their populations are declining severely due to extraction of underground parts. The densities of rare medicinal herbs such as *Dactylorhiza hatagirea, Picrorhiza kurrooa, Meconopsis aculeata, Rheum australe, Aconitum violaceum, Aconitum balfourii,* and *Fritillaria roylei* were higher (1.00 ± 0.84, 4.50 ± 0.00, 1.44 ± 0.36, 0.24 ± 0.11, 2.05 ± 0.11, 0.34 ± 0.16 and 6.14 ± 9.68 respectively) in the protected area compared to unprotected areas viz., Khiron valley and buffer zone of the park (Table 4.1). Exploitation of rhizomes and tubers at commercial scale has led to substantial loss of medicinal plants from their habitats in many parts of the Garhwal Himalaya. Although, Khiron valley had lowest number of medicinal plants yet, their densities and frequencies were higher compared to the buffer zone of the National Park, which may be due to lower grazing pressure in Khiron than the buffer zone. The low density of medicinal herbs in the buffer zone may also be attributed to high tourism pressure and grazing of livestock (mule, horses, and cattle).

Activities such as human interferences in the form of deforestation, uncontrolled tourism and construction of new roads and buildings are also badly affecting the natural flora and fauna of this fragile ecosystem. The mode of grazing also affects the plant population. The mules graze very close to the ground and also their dung is not considered as good manure thus leading to the adverse effect on regeneration of plants. The construction of dam across the Alaknanda river (Vishnu Prayag Project) in the lower areas outside the park is likely to affect the population of some of the medicinal plants such as *Hedychium spicatum, Dioscorea deltoidea,* and *Hippophae rhamnoides* as these species grow mainly in the sub-alpine and temperate forests. Very few individuals of the *H. rhamnoides* occurred in the buffer zone of the park (2,500-2,800 m asl) whereas it was common on the way to Badrinath at similar elevation.

Taraxacum officinale, Anemone rivularis, and *Plantago major* had higher density in the sub-alpine meadows (buffer zone of the park) where livestock grazing continued. These are some very rare herbs. Their high density in the grazed area indicates that these herbs are less affected by grazing. The high density of *Iris kumaonensis* in the Khiron valley but its poor representation inside the park area reveals that sheep and goats grazing may help this species. There were several other herbs, which were sensitive to various anthropogenic pressures. Such species had low population size in terms of density and frequency outside the park. Medicinal herbs such as *Fritillaria roylei* and *Dactylorhiza hatagirea,* which have been assessed as a critically endangered species in the CAMP meeting, were common within National Park but very few outside the park area.

Picrorhiza kurrooa, which has been placed in the CITES was found only in the park inspite of its habitat availability outside the park. Similarly, *Arnebia benthamii* had very few individuals in the treeline zone of the park but not seen in the buffer zone of park and Khiron valley. These facts collectively indicate the over harvesting of selected high value medicinal plant species. The density of *Potentilla atrosanguinea* and *Geranium wallichianum* was highest in the park and also both the herbs were distributed in all pressure zones because of their wide range of adaptability in the alpine meadows. In the Khiron valley, the collection of medicinal herbs was mainly done by the people of nearby villages viz., Khiron, Paturi, Benakuli, and Binayakchatti, who were mostly dependent on these resources for their subsistence besides some minor agricultural practices.

In addition to the collection of *Dactylorhiza hatagirea, Picrorhiza kurrooa,.Allium humile, A. wallichi, Arnebia benthamii,* and *Areseama jacquemontii*, villagers also collected *Origanum vulgare (ban tulsi)* at a large scale. Although, this perennial herb has medicinal properties, its demand is very high for the religious purpose as it is offered to Lord Vishnu's temple at Badrinath. The other herbs, which have medicinal properties but their collection have made mainly for the spices, were *Allium humile* and *A. wallichi.* There was a common belief among the local people that *Allium* spp of Khiron valley had better taste with more aroma than the Alliums of side valleys. As a result inhabitants of other villages such as Mana, Chang, Thang, Raigaun, and Pinaula in Chamoli district visit Khiron valley to collect these herbs.

Tourism was the mainstay of village. It had better economic status mainly due to tourism. But this sudden spurt in tourism had taken its the traditional practices in Bhyundar valley were declining

Table 4.1 Frequency (F) and density ±SD (Standard Deviation) of Medicinal Plants in Various Pressure Zones

Species name	*Inside park*		*Butter of park*		*Khiron valley*	
	F	*Density ±SD*	*F*	*Density ±SD*	*F*	*Density ±SD*
Aconitum balfourii Stapf	15	0.34 ± 0.16	5	0.02 ± 0.00	-	-
A. violaceum Jacq. Stapf	10	2.05 ± 0.11	5	0.95 ± 0.00	-	-
Allium humile Kunth.	25	5.54 ± 5.56	-	-	5	13.28 ± 0.00
A. wallichi Kunth	5	1.12 ± 0.00		-	-	-
Anemone rivularis Buch-Ham	25	5.70 ± 6.32	65	16.59 ± 9.8	90	10.61 ± 7.55
Angelica glauca Edgew.	50	1.03 ± 0.74	15	0.91 ± 0.61	-	-
Areseama jacqemontii Bl	50	1.18 ± 1.44	40	0.62 ± 0.41	55	1.47 ± 1.37
A. torulosum (Wall.) Scholl	10	0.24 ± 0.11	15	0.32 ± 0.16	-	-
Artemisia absinthiam L.	-	-	25	2.75 ± 3.43	-	-
Bergenia stracheyi (Hk. f. & Th.) Engl.	10	0.85 ± 0.23	-	-	-	-
Bupleurum longicaule Wall ex DC	30	13.60 ± 9.2	30	3.31 ± 3.68	30	1.97 ± 1.89
Caltha palustris	10	0.80 ± 0.00	5	0.64 ± 0.00	-	7
Capsella bursa-pastoris Medic.	-	-	10	0.67 ± 0.23	5	0.75 ± 0.00
Cardemine impatiens L	-	-	10	0.86 ± 0.26	-	-
Cassiope fastigiata Don	20	1.22 ± 0.98	-	-	-	-
Cerastium cerastoides (L) Britt.	-	-	40	7.57 ± 5.89	75	2.68 ± 1.87

(*contd...*)

Species name	Inside park		Butter of park		Khiron valley	
	F	Density ±SD	F	Density ±SD	F	Density ±SD
Cortia depressa (Don) Norm.	25	9.76± 7.64	-	-	-	-
Corydalis meifolia Wall.	25	0.35 ± 0.21	-	-	-	-
C. govaniana Wall.	10	1.04 ± 1.02	-	-	-	-
Cotoneaster microphyllus Wall. ex Lindl.	5	0.19 ± 0.00	30	0.56 ± 0.57	55	2.81 ± 4.97
Cuscuta reflexa Roxb.	15	0.43 ± 0.18	-			-
Cyananthus integer Wall ex Benth	20	6.24 ± 4.42	-	-	-	-
Cyanoglossum glochidiatum Wall.	-	-	10	1.20 ± 1.02	10	0.56 ± 0.34
Dactylorhiza hatagirea (D.Don) Soo	75	1.00 ± 0.84	-	-	5	0.16 ± 0.00
Euphorbia pilosa L.	-	-	25	1.56 ± 0.95	5	0.32 ± 0.00
Frageria nubicola Lindl. ex Lacaita	40	1.36 ± 0.92	65	8.68 ± 6.20	5	0.68 ± 0.00
Fritillaria roylei Hook	25	6.14 ± 9.68	-	-	5	0.64 ± 0.00
Galium aparine L.	10	1.44 ± 0.91	60	8.99 ± 8.64	45	10.60 ± 12.52
Gaultheria trichophylla Royle	5	16.08 ± 0.0	5	4.32 ± 0.00	5	0.32 ± 0.00
Geranium nepalense Sweet	35	1.81 ± 2.89	55	11.40 ± 10	55	7.45 ± 3.94
G. pratense L.	65	5.08 ± 5.99	10	4.40 ± 3.96	-	-
G. wallichianum D. Don	95	28.56 ± 10	45	7.31 ± 6.30	90	14.80 ± 11.26
Geum elatum Wall.	10	0.16 ± 0.00	-	-	-	-
Gymnadenia orchidis Lindl	-	-	-	-	5	0.32 ± 0.00
Iris kumaonensis Wall	35	3.47 ± 3.73	30	9.65 ± 8.01	40	41.30 ± 38.9

(contd...)

Species name	Inside park		Butter of park		Khiron valley	
	F	Density ±SD	F	Density ±SD	F	Density ±SD
Juniperus communis L.	10	0.48 ± 0.23	-	-	5	0.32 ± 0.00
Jurenea macrocephala (Royle) Aswal & Goal	-	-	-	-	10	1.28 ± 0.91
Meconopsis aculeata Royle	10	1.44 ± 0.36	-	-	-	-
Ophioglossum vulgatum L.	10	1.12 ± 0.00	5	0.16 ± 0.00	10	0.56 ± 0.34
Origanum vulgare L.	20	0.40 ± 0.31	75	16.62 ± 15	60	8.72 ± 9.61
Oxyria digyna Hill	5	0.48 ± 0.00	5	1.12 ± 0.00	-	-
Paris polyphylla Sm.	-	-	-	-	30	5.17 ± 2.59
Parochaetus communis Don	-	-	40	4.14 ± 3.48	-	-
Pedicularis pectinata Wall	35	1.44 ± 1.21	30	1.68 ± 2.06	15	4.32 ± 3.60
Phlomis bracteosa Royle	55	1.37 ± 0.94	25	0.70 ± 0.68	25	3.17 ± 3.93
Picrorhiza kurrooa Royle ex Benth	5	4.50 ± 0.00	-	-	-	-
Plantago major L.	25	3.23 ± 2.97	55	2.14 + 2.82	10	1.36 ± 1.47
Polygonatum cirrhifolium (Wall.)Royle	5	1.12 ± 0.00	5	0.48 ± 0.00	5	1.44 ± 0.00
P. verticillatum (L) All.	35	2.56 ± 1.58	10	1.10 ± 0.81	20	0.72 ± 0.77
P. recumbans Royle ex Beb.	-	-	10	8.64 ± 5.88	-	-
Potentilla atrosanguinea Lodd	85	32.20 ± 12	50	8.53 ± 7.92	85	16.24 ± 11.5
Prunella vulgaris L.	15	0.69 ± 0.92	60	25.20 ± 20	15	18.93 ± 15.61

(*contd...*)

Species name	*Inside park*		*Butter of park*		*Khiron valley*	
	F	*Density ±SD*	*F*	*Density ±SD*	*F*	*Density ±SD*
Rheum australe D. Don	10	0.24 ± 0.11	10	0.16 ± 0.00	-	-
Rhododendron anthopogon D. Don	15	4.00 ± 4.12	10	2.00 ± 1.92	-	-
Roscoea pupurea Royal	-	-	-	-	75	7.91 ± 4.71
Rumex acetosa L.	85	5.49 ± 3.63	60	2.47 ± 1.62	65	1.91 ± 1.21
Saussurea obvallata (DC.) Sch. Bip.	10	0.32 ± 0.18	-	-	-	-
Senecio crysanthemoides DC	35	0.87 ± 0.56	80	5.93 ± 4.56	47	1.10 ± 0.64
Solidago virga-aurea L.	15	0.27 ± 0.09	20	2.48 ± 3.56	-	-
Swertia alata Royle ex D. Don	10	0.40 ± 0.34	25	0.99 ± 0.61	-	-
Thalictrum foliolosum DC.	-	-	10	1.28 ± 0.06	-	-
Taraxacum officinale Weber	5	0.16 ± 0.00	60	19.40 ± 33	55	5.24 ± 7.67
Thymus serphyllum L.	10	17.68 ± 0.1	20	7.57 ± 7.24	40	6.64 ± 6.66
Urtica dioica L.	15	4.14 ± 3.95	25	23.55 ± 14	20	2.48 ± 2.28
Viola canescens Wall.	-	-	60	4.91 ± 3.35	15	0.75 ± 0.24

rapidly due to sudden increase in the number of tourists and pilgrims. As a result there was also a decline in the collection of medicinal herbs by the local people. With the rapid socio-economic changes, the villagers of Bhyundar valley have now shifted their traditional practices towards market economy.

Awareness on Use of Plants as Medicine

To assess the traditional knowledge on the medicinal plants among various age groups, the local people were categorised into 4 age classes 1-12 (infants who are not in the process of learning), (ii) 13-25 (youths), (iii) 28-45 (adults) and >46 (old or veterans). Further, the degree of knowledge occupied by each individual was categorised into three ranks based on the person's knowledge on the number of medicinal plants. If the person had no knowledge then he/she was ranked 0, if he/she knew the commonest medicinal plants then they ranked 1, and if he/she knew most of the medicinal plants then they were given rank 2. Attitude of various age classes towards learning on medicinal plants were analysed using the semi-structured interviews.

In the Bhyundar valley, the attitude of young generation towards traditional healing system was in middle of the road. The younger generation was keen to do other business, as they felt it less tedious than the pastoral and agricultural practices. Among the youths who formed 23% of the total population, 95% had no knowledge on medicinal plants. Adults formed the 29% of the total population, of which 68% had no knowledge, 27% possessed adequate knowledge and 5% had good knowledge on medicinal plants. Old people formed only 19% of the total population, of which 35% had no knowledge, 52% had adequate knowledge and 13% had very good knowledge on medicinal plants (Table 4.2). The old people had more knowledge on the medicinal plants compared to younger generation.

The elder people (>46 years old) in some families knew the healing properties of plant species and treated the patients free of cost. They did not disclose the name and uses of medicinal plants to others, as they believed that the desired effect of medicinal plant reduces if its name is revealed to others. This belief and practice helps in conserving the rare plants but at the same time if knowledge is not transferred to appropriate person at the right time it results in the downfall of the traditional knowledge through generation. There was not well-recognised vaidya in the Bhyundar valley as such.

For ancient time, the bark of Bhoj Patra *(Betula utilis)* has been used as a paper. Still today, the priest or saint writes sometimes 'mantras' or spells on the bark of this tree in red ink. It is given to the devotee preserved in the small casket, which is believed to cure certain diseases. It is regarded as a magic box possessing the power of warding off demons and devils. No evil eyes can harm a child/person bearing this amulet. This sort of amulet (Tabeej) is tied invariably around the neck or the right hand of young children. *Cannabis sativa* is another religious plant. Hindu devotees regard the Lord Shiva as *Bhangeri Baba* and relish the drink prepared from its dried seeds.

The flowers of *Jasminum humile* are especially offered to Lakshmi (the wife of Lord Vishnu) in the months of *Chaitra* (March-April) and *Baisakh* (April-May). Devotees write the name of God or deities on leaves, sometime count the flowers, prepare garlands and offer them to God and Goddesses. That way, besides medicinal plants, the villagers had a considerable faith in the medico-religious and religious plants. *Saussurea obvallata* was collected on the occasion of worship of local deities, especially the offerings of a local deity, Goddess Nanda Devi.

Table 4.2

Transfer of Knowledge on Medicinal Plants Through Generation

Age class	*Degree of knowledge*	*Male*	*Female*	*Total*
13-25	0	33 (89)	40 (100)	73 (95)
	1	4 (11)	-	4 (5)
	2	-	-	-
26-45	0	35 (63)	31 (76)	66 (68)
	1	16 (28)	10 (24)	26 (27)
	2	5 (9)	-	5 (5)
>46	0	13 (35)	9 (35)	22 (35)
	1	20 (54)	13 (50)	33 (52)
	2	4 (11)	4 (15)	8 (13)

Values in parenthesis are in percent. Degree of knowledge
0 = No idea at all; 1=Know only about commonest medicinal herbs;
2 = Know majority of medicinal herbs

There is an old tree of *Morus serrata* located in the middle of Joshimath town had a special significance in this region. It was called as *Kalpavriksha* (tree of eternity). The Sankaracharya is said to have meditated under this tree c. 800 years ago. The root of *Hedychium spicatum* had a special religious significance on the occasion of marriages. Its decoction was applied on the body of bride and grooms to keep the body cool. *Origanum vulgare* was another medico-religious plant, which was offered to Lord Vishnu and Shiva in Badrinath and Kedarnath temples.

Villager's Dependency on Medicinal Plants

There are mainly three medicinal herbs viz., *faran (Allium humile)*, *choru (Angelica glauca)* and *dolu (Rheum australe)* which the residents of Bhyundar valley collected from the adjacent areas viz., Kahbhusandi, Khiron valley, Semertoli, Hemkund and the Valley of Flowers. These herbs were collected for their own use and at times villagers offered them to their relatives and friends as gift. Out of 63 families of Bhyundar village, 46 were involved in the collection of *faran,* 37 in *choru* and 15 in *dolu* (Table 4.3). The average collection of *faran, choru* and *dolu* by each family was 20 kg, 4.40 kg and 370 gm respectively. *Faran* was collected in highest quantity (19.70 ± 0.35 kg per family), followed by *choru* (4.40 ± 0.14 kg per family) and *dolu* (0.37 ± 0.09 per family). The availability of these herbs in the wild was generally low in the buffer zone. The density (individuals mv^{-2}) of *faran* in Khiron valley was higher (13.28) compared to the Valley of Flowers (5.54 ± SD 5.56). The *chorus* densities in park and buffer zone of the park were 1.03 ± 0.74 and 0.91 ± 0.61 respectively. The dolu's densities in park and its buffer zone were 0.24 ± 0.11 and 0.16 respectively.

Table 4.3
Extraction of Three Major Medicinal Herbs by Villagers of Bhyundar (in kg)

Parameters	*Faran*	*Choru*	*Dolu*
No. of families involved	46	37	15
Minimum quantity (kg)	10.00	2.00	0.20
Maximum quantity (kg)	25.00	5.00	1.50
Variance	5.68	0.69	0.14
Mean quantity ± SE	19.70 + 0.35	4.40 + 0.14	0.37 ± 0.09
Total	**906.00**	**163.00**	**5.50**

Faran was collected every year. It was not uprooted and only leaves and flowers of this herb were harvested. Such a practice might be better for the conservation of this species compared to uprooting. Some of the families, who either earned good income from tourism or who didn't have manpower to collect these herbs had left this traditional practice of medicinal plants collection. Mainly women folk of Bhyundar valley were responsible to collect *faran.* In July when the *faran* had flowers, women of Bhyundar valley in groups of 15-20 went for its collection in the alpine meadows. They took *kandi* (bamboo made local baskets) and each woman collected around 15-20 kg of *faran.* Man collected *dolu* and *choru* during September-October. Besides these herbs, men also collected *mitha (Aconitum balfourii), balchhadi (Arnebia benthamii), hathajari (Dactylorhiza hatagirea), salammishri*

(Polygonatum verticillatum), mamira (Thalictrum foliolosum), etc. The bark of *thuner (Taxus baccata)* was also collected mainly for making tea. *Thuner* was severely exploited for firewood and construction of temporary sheds on way to Hemkund.

Due to easy availability of allopathic medicines in the market and rapid socio-economic changes in this region the dependence of local people on medicinal plants has decreased. The younger generation had more belief on allopathic medicine. Notwithstanding, they had some faith in medicinal plants for curing diseases, for instance, the use of *Thalictrum foliolosum* was in practice for curing eye complaints and skin diseases, *Dactylorhiza hatagirea, Eulophia dabia* and *Gymnadenia orchidis* were used as health tonics as well as for curing gynaecological disorders, *Picrorhiza kurrooa* for fever and headache etc.

The quantity of extraction of certain important species, such as *Dactylorhiza hatagirea, Picrorhiza kurrooa, Nardostachys grandiflora* etc. could not be assessed because the local people of Bhyundar didn't admit their collection. One of such species, i.e., *Dactylorhiza hatagirea* was very popular and the popularity of this herb can be judged by the fact that all people of the study area knew its uses and were able to identify this herb. However, there were reports on the illegal trade in these species as some informants mentioned that people from the adjacent district had been collecting these herbs along with musk from this region.

Cultivation of Medicinal Plants

A need is felt to develop a scheme for utilization of steeper and marginal land around villages lying in the Bhyundar valley so that native medicinal herbs, which have become rare in wild, could be made available to the consumers by farming. The collection of medicinal plants for commercial purposes has exerted a tremendous pressure on the existing plant populations and their habitats. At the same time, there was a tendency to neglect the use of less important herbs resulted in the loss of traditional knowledge. Since law prohibited collection of medicinal herbs from the National Parks, the local people were forced to over-exploit the unprotected areas for the collection.

Some prospects of raising nurseries for wild medicinal herbs in the village wastelands were studied and therefore, this discussed with the villagers of Bhyundar valley. About 80% of them were enthusiastic of this approach. One of the villagers willingly offered his land for the initial experiments. Two plots of 20 × 20 m were fenced with rubble wall at 200 m distance from village boundary. Fencing was done for prohibiting the livestock entry into the plots. The upper surface of land in both the plots were dug out and about 50 kg of manure (cow, sheep and goats dung) were added uniformly on one plot to observe the effect of manure. Seeds, rhizomes and tubers of three rare medicinal herbs viz., *hathajari (Dactylorhiza hatagirea), bankakri (Podophyllum hexandrum)* and *dolu (Rheum australe)* were collected from the wild for sowing. The selection of medicinal herbs for cultivation was based on the local people's choice. They had utilized the selected species for their own use and also the demand of those species were high in the market. Before sowing, the seeds were dried in the sun for three days. The seeds of *Dactylorhiza hatagirea* being powdery were mixed with sand and then sown, as it was difficult to disperse the powdery seeds uniformly on the ground. The area remained under snow during winter and the propagules (tubers, rhizomes and seeds) were iikely to remain dormant till the snow melt.

Some more information are given below for the farming of selected species:

Dactylorhiza hatagirea: It grows well in the open stable meadows requires well-drained soil. This rare medicinal herb is found in open moist slopes between 3,500-4,500 m in western as well as eastern Himalaya. Its seeds should be sown in October and November. Two times manure and frequent weeding is considered to be good for better tuber growth. This herb is propagated through seeds or tuber cutting. Harvesting of tubers after 4-5 years of its cultivation may yield good crop. It may be harvested after 2-3 years.

Rheum australe: This medicinal herb requires cool and temperate climate and rich porous soil. This is found between 2,800-3,600 m. October and November are the best months for sowing of seeds. Planting may be done in moisture retentive exposed rocky soil. For its better yield, it needs moderate input of sheep and goats dung. Its root can be harvested biannually.

Podophyllum Hexandrum: This herb requires cool and temperate climate with humus rich loamy soil in partial shade. It found in nature between 2,500-3,200 m. Seed sowing should be done in May and June. For its better yield heavy inputs of manure, particularly of sheep and goat, is required. Its fruits could be harvested annually and roots once in 3-4 years.

There was keen interest amongst the farmers of Bhyundar valley. They have shown interest to take up more trials and follow other methods in the event of failures. There is technology available elsewhere (High Altitude Plant Physiology Research Centre, Srinagar Garhwal, and G.B. Pant Institute of Himalayan Environment and Development, Almora) that can be used to improve the economy of the hill people.

Enterprise Development

Local communities, Forest Department, Block Development Authorities, Herbal Research and Development Institute, Gopeshwar, High Altitude Plant Physiology Research Centre, Srinagar Garhwal, Environment and Mountain Development Institute, Sumari, co-operative societies and many local social workers were approached for enterprise development. The following points emerged during discussions with them.

After 1992, the collection of many herbs has been banned from the Nature Reserves as per the Forest and Wildlife Acts. But before were interviewed 1992, about 12-15 medicinal herbs were collected by the villagers in district Chamoli from the wild and supplied to the Co-operative societies (Table 4.4) without any restrictions from the Government. As a result, only 4 species viz., *reetha (Sapindus mukorossi), guchchi (Morchella esculenta), indrayan (Trichosanthus tricuspidata)* and *jhula* (lichens) are being collected and sold to the co-operative societiės at present. The rate of these medicinal plants varied from Rs. 2.50-2,600 per kg. There was a marked difference in the prices of purchase and sale of the medicinal plants by co-operative societies, e.g., the buying cost of *guchchi* was Rs. 1,200 per kg and selling cost Rs. 2,600 per kg, *jhula* was purchased at Rs. 30 per kg and sold at Rs. 25 per kg, in 1997.

The cost of these plants was higher in the local markets compared to co-operative society. Therefore, the medicinal plant collectors prefered to sell these plants in the local and regional markets rather to middle man, contractors and co-operative societies. Since there was no legal trade allowed in Bhyundar and adjoining valleys on these medicinal plants, there were indications of illegal trade particularly in species such as *hathajari, atis* and *jatamansi.*

Hathajari (Rs. 800-1200 per kg), followed by *atis* (Rs. 180-250 per kg) and *jatamansi* (Rs. 85-100 per kg) during 1997-98, the cost of these rare species was highest at Joshimath. Some of the medicinal plants are being traded to India from Nepal at much cheaper rate resulting the devaluation of indigenous products. Similarly in the neighbouring state Himachal Pradesh Forest Department issued permits to the local medicinal herb collectors even from few of the National

Table 4.4 Trade Value of Medicinal Plants. Serial 1-13 Species were Sold in Co-operative Societies before 1992

	Species	*Local name*	*Rates (Indian Rs/kg)*	
			Purchase	*Sale*
1	*Paris polyphylla*	Mithi buch	20.00	25.00
2	*Hedychium spicatum*	Kapoor kachri	3.00	5.00
3	*Dioscorea deltoidea*	Dioscorea	2.50	5.00
4	*Swertia chirayita*	Chiraita	7.50	16.00
5	*Bergenia ligulata*	Pasanbhed	3.50	5.00
6	*Zanthoxylum armatum*	Timur	18.00	25.00
7	*Valeriana hardwickii*	Samewa	12.00	18.00
8	*Centella asiatica*	Brahmi	8.00	12.00
9	*Saussurea costus*	Kut	650.00	700.00
10	*Trichosanthus tricuspidata*	Indrayan	-	-
11	*Jhula (All lickens)	Jhula	13.00	25.00
12	**Sapindus mukorossi*	Reetha	5.00	12.00
13	**Morchella esculenta*	Guchchi	1200	2600
14	***Aconitum heterophyllum*	Atis		180-250
15	***Angelica glauca*	Choru		55-75
16	***Dactylorhiza hatagirea*	Hathajari		800-1200
17	***Nardostachys grandiflora*	Jatamansi		85-100
18	***Picrorhiza kurrooa*	Katuki		60-85
19	***Rheum australe*	Dolu		30-50
20	***Taxus baccata*	Thuner		15-25
21	***Polygonatum verticillatum*	Salam misri		15-20
22	***Allium humile*	Faran		75-90
23	***Pleurospermum angelicoides*	Choru		18-20
24	***Podophyllum hexandrum*	Bankakri		50

* Species currently sold through co-operative societies.

** Species sold only in local market.

Parks. There was no such provision in Chamoli district and even to cultivate some of the rare medicinal plants the cultivators had to have the permission from the government, the procedure for which was sometimes lengthy and troublesome.

Earlier, some of the inhabitants in the buffer zone of the NDBR cultivated *dolu* in the surrounding wastelands of villages and fortunately the yield was very good but due to lack of market they could not sell it. Therefore, they stopped to cultivate it. Marketing in fact has become a problem in medicinal plant trade. Some of the plants of *dolu* were still growing in those wastelands. The farmers of Mana village, 3 km after Badrinath, had to face a similar problem in marketing of Kut *(Saussurea lappa). Allium carolinianum* is being cultivated in the buffer zone of NDBR but it is used for own consumption. Third problem, which is being faced by the cultivators, is the cheap rates of many medicinal plants, which are even lower than the prices of seasonal vegetables. The medicinal plants collectors in Himachal Pradesh are facing the similar problem.

Still, the farmers of Bhyundar valley and NDBR are keen to cultivate the medicinal herbs. Many more villagers have now realised the potentiality of medicinal plants and they are willing to propagate more herbs if cultivation technology is made available to them. Some experiments at Tungnath have carried out on the cultivation of medicinal plants by High Altitude Plant Physiology Research Centre. The local people were advised to visit Tungnath area for learning the cultivation techniques of other medicinal plants. Once the transfer of technology gets over the genuine prices of these medicinal plants can be fixed up keeping the small farmers in mind.

Almost all the approached government and non-governmental organizations had consensus on the economic development of farmers through medicinal plant farming by providing some kind of subsidies to them. This may help in mitigating the pressure on these medicinal plants. Moreover, since the Uttaranchal has been declared as a separate state, many voices have been coming up for making the Uttaranchal as an herbal state. If it does take shape, the marginal farmers of the high altitudes may be benefited through this policy. In such elevation ranges only the medicinal herbs can grow in abundance.

5

The Lepcha Medicobotany of Dzangu in the Sikkim Himalaya

The Lepchas are the oldest inhabitants of Sikkim. Approximately 30 per cent of the population of the state is Lepcha, and mostly concentrates in the North District in the Lepcha reserve of Dzangu. They are the oldest inhabitants of Sikkim Rong– a language of the Tibeto-Burman group– which is spoken by the Lepchas is very rich in vocabulary that relates to flora and fauna, representing a way of life that is close to nature and makes extensive use of plants for medicinal purposes. The study documents 41 such medicinal plants used by the Lepchas for treating various ailments, which speak for the traditional knowledge accumulated by the community.

The Lepchas in Sikkim

Sikkim was virfually seraled from the outside would till its merger with India in 1975. It is one of the most beautiful of the Himalayan state because of ethereal presence of Kangchendzongha. But this attraction belies the toughress of the life its native peoples have had to follow. When these people had migrated into the area from tibet many centuries ago, they met a tract of continuous forest interspersed here and there by several streams and rivers, where they gradually established settlements unlinked by any system of communication. Adjusting to their new environment, they began testing locally-available materials to meet their needs for food, fodder and clothing. As for medicine, they started accumulating ethnic knowladge.

Which ever people later on settled in Sikkim they brought with them whatever they knew of ethnomedicine. There where Lepchas sherps Bhutias and Nepalese. While sporadic mention of the ethnomedicine practised by these peoples is found in the literature

(Bennet, 1983,1985; Hajra and Chakravorty, 1981; Krishna and Singh, 1987; Kumar *et al, 1994;* Raju and Krishna, 1990; Panda, 1996; Saklani & Jain, 1994), no comprehensive effort has so far been made to detail the ethnomedicine of any given community. The present study makes this effort in case of the Lepcha settlements of Dzangu.

The Lepcha reserve of Dzangu (also called Lepcha Gaon) is located 15 km downhill from Mangan in North Sikkim in an altitudinal range from 900-2100 m, and is hemmed in by impassably high mountains. The rivers Dikchu, Tallung and Rongnyu that demarcate the area are only crossed by suspension bridges at Sankalang and Pheedong. The Lepchas of Dzangu thus still maintain the racial and tribal sanctity that has come down to them with their stock, and are shy and avoid strangers. Dzangu is characterised by great floristic diversity. Like other tribal peoples in the country, the Lepchas living there worship the spirits of the mountains, rivers and forests with whom they have coexisted in natural surroundings. Interestingly the name *Rong-pa* given to the Lepchas by the Tibetan people which means "ravine-folk", carries the connotations of the Lepcha lifestyle which encourages them to live at a distance from roads, and to depend extensively on wild plants as sources of food, fibre, fodder, fuel, and for medicinal and other aromatic purposes.

Besides gathering these products from forests, the Lepchas still practise slash and burn cultivation (*jhum* agriculture) in the upper reaches of Dzangu, where they grow rice, buckwheat, millet and barley, following a seven-year rotational cycle. More than the other ethnic peoples of Sikkim, the Lepchas are familiar with the medicinal properties of numerous plants which grow around them, which they use to treat their own ailments and those of their cattle. It is not the *Bungthing* (Lepcha herbalist) alone who is well versed in the use of plants in the treatment of ailments, since ethnic knowledge in this respect has been inherited by the community from its forefathers. As a result, the Lepchas partake of various plants and roots known to be poisonous) as food, since they know the art of freeing the poisons.

In this study are consedered the medicinal use of various plants by the Lepchas, identifying these by their scientific and local names, and the areas and elevations where they occur. The parts used and modes of application are also mentioned along with dosage and plants used in combination. The authors have followed the usual standard methodology of collection for ethnobotanical data (Rao, 1989). Voucher specimens of the plants used are deposited with the BSHC at Gangtok.

Botanical Names	*Family*	*Vernacular Name*	*Area of Occurrence and Specimen*	*Elevational Range*	*Mode of Application*
Abies densa Muell	PINACEAE	L. Chandenkung; N. Gobreysalla	Ravongla, Hilley, Dzongri S.K. Jana 2483 [BSHC]	2100-3500 m	Oleoresin extracted from cones used to treat toothache
Aconitum ferox Wallich	RANUNCULACEAE	L. Bikhuma	Kishong-la, Chhangu, Sherathang, Nathu-la S.K. Jana 18304 [BSHC]	3700-4200 m	Crushed tuberous roots applied externally on gum and tongue sores; paste of the same administered orally in case of food poisoning
Aegle mermelos (L) Currea	RUTACEAE	L. Belpot; N. Bel	Rhenok, Reshi, Rongli, Rangpo, Melli Singtam (Dikchu) S.K. Jana 1839 [BSHC]	250-1130 m	Crushed tender leaves in aqueous solution administered orally to control excessive seminal discharge
Artemisia Indica Wild	ASTERACEAE	L. Tail; N. Titapat	Throughout Sikkim S.K. Jana 15762 [BSHC]	1100-2600 m	Macerated leaves in aqueous solution administered orally to control excerrive seminal discharge.
Astilbe rivularis Buch.-Ham. ex D. Don	SAXIFRAGACEAE	L.Burhokhati	Hilley, Ribdi, Sherathang S.K. Jana 15762 [BSHC]	2700-3100 m	Powdered or pasted roots applied externally to cure acute body pains; the same administered orally with warm milk to arrest excessive bleeding during childbirth

Botanical Names	*Family*	*Vernacular Name*	*Area of Occurrence and Specimen*	*Elevational Range*	*Mode of Application*
Bergenia purpurecens (Hook.f. & Thomson) Engl.	SAXIFRAGACEAE	L. Pashanbed-reep; N. Pakhanbed; Peyogokhum	Dzongri, Lachen, Lachung, Bakhim S.K. Jana 18084 [BSHC]	2700-3700 m	Crushed rhizome administered orally with egg yolk to relieve fever, and body and chest pains; rhizome pasted with *Viscum articulatum* Brum f. applied externally to sprained joints, cuts and wounds
Bischofia javanica Blume	BISCHOFIACEAE	L. Sunong-kung; W.Kainjal	Dzongu S.K.Jana 17901 [BSHC]	1420 m	Bark used to treat gastric disorders, oleous extract of the seed applied externally to relieve muscular pain
Boehemeria clidemioides) *Miq.(=B. platyphylla* var. *cinerascens* Hook.f.	URTICACEAE	L. Kamley-ruy; N. Kamley	Dzonigu.'Tashiding, Geyzing, Sombarey S.K.Jana 2560 [BSHC]	1120-1720 m	Macerated leaves applied externally to cure skin disease
Brassalopsis hainla (Buch-Han ex D. Don) Seem	ARALIACEAE	L.Sunong-kung; N. Chiletro	Chungthang, Tashiding, Lingtam B. Krishna 2560 [BSHC]	1300-1800 m	Ground sun-dried roots administered orally in controlled dosage in case of dysentery

Botanical Names	Family	Vernacular Name	Area of Occurrence and Specimen	Elevational Range	Mode of Application
Calotropis procera (Aiton) Dryand.	ASCLEPIADACEAE	L. Anakh-mukh; N. Anakh	Tashiding, Rhenok, Dikchu, Mangan S.K.Jana 18097 [BSHC]	900-1500 m	Fresh leaves heated for a few seconds over a flame applied as a warm poultice to affected region to relieve pain from rheumatism and gout
Coelogyne assamica Lindley and Reichb.f.	ORCHIDACEAE	L. Sunong-reep; N. Sunakhari	Dentam, Okhrey, Gangtok, Tingyong, Sakyong P.K.Hajra 695 [BSHC]	1500-1980 m	Macerated pseudobulb administered orally in case of stomach ailment
Colebrookea oppositifolia Smith	LAMIACEAE	L. Dhusurey-kung; N. Dhusur	Tashiding, Rongli, Rhenok, Lingtam S.K.Jana18908[BSHC]	910-1700 m	Fresh leaves macerated by hand smelt to reduce sneezing in case of cold
Costus speciosus (Koenig) Smith	COSTACEAE	L. Roo-pa-tong; N. Betlauri	Throughout Sikkim S.Kumar 11453 [BSHC]	560-1820 m	Crushed rhizome mixed with leaf-juices of *Drymeria diendra* Blume and pasted roots of *Bombax ceiba* L. sapling administered orally in case of urinary disorders

Botanical Names	Family	Vernacular Name	Area of Occurrence and Specimen	Elevational Range	Mode of Application
Cuscuta refelexa Roxb.	CUSOUTACEAF	L. Mankam; N. Binajari	Rongli, Chujachen, Dzongu, Namchi S.K. Jana 17925 [BSHC]	850-1460 m	Pasted stem administered orally in case of menstrual disorders; the same also administered orally in case of jaundice
Dicentra scandens (D.Don) Walp.	FUMARIACEAE	L. Kundley	Hilley, Lachen, Tallung S. Kumar 7326 [BSHC]	2200-2902 m	Powered dried root administered orally with cold water in case of gastric disorders
Elatostema platyphyllum Wedd.	URTICACEAE	L. Behay; N. Gogleto; B. Dambrumbchoem	Gangeep, Dzongu, Pelling S.K. Jana 18924 [BSHC]	1580-2220 m	Shoot consumed as vegetable in case of gastric disorders
Entada purssetha DC.ssp.sinoghimalensis Grierson & Long	LEGUMINOSAE	L. Kluk-pot; N. Pangra	Tashiding, Darap, Soreng S.K. Jana 18386 [BSHC]	1300-1800 m	Pasted cotyledons applied externally on swollen parts in case of mumps
Eupatorium adenophorum tSprengel	ASTERACEAE	L. Banmara-mukh; N. Banmara; S. Kaleyjharh	Throughout Sikkim B. Krishna 2700 [BSHC]	1100-2400 m	Pasted cotyledons applied externally on swollen parts in case of mumps

Botanical Names	*Family*	*Vernacular Name*	*Area of Occurrence and Specimen*	*Elevational Range*	*Mode of Application*
Fagopyrum esculentum Moenech	POLYGONACEAE	L. Ruhru; N. Phaphar	Cultivated throughout Sikkim S.K.Jana 17984 [BSHC]	100-2200 m	Leaf-juice administered orally in case of stomach ailments and gastric disorders
Galinsoga quadriradiata Ruiz & Pavon	ASTERACEAE	L. Mukh-nock	Chandmari.Gangtok, Tumin, Dzongu B.Krishna 1598 [BSHC]	1120-1980 m	Pasted leaves applied externally to snakebites
Gynocardia odorata R.Br.	FLACOURTIACEAE	L Kothor-pot; N. Gantey	Tashiding, Dzongu, Gangeep S.K.Jana 1890 [BSHC]	1400-2100 m	Oleous extract of seed used for massaging infants
Hedychium coronarium Koenig	ZINGIBER ACEAE	L. Sleeek; W. Phacheng	Ribid, Kabi S.K. Jane 17964 [BSHC]	1300-2100 m	Pasted fresh rhizome applied externally to sprained joints
Hemiphragma heterophyllum Wallich	SCRO-PHULARIACEAE	L. Leh-reep; N. .Kanakmala, Malager	Phadamchen, Hilley, Ribdi, Sombarey S.K.Jana 18069 [BSHC]	1800-2920 m	Fresh Fruit consumed, or else chewed and the juices swallowed, to relieve sore throat paints.
Heracleum nepalens D. Don	APIACEAE	L. Chimping	Hilly, Zuluk, Lachen D.C.S. Raju & S. Singh 7705 [BSHC]	2600-3200 m	Pasted Seeds administered orally in case of fever, headache and stomach ailment.
Kaempferia sikkimensis. (King &Baker) Larson	ZINGIBERACEAE	L. Bhunichampa	Dzongu, Chungthang S. K. jana 17933 [BSGC]	1320-1800 m	Pasted rhizome applied externally to sprained joints; juice from paste applied externally on burns

Botanical Names	*Family*	*Vernacular Name*	*Area of Occurrence and Specimen*	*Elevational Range*	*Mode of Application*
Mimosa Pudica L.	MIMOSACEAE	L. Buarey-mukh; N. Buarey-jharh	Reshi, Rongli, Melli, Dzongu P. K. Hajra 1085 [BSHC]	500-1300 m	Pasted tender shoot-tips applied externally to the forehead in case of headache
Oroxylum indicum sore	BIGNONIACEAE (L) Vent.	L. Pago-reep;	Rhenok, Lingtam, N. Tatala Dzongu (S.K. Jana 18988 [BSHC])	600-1500 m	Burnt and powdered seeds applied externally with lime to the throat to relieve throat pains; pasted fresh seeds administered orally to relieve menstrual pains
Rhododendron arboreum smith	ERICACEAE	L. Khenio; N. Laligurans	Lachen, Gangeep, Varshey G. P. Sinha 17454 [BSHC]	220-3200 m	Fresh or dried petals administered orally in case of acute blood dysentery, in a dosage of 3-5 petals at a time thrice daily for 2-3 days
Rhus semialata Murray	ANA CARDIACEAE	L. Tungrit-kung; N. Bhakimlo	Tashiding Dzongu Rongli, kabi S.K. Jana 17936 [BSHC]	900-1780 m	Oleos extract of Seed administered orally in a dosage of 2 tsp twice daily in case of blood dysentery till symptoms disappear.
Rubia cordifolia L.	RUBIACEAE	L. Bhyemi; N. Manjeto	Throughout temperate Sikkim S.K. Jana 15733 [BSHC]	-	Extracted Juice of macerated root applied as an astringent to cuts and wounds.
Rumex nepalensis Sprengel	POLYGONACEAE	L. Palu; Isomo N. Halhalay	Dzongu, Gangtok, Yoksum B. Krishna 4040 [BSHC]	1500-2900 m	Tea made from cut boiled roots administered orally in small tumbler-fulls twice daily upto 3days in case of food poisoning

Botanical Names	*Family*	*Vernacular Name*	*Area of Occurrence and Specimen*	*Elevational Range*	*Mode of Application*
Schima wallichii (D.C.) Korthals var. wallichii	THEACEAE	L. Sambrumb-Kung; N. chilauni	Dzongu, Gangeep, Tashiding S. K. Jana 17907 [BSHC]	1500-1800 m	Bark pasted with bark of Bridelia retusa Sprengel (Penji) applied externally on deep cuts and wounds
Siejesbeckia orientalis L.	ASTERACEAE	L. Mong-reep	Dzongu, Tashiding, Burtuk S. K. Jana 17943 [BSHC]	1400-1800 m	Leaves applied as an external poultice on sores
Solanum viarum Dunal	SOLANACEAE	L. Jaiu; N. Kachingre-Kanra	Dzongu, Dentam, Khechopalri D.C.S. Raju 3307 [BSHC]	1400-1820 m	Burnt fruits administered orally to check tooth decay
Symplocos theifolia D. Don	SYMPLOCACEAE	L. Singhum; N.Kharaney	Okhrey, Ribdi, Sombarey, Dzongu S.K. Jana 15765 [BSHC]	1600-2600 m	Fruit juice in aqueous solution administered orally in case of loose bowel motions
Terminalia myriocarpa Heurck. & Muell.-Arg.	COMBRETACEAE	L. Songlok-kung; N. Panisaj	Okhrey, Ribid, Sombarey, Dzongu S.K. Jana 18008 [BSHC]	1100-1700 m	Bark administered orally as laxative and in case of liver ailments
Thysanlaena maxima (Roxb). O. Ktze.	POACEAE	L. Pursuer; N. Amlisho; Chakula	Geyzing, Dentam, Rhenok, Gangtok, Dzongu G.P. Sinha 8548 [BSHC]	950-1820 m	Pasted root applied externally as a poultice on sores and boils

Botanical Names	Family	Vernacular Name	Area of Occurrence and Specimen	Elevational Range	Mode of Application
Trichosanthes tricuspidata Lour.	CUCURBITACEAE	L. Tong-kung-pot; N. Indrani-Lahra	Tumin Tullung (Dzongu) S.K. Jana 16727 [BSHC]	1880-2700 m	Root administered orally in case of food poisoning; oleos extract of seed applied externally to cure skin diseases; stem used by '*Bungthings*' in case of snakebite
Urtica ardens Link (=U. parviflora Roxb.)	URTICACEAE	L. Sorong; N. Gharia-sisnu	Throughout temperate Sikkim G.P. Sinha 15762 [BSHC]		Leaves consumed as vegetable to control high blood pressure
Viola diffusa Ging. ex DC	VIOLACEAE	L. Dambrum-pot; N. Heeley	Dzongu, Gangtok S.K. Jana 17978 [BSHC]	1500-1900 m	Pasted leaves applied externally to treat allergy
Vitex negundo L.	VERBENACEAE	L. Simbrek-kung; N. Sewli	Chujachen, Melli, Reshi, S.K. Jana 18053 [BSHC]	750-1080 m	Macerated leaves applied externally as a warm poultice to treat rheumatism
Zanthoxylum acanthopodium DC.	RUTACAE	L. Nangrupot; N. Bokey-timboor	Ribdi, Gangtok S.K Jana 15741 [BSHC]	1900-2700 m	Powdered fruit administered orally to check tooth decay.

Their preservation Knowledge Systems

Previously they has beliefs which attributed most of the ill of life to spirits and often sought magicoreligious remedices for such problems. Over many years, with the accumulation of experience, Lepchas they have learnt that many ailments and illnesses can be cured by proper application of plant remedies. Many common diseases, although believed to have originated in malevolent spirits, are considered curable through the use of herbal medicine. However, as more and more Lepchas acquire education and training and resettle themselves in the towns and cities, the traditional knowledge they have carried with them slowly gets lost. Documentation of their medicobotany can therefore make their healing knowledge accessible to all. Modern medicines of chemical origin. But compared to the herbal medicines used by them are cheap and have minimum side-effects

Secondly, creation of awareness among the people that all living resources are in limited stock and should be conserved instead of being squandered away can preserve the values of biodiversity. Because of prolonged and increasing exploitation, the medicinal plants used have undergone depletion and are consequently under threat. Implementation of the Ethnobiological Education Spectrum [EES] involving awareness of practical life situations, judicious utilisation and *ex situ* and *in situ* conservation of local biological resources can ensure their long-term sustainability.

The authors are grateful to the Director, BSI, Calcutta, and to Dr. V.Mudgal, Jt.Director, BSI, Calcutta, for encouragement. They are also grateful to the Ministry of Environment and Forests, New Delhi, for providing financial assistance to the study.

References

1. S.S.R. Bennet [1983]: 'Ethnobotanical Studies in Sikkim'. *Ind. For.* 109 (7): 477-481.
2. S.S.R. Bennet [1985]: 'Ethnobotanical Studies in West Sikkim'; J. Econ.Tax.Bot. 7(2): 317-321.
3. P.K. Hajra, P. Chakravorty [1981]: 'A Survey of Wild Plants Sold in the Lal Market of Gangtok', *Ind.Jour. forestry* 4 (3): 217-220.
4. S.K. Jain [1991]: *Dictionary of Indian Folk Medicine and Ethnobotany, Deep*, New Delhi.
5. B. Krishna, S. Singh [1987]: 'Ethnobotanical Observation in Sikkim'; *J. Econ. Tax. Bct.* 9(1): 1-7.

6. S. Kumar, P. Singh, V. Singh [1987]: 'Ethnomedico-aspects of some Arboreal and Arborescent Taxa of Sikkim', in Higher Plants of the Indian *Subcontinent,* Vol. 3, pp. 164-166.

7. D.C. Pal, S.K. Jain [1997]: *Tribal Medicine,* Naya Prakash, Calcutta.

8. S. Panda [1996]: 'Plant Use: A Recent Perspective from Eastern Himalaya', J.E con. Tax Bot. (addl.ser.) pp. 332-337.

9. D.C.S. Raju, B. Krishna [1990] 'Less-known Edible Plants of Sikkim'; in R.P. Purkayastha (ed): *Economic Plants,* Vol. 7, Microbs, New Delhi, pp. 83-86.

10. R.R. Rao, P.K. Hajra [1987] 'Methods of Research in Ethnobotany'; in S.K. Jain (ed.): A Manual of *Ethnobotany.*

11. H.H. Risley [1894]: *Gazetteer of Sikkim,* Bengal Government Secretarit Press, Calcutta.

12. P. Sensarma [1997]: *Ethnobiological Information in Kautilya Arthasastra,* Naya Prakash, Calcutta.

6

Ethnobotany of the Darjeeling Himalaya

A special feature of the Darjeeling Himalaya has been a mixing of ethnic communities, and therefore also of ethnobotanical traditions. Himalayan communities resident in the Darjeeling Himalaya are a repository of undocumented knowledge on the indigenous uses of plant specimens endemic to the area. The paper documents certain little known plants in use by the community in terms of their genus, species and methodology of use.

Ethnobotany in the Region

The Darjeeling Himalaya is over tropical, temperate and sub-alpine climate zones. It is extremely rich in biodiversity as well as in ethnobotany. It has a geographical spread of 3149 sq. kms. Ethnobotanical studies of around 6000 plant species found in the region have however only commenced recently. Unnumbered species have been used in unnumbered ways by tradition, and use of the same species in different ways over different localities is also observed. However, onslaughts from the modern way of life and the easy substitutes it offers have pushed the practice to ethnobotany back to far flung villages where the facilities of modern life are lacking. Meanwhile, it stands to reason that several valuable ethnobotanical traditions have been lost with the passage of time as there is still lack of an organised effort to document them into archives. Except for plants that only see use in festivities, worship, marriage and death rituals, others that serve food and medicinal purposes need phytochemical analysis in order to ascertain their worth for wider use. It appears that only a fraction of the available ethnobotanical wisdom has been recorded.

This paper high lights some of the lesser-known plants in ethnobotanical use by tribal communities in the Darjeeling Himalaya.

Materials and Methods

Interviews were conducted of herbalists and of persons who had been treated by them and the actual usage of plants was recorded. Visits were made to the *haats* (weekly markets) to identify and record plants brought for sale from the villages. Visits were also made to rural homes to observe ethnotechnology. The plants identified are deposited with the Kalimpong College Herbarium for further study.

Summarised Findings

Yonzone *et. al.* [1984 a, b; 1985 a, b] have reperted many plants but they failed to cover certain aspects. have reported 118 ethnomedicinal plants, 46 wild edible plants and 47 poisonous plants from the Darjeeling Himalaya in their study on natural resources in the region. The present paper covers to additional instances and aspects not reported so far, which are summarily listed below.

Name and Local Name	*Family*
Daphne cannabina Hook. F. N. Argeli or Kagatey [Location: Lava, Kalimpong]	THYMELEACEAE
A high quality insect-resistant paper is made from the bark of serial parts by a remarkably eco-friendly traditional method in which no chemical is used. The product, locally called *Paharay Kagach* is the traditional folk paper. The plant coppices well and continued supply of bark is ensured. The plant grows abundantly in the temperature Himalaya.	
Dicentra scandens (D. Don) Walpers N. Makuray jhar [Location: Birch Hill, Darjeeling]	FUMARIACEAE
The leaves of the climbing plant are used in cardiac ailments.	
Equisetum diffusum D. Don N Kurkuray jhar [Location: Bong Busty, Kalimpong]	EQUISETACEAE
Young shoots are made into a paste and directly applied for the removal of warts. Extracted juice has also been found to act as biological pesticide. The plant grows well in damp wastelands of the temperate Himalaya.	
Emblica officinalis Gaertn. N. Amala [Location: Sinji Busty, Kalimpong]	EUPHORBIACEAE
The fruit is eaten raw in case of indigestion.	

Name and Local Name	*Family*
Elsholtzia blanda Linn. N. Chhinik; Sherpa. Lenza [Location: Sonada, Darjeeling]	LAMIACEAE

The powdery seeds of the plant swell and become sticky when boiled and are eaten as pulses *[dal]*, an important constituent of the Indian. The discovery of the plant as a new dal-substitute was mad a few years ago, even though it has been in traditional use by Sherpas in Darjeeling. The seeds are extremely light, so that 500g provide the same quantity of cooked *dal* as 1 kg of the usual pulse seed. The Sherpas use the plant at high elevations. Seeds are sown in *jhum* (swidden) fields at 1800 m and above. Black soil and Cowdung manure are found to favour the growth of the plant.

Mahonia nepalensis DC N. Citray, Chutro or Kesari [Location: Birch Hill, Darjeeling]	BERBERIDACEAE

The ripe yellow berries are crushed in water and the filtrate is orally imbibed in case of dysentery and urinary problems.

Urtica dilica Linn. N. Gharia Sisnu	URTICACEAE

A savoury nettle soup is made by boiling the young inflorescence in water with a little salt. Addition of a little flour improves the consistency to a thick soup.

Oroxylum indicum Vent. N. Totala [Location: Seokbir Busty, Kalimpong]	BIGNONIACEAE

Juice of the bark is used in the treatment of diabetes.

Ophiopogon intermedius D. Don. N. Nakima [Location: Pedong, Kalimpong]	LILIACEAE

The young inflorescence of the stemless plant with a cluster of leaves makes a fine curry.

Rhododendron arboreum Smith N. Rato Gurans [Location: Senchal, Darjeeling]	ERICACEAE

The young leaves are used to poison fish. The red flowers find medicinal use in case of dysentery accompanied by gastrointestinal bleeding and against throat infections.

Strobilanthus petiolaris Nees. N. Sharpa Aushadhi jhar [Location: Bong Busty, Kalimpong]	ACANTHACEAE

The plant is used as an antidote to snake venom. The aerial parts are made into a paste with the addition of water and applied as poultice for several hours at the location of the snakebite.

Name and Local Name	*Family*
Tagetes patula Linn. N. Saipatri phul [Location: Bong Busty, Kalimpong]	COMPOSITAE
A decoction of flowers in water is orally imbibed in case of ordinary fever and pneumonia. The plant is grown commonly as an ornamental, and its flowers find wide festive and ceremonial use.	
Thysanolaena maxima (Roxb.) O.Kuntze N. Kuchcho [Location: All over the hills]	GRAMINEAE
A decoction of the root in water is used to induce abortion and to treat mumps, boils and abscesses. The plant finds multifarious uses. Ideal when grown along hill slopes to anchor the soil against erosion, its mature terminal inflorescences make indigenous brooms, while its leaves are a good fodder for cattle.	
Solanum khasianum Clarke N. Rambhenri kanra [Location: Birch Hill, Darjeeling]	SOLANACEAE
The seeds are burnt and their smoke is wafted onto aching teeth to relieve pain	
Cardamine hirsuta Linn. N. Simraya [Location: Rajbari, Darjeeling]	CRUCIFERAE
The leafy stems which are eaten as green-spinache are also valued as health food that counteracts jaundice, cardiac disease, low blood pressure and gout.	
Capsicum frutescens Linn. N. Dallay Khorsani [Location: Cultivated in the villages of Kalimpong]	SOLANACEAE
The fruits which are used as a spice also relieve gastric problems.	
Zanthoxylum armatum DC. N. Bhale Timur [Location: Pedong, Kalimpong]	RUTACEAE
The red fruit is eaten in pickled form in case of indigestion.	
Gynocardia odorata R. Br. N Gantay [Location: Foothills of the river Tista, Kalimpong]	FLACOURTIACEAE
Oil extracted from the seeds is used in the treatment of leprosy and skin diseases. The fruits are used to poison fish and also yield a biological pesticide.	

Future Course of action

An estimated 20 per cent of rural people and 5 per cent of urban people residing in the Darjeeling Himalaya still use traditional herbal medicine in treating diseases. Of 118 plant species covered by the extended study, the use of organic parts stands as follows

Whole plants	10 species
Young shoots	12 species
Stems	24 species
Leaves	21 species
Roots	22 species
Flowers	8 species
Fruits	21 species

The cultivation of traditional agricultural crops such as rice, maize and wheat on hill slops has taken its toil on the soil. It has led to excessive soil erosion. Investigation of biochemical, pharmaceutical and pharmacological aspects of the listed plants would therefore aid their evaluation as potential economic crops for hill farmers. There is now an urgent need for replacement of these by recourse to high-valued cash crops such as medicinal plants.

The integration of all aspects and implications of ethnobotany into development planning for the Himalaya with conservation and protection of all species of plants and animals in traditional use has emergelous the future focus area. The wisdom concealed within the vast realms of ethnobotany is inestimable and invaluable, and essentially rests with the rural folk. In the development of ethnobotany, three minimal components, namely, planning, motivation and active people's participation are involved, with education playing the pivotal role in arousing mass consciousness. The following measures might therefore be suggested for the promotion of ethnobotany:

(i) organisation of village-level workshops, training camps and awareness campaigns.
(ii) demonstrations and promotion of the use of traditional plant products.
(iii) provision of financial and technical assistance as a promotional measure, in view of the fact that ethnobotany is very often related to the ethno-economy.
(iv) preparation of an inventory of endangered plants.
(v) establishment of ethnobotanical gardens, museums and research institutes.
(vi) establishment of a network of local, national and global marketing chains for sales and purchase of ethnobotanical products.

(vii) introduction of ethnobotany as full-fledged discipline in educational institutions.

(viii) enactment of legislation for conservation of rare plants of ethnobotanical importance.

Toxic Plants of Darjeeling Himalaya

The papers makes an analytic study of certain toxic plant species in the Darjeeling Himalaya and identifies the alkaloid and toxic reactions to them. These plants are endemic to the hill region, which are extremely harmful to livestock and human beings alike. Lack of proper identification of these species and their physiological effects makes it difficult to adopt preventive and curative measures. Further studies on the plants may prove them of economic value.

The Himalayan ecosystem is known for its richness in biodiversity. The flora of this region not only maintains ecological balance but serves essential medicinal uses too. While there are several plants which contain curative principles, several other species are very lethal to human beings as well as to animals. Poisonous plants are often found to produce acute toxicity in livestock. However, in the hill areas, although cases of poisoning are a frequent occurence, diagnosis of cases becomes very difficult, because of the lack of proper knowledge. Three yaks died at the Padmaja Naidu Himalayan Zoological Park in 1994 without giving any time for treatment. Post-mortem examination failed to identify the cause. In the past too, incidences of this sort have been recorded in the zoo, where in most cases due to lack of information about the toxic plant and its toxic effect, prevented the rendering of treatment. The present paper seeks to identify different toxic plants in Darjeeling alongwith their toxic effects on livestock.

The Bracken Fern *(Pteridium Equilinum)*

This common fern, locally known as *'Unew'* is integral to the Himalayan ecosystem, growing in highly humid areas at altitudes of 1500 ft. and above. The poisoning caused by this plant is of complex nature as the species contains several potentially harmful toxic agents, namely:

(i) a cyanogenetic glycoside

(ii) a thiaminase

(iii) an 'anaplastic anemia' factor

(iv) a factor causing haematuria

(v) Ptaquiloside, a mutagenic carcinogen

In the Darjeeling Himalaya, the chronic form of poisoning from this plant, i.e. enzootic bovine haematuria is commonly seen in cattle.

Toxicity of this plant varies with the stage of growth, the younger plant being more toxic. Poisoning caused by ingestion of the plant occurs commonly and is highly fatal to large herbivorous animals, with toxicity depending on the quantity ingested and the time elapsed. In rare cases, acute illness is noted, which may start suddenly with sharp rise in body temperature, haemorrhaging from body openings with delayed clotting time, diarrhoea and inflammation of the upper respiratory tract. Blood tests reveal thrombocytopenia, neutropenia and anemia with death occuring within one to three days.

Marked lesions are noted in bovine species with widespread haemorrhaging in mucous and serous membranes of different visceral organs including the muscles. In the chronic form of poisoning known as enzootic haematuria, The main lesion is found in urinary bladder where the carcinoma of the blood vessels develops and is the source for the blood in the urine.While being highly poisonous to cattle, the symptoms are not so serious in other species. In the horse for instance, they can be cured by administration of thiamine. Ingestion of the plant by sheep and goats causes neoplastic growth of the alimentary tract and liver.

The plant is thought to have indirect health significance on human beings, the plant toxins are excreted through the milk in lactating animals, and may thus be transmitted to the offspring of animals and humans, who drink this milk.

Rhododendron Sp

The rhododendron is also integral to the Himalayan ecosystem as a very common flowering plant. 42 species are found in the Darjeeling region ranging between 4000 to 15000 ft of which the following are lethal to Live stock.

R. auklandii.
R. dalhousie.
R. falconeri.
R. lindleyi.
R. nivale.
R. anthopogon.
R. ciliatum.
R. hodgens.
R. obovatum.
R. setosum.
R. arboreum.
R. Lepidotum.
R. niveum.
R. triflorum.
R. fulgens.
R. grande.
R. camelliaeflorum.
R. edgeworthii.
R. hodgsonii.
R. pumilum.
R. barbatum.
R. campanulatum.

R. cinnibarium
R. decipiens.
R. eleagnoides
R. glaucum.
R. griffithianum.
R. lanatum.
R. maddenii.
R. wightii.
R. virgatum.
R. wallichi.

The active toxin in this plant is tetracyclic polyol andromedotoxin known also as grayanotoxin or acetylandromedol. This causes hypotension as well as respiratory and central nervous system depression after an initial transient period of excitement. Clinical signs commence a few hours after the plant is eaten and include dullness, depression, salivation, nausea, colic, depression of respiration, weakness, staggering gait and convulsions with opisthotonus. Trachycardia and cardiac irregularity occur in some cases. The course of poisoning may extend to several days and may lead to death. Post-mortem change is not remarkable except for pneumonic lungs.

***Bhik Jhar* (*Cestrum aurantiacum*)**

This is another common plant of the Darjeeling hill region and is poisonous, as its name suggests. The plant belongs to the Solanum or Nightshade family. Poisoning due to ingestion of this plant is very common in Darjeeling. On two occassions, deaths have also been recorded among the herbivores in Darjeeling zoo. In 1994 for instance three yaks died following ingestion of this plant. The active toxin in this plant is Atropine. Leaves and berries contain atropine with the latter being most dangerous when unripe. Symptoms noted are anorexia and excitement, followed by uncoordination in movement. Gastro enteritis is also seen sometimes, with bloating due to indigestion also being observed. Post-mortem pathological changes include haemorrhagic gastroenteritis, with degenerative changes in the liver and kidneys.

Euphorbia Sp

The genus *Euphorbia* has 1000 different species all over the world. In the Darjeeling Himalaya, two species, i.e., *Euphorbia himalayensis* and *Euphorbia sikkimensis* are commonly found. This plant belongs to the Spurge family and the local name is *Syalmutey*. These species contain high concentrations of nitrates which are very poisonous, since they convert haemoglobin in the blood into methaemoglobin, which can not act as an oxygen carrier. Death occurs mainly due to tissue anoxia.

Symptoms include abdominal pain and diarrhoea owing to the irritant action of the nitrate ion, muscular weakness and uncoordination, convulsions, accelerated heart beat and dyspnoea. Progressive cyanosis is visible as a bluish discolouration of mucous membranes and unpigmented areas of the body, leading to death in severe cases. Among livestock, pigs are more susceptible to this form of poisoning than cattle, sheep and goats. Post-mortern changes observed include discoloured and tarry blood, and blush colouration of mucous membranes of the body.

Lobelia Pyramidalis

The local name for the plant is *Eklaybir. Lobelia pyramidalis* is found at altitudes of 14000 feet. The active toxine of this poisonous plant is piperidine alkaloid lobeline. Ingestion of the plant causes erosion of the mouth, salivation and diarrhoea. On post-mortem observation enteritis is evident.

Aconitum Sp

The plant has medicinal value. Species recorded in this region are *Aconitum napellus*. The plant causes poisoning in grazing animals. The toxins in the plant are diterpenoid alkaloids of five types, namely aconitine, barbitine, lycoctinine, delphinine and heteratisine. Incidence of this poisoning varies widely according to season and climate, probably due to wide variations in the concentration and chemical composition of specific alkaloids in the plant. The plant is common to the Darjeeling region and is known locally as *Bikma*.

All animal species are susceptible to this plant. Among them, cattle are found to be most affected. Sheep are much less susceptible, and among horses too toxicity rarely occurs. These toxines cause malfunctioning of the neuro-muscular junction and interference in other parts of the neuro-muscular arc. If ingestion of the plant is stopped, the signs and changes are reversed after 4/5 days.

With weakness, muscle tremors and staggering gait in animals there are the symtons indicates this poesoniog, followed by paralysis of the limbs and recumbency. Salivation vomiting and bloating are common signs, caused the paralysis of the oesophageal muscle. Constipation is noted, followed by diarrhoea. Overall symptoms and the course of illness is directly related to the quantity of the plant ingested by the animal. Death may occur due to respiratory failure. Post-mortem changes are not specific enough to be conclusive about the cause of death.

Pieris Sp

It is found in the Darjeeling Himalaya between the range of 5000 to 10000 feet, Its local names is Angeri. The three species found are *Pieris ovacifolia, P. villosa* and *P. fermosa*, which are all poisonous to livestock. The toxin in this plant is Andromedotoxin, a resinoid substance. Which is a member of the deterpenoid group of alkaloids.

Albizia Sp

Several species of the plant found in the Darjeeling region and are known locally as *Siris. Of* these *Albizia lebbeck, A. gamblei, A. stipulata* are toxic. The toxin in this plant is 4-Methoxypyridone, a pyridoxine analog. Clinical signs include hypersensitivity, hyperthermia, dyspnoea, ataxia and tetenic conulsion. After death, the heart shows cardiomyopathy. Pulmonary edema and degenerative changes in other organs are also noted.

Arum Sp

A plant which occurs commonly over the Himlayan region is known buy the local name of Darshany. All species are toxic. Species recorded are *Arum costatum, A. cavatum, A. echinatum, A. erubescens, A. flavum, A. guttatum. A. nepenthoides. A. tostuosum, A. venosum and A. italicum.* The toxic principle varies from species to species. In some species, the toxin present is saponin, while others contain insoluble calcium oxalate crystals. In cases of saponin poisoning, clinical signs include violent purgation, vomiting and general collapse. Post-mortem examination may show hyperemia of the gastrointestinal mucosa and Erosive stomatitis, resulting profuse salivation, swelling and protrusion of the tongue is caused by ensobuble kidney, and fatty degeneration of the liver. Insoluble calcium oxalate crystal in high concentrations.

Indigofera Sp

Several species occur in the Darjeeling region including *Indigofera dosua, I. pulchela, I. pulchella, I. rotundifolia, I. trifoliata* and *I. stachyodes.* Of these species, only *Indigofera dosua* is toxic, and contains the toxic amino acid indospicine and the nitrocompound karkin. Indospicine was previously ascribed as factor responsible for poisoning, but now the nitrocompound has been identified to be the etiologic agent. The plant may cause either acute or chronic poisoning. In the acute case symptoms are dyspnoes, tremors and sudden death, and the course of illness may vary from 3 to 24 hours.

In chronic poisoning, the animal loses weight. Develops a poor hair coat, and shows nasal discharge and poor exercise tolerance. Uncoordination followed by paraplegia is common. Mortality from this type of toxicity is very high and the course of illness may extend over several months. In case of animals that recover, permanent nervous disorder may be noticed.

Datura SP

The only species found in the Darjeeling Himalayan is *Datura stramonium*, locally called *Datura*. Cases of poisoning of livestock by this plant are comparatively less because of its unpalatibility and high toxicity. Animal fed with this plant show nervous symptoms.

Arisaema Sp

A. Jackquimonti known locally as *Laruwda*, occurs in the Darjeeling region It includes *Arisaema verrucosum*, *A. vituperatum*, *A. allichianum*. *A. sikkimense*, *A. propinquum*, This plant is lethal to animals. Salivation and swelling of the tongue are the common clinical signs noted. Besides the toxic plants identified and analysed here, there are many plants like *Acoriatum Sp* (*Acoriatum ferox*, *A. leuridami*, *A hookerii*), *Bupleurum candollii* and *Ostodes paniculata*. Which are also poisonous. Details on their toxic principles and clinical effects need further study.

References

1. G.S. Yonzone *et. al.* [1984 a]: 'Medicinal Plants of Darjeeling district,' J. Econ. Taxon. Bot. 5: 605-16.
2. G.S. Yonzone *et. al* [1984 b]: 'Paisonous Plants of Darjeeling District,' J.Him. Res. And Dev. 31-34.
3. G.S. Yonzone *et. al.* [1985 a]: 'Wild Edible Plants of Darjeeling District,' J. Beng. Nat. Hist. Soc. (New Series) 3(1): 76-83.
4. G.S Yonzone *et. al.* [1985 b]: 'Ethnomedicinal Plants of Darjeeling Sikkim Himalayas,' Fifth Int. Soc. Hort. Sc. [Special Issue] 202.
5. G.S. Yonzone, S.K. Chatterjee [1986]: 'Cultivation of Medicinal Plants in Darjeeling District: its Future Potentialities,' J. Act no. 188.
6. G.S. Yonzone *et. al.* [1996]: 'Contribution to the Ethnobotany Darjeeling District, India, in S.K. Jain (ed.): Ethnobiological Human Welfare, Deep, New Delhi, pp. 388-89

7

Bon Medicine among Monpas in Western Arunachal Pradesh

Introduction

Modern medicine appeals to the dominant social institutions and imagery of 'science' is a source of legitimacy, probity and integrity. Important to the legitimating of science, in contrast to religious and other systems of knowledge, its procedure are regarded as objective and value free. The conduct of objectivity, as sociologist Will Wright (1992: 23) has explained, gives science a 'desperate privilege,' so that in Western societies, knowledge is virtually equated with the achievements of science.

While other systems are constructed as other by being treated (by social scientists, biomedical practitioner) as 'folk' 'ethno' 'alternative' 'unorthodox' 'quack' and so on, the anthropologist of medicine reverses the polarity. For now it is the conventional and dominant system of medicine that is treated as other (Atkinson, 1995: 28). Inevitably, the world can not be reduced into sole line of thought or enlightened mode of Western value system in this plural multicoloured world. The coercive degradation of another knowledge by making it 'Other' cannot be granted uncritically by those who touched the world of the knowledge of which purview is more than the modern framework.

It is only in recent years, that anthropologists of medicine have attempted to characterize contemporary medicine as a cultural system (Atkinson 1995: 21). Not only practitioners of biomedicine, it is common place in this side of the 'modern world' to assume biomedicine as essentially and exclusively in theory and practice, as a 'true science', which professes the cellular, biochemical basis of pathology. Hence, anything that is said or done by a professional practitioner of contemporary orthodox medicine is assigned to 'scientific' culture of 'biomedicine' that culture is seen indeed a dominant and all encompassing (Atkinson 1995: 28). Thus, traditional unorthodox medicine is assigned here to be 'scientific' to secure a room in the 'modern' culture.

Thus, for the most recent anthropological studies, biomedicine is itself an ethnomedicine. It is 'the pre-eminent professional ethnomedicine of Western cultures' (Gains and Hahn, 1985: 18, n.l), although anthropologists began by defining the scope of their interest as ethnomedicine and originally excluded biomedicine from that categorization (Atkinson 1995: 21).

As Gains and Hahn articulates (I985: 3), anthropological and medical critics have been struck by the reductionism, which excludes alternatives. It asserts biological universalism and individualism. It ignores if not deny, basic anthropological understandings which see cultural and social forces as wellspring of human behavior, including healing and suffering (Gains and Hahn, l985: 3). Arnold (1988: 18) also delineates in same manner in relation to medicine in European colonies, 'seeing it as rational, scientific and universalistic, western medicine defined itself in opposition to the presumed irrationality and superstition of indigenous medicine. The customs and beliefs of the people were treated as obstacles to overcome, obscurantism to be brushed aside by the new scientific age' (Collins, 1999: 182-183).

Therefore to have the garb of 'scientific' seems to be the only left solution for the 'obstacles' in this perspective to avoid being labeled as 'uncivilized'. This force of knowledge colonization and the rhetoric of biomedical supremacy may be persuasive because it forms part of larger discourse, which has dominated Western thinking since the birth of the industrial era (Gordon, 1988)—a discourse which assures by means of accurate observation and rational deduction human beings can attain an objective knowledge of the nature of reality that will enable us to predict and control nature (Lupton, 1994: 87).

Bon Medicine is not as complemented to the biomedicine, but is one distinguished system of knowledge in its own right. In other words, as an application of this trend of decentralisation, this paper is not attempting to examine through biomedical standard, but to describe the thickness of the causality and efficacy beyond scientific proof through the logic of Bon world view. For being inside the logic and frame of the science can not help involving oneself with reproduction of same prosaic discourse.

This principle of symmetry in this context insists that it is necessary— as a methodological imperative—to apply the same anthropological analyses to domain of knowledge that are conventionally regarded as 'orthodox' as to the 'rejected,' the 'failed' or the heterodox (Atkinson, 1995: 45). In the field of medical knowledge, the anthropologist has to pay serious attention to the practices of orthodox cosmopolitan medicine as also non-western, non-orthodox medice.

Against that background of methodological precept, therefore, there is no difficulty in recognizing that all knowledge— including scientific and medical— is socially produced.

It would be ludicrous not to acknowledge the existence of organic diseases that require 'treatment' at both the biological and the social levels. However, she warns, mislocation is more likely to occur from lack of clarity about the term 'social.' The danger is in assuming that the interesting sociological issues— of cultural variation, of belief, practical reasoning— are to be found only in the interaction of the patient's biography and the practitioner's expert knowledge. This bias therefore parallels the classic anthropological preoccupation with illness behaviour. Of course, says Kenwood (1999: 180), no social constructionist denies the existence of true organic problems and diseases (e.g., epilepsy, Alzheimer's).

The principal of symmetry requires that we acknowledge how knowledge is made, legitimated, shared and transmitted within socially organized contexts. The anthropological literature tell us far too little about how medical knowledge and practice are produced and reproduced, how it is shared and transmitted, how it is legitimated in practice. Since health and its promotion may be seen to be universally valued end, it is widely recognized that medicine serves sectional interests (Atkinson 1995: 34) like between religious group such as Bon and Buddhism.

Background

Process of Bon: Bon religion was being practised widely in Tibet. In pre-Buddhist Tibetan cultural sphere, Buddhism reached in there in the seventh century and became state religion in the year of 762 A.D. Since then, though, once there was severe persecution at the initial stage in eighth century, the configuration of life, culture and discourse in the world of Tibetan culture has been centering Buddhism value system. Though Bon elements have been underpinning of their version of Buddhism, which colours originality of it.

To our interest, some of the pockets of this cultural sphere fall in the land where a 'tribe' of India settles. It covers Ladakh, Kinnor district of Himachal Pradesh, and Tawang and West Kameng District of Arunachal Pradesh, the vicinal area of Tibet. The inter-exchange of people and goods with ambient culture has configured the multicolored medical knowledge and healing practice on its own right in each different geographical and cultural context. Although people living there are linguistically and historically distinct from mainland Tibetan, the spatial continuity exposed people into profound influence of Tibetan Buddhism culture.

Although both exiled from main Tibet in different historical phases, the former Bon, which is practiced among indigenous communities in India, is a healing tradition, dealing with the ailments of the locals through ritual performances. The Monpas of Tawang and West Kameng district of Arunachal Pradesh take part in the fabric, and this is the community, which this paper focuses on. They have been less exposed not only to Buddhist influence, to any other outer force due to geographical location, thus Bon among them remains in the art of healing. Therefore, in the present day were modality of the Bon differs between these two kinds of communities.

Besides these autochthonous communities, India also embraced the very community of Tibet fled from main Tibet after the Chinese uprising in 1959. Among them, Bon forms institutionalized religion still followed by the people now reduced to minority in Tibet. To the Tibetans in general, Bon is identical to this form of legitimate 'Yungdrung (Nine Swastika), Bon' which officially recognized as one of the five tradition by Tibetan government in the year of 1988, hence highly in Buddhist garb.

The term 'Bon' has variant meaning and depends on the interpretation in historical sources and understanding of the interpreter, one of them means to invoke, being related to 'bod pa' (to invoke or to invite in Tibetan), another one means "seed". In Zhang Zhung term, it is identified with 'gyer' means to chant (Bansal 1994). Zhang Zhung was a kingdom where Bon religion originates and flourished before it was conquered and incorporated by Tibet in 7th century. According to Namkhai Norbu, it is identical with ancient word 'bzla', to recite mantras or magic formulae (*sivgag*) (Namkhai, 1980).

On the other hand, Ekval says, it is not certain that the word 'Bon' referred to one unified religion, for there is some evidence which suggests the possibility that the early religion of Tibet was not a unified system (Ekval, 1964), it was rather belief system of population, which seek the service for riddance of ills and misfortune of everyday life, also in the court for kings and country's well-being. Later on, this form of belief acquired 'unified' shape in the course of encounter with 'international' 'organized' foreign religion, i.e., Buddhism.

In Tibetan term, Bonpo is follower of Bon religion (Bon = Bon religion, po= of people), however bonpo in these community of pre-Buddhism Bon denotes medicine man or faith healer, more precisely, it often referred to 'pujari', priest or ritual conductor in Hindi. In the area covered by Tibetan Buddhism, bonpo commonly is used (though there is slight alteration such as bonpo in Ladakhi, mun in Lepcha), and it does not mean the follower of Bon religion, hence their creed is Buddhism in basic. The term 'bonpo' represents this crucial difference between these two forms of Bon.

They are succeeding the popular tradition of healing art of pre-Buddhism Bon till present day, as it remains in the designation. Or it may be actually continuation of Bon as aristocratic priests in Yarlung Dynasty, as Sammuel emphasises the bon priest in the earlier 'court religion' of Zhang Zhung, which were merely one kind of various court priests at this time (Sammuel, 1993). Whether this hypothesis is veracious or not, it profoundly comprises the vestiges of pre-Buddhism knowledge and practice. To them, pre-Buddhism Bon is contemporary living experience, not the past relics confined within the texts and historiographies. However, this form of continuation is not tangible to the authority of 'official' Bon, viz. 'Yung Drung Bon', of which headquarter locates in the Tashi Men-ri monastery in Sirmour District of Himachal Pradesh.

To the supremacy of this version of tradition, 'unorganized' pre-Buddhism belief and practice in those periphery is not their 'sophisticated' Bon, in fact the existence of this mode of Bon itself is not much known to them. Rinpoches, who are the source of knowledge of Yung Drung Bon does not accept the 'older worship' as the part of 'modern' Bon teachings (Crossette 1995: 77). However, according to the oral history of Tashi bonpo in Zung village of Lumla circle, Tawan district of Arunachal Pradesh, they are descendants of the exile who were expelled at the time of Buddhist persecution during eighth century. Moreover, his written texts in Tibetan script which he succeeded from his forefather do tell the name of 'Tonpa Shenrab' as the source of their knowledge for healing rituals. (Tonpa Shenrab Miwo is the name of the founder of Bon religion, who occupies equivalent status as Buddha).

It is said in some chronicles that the Bon looked after the life (tsho) of the king or aid his ministers with the word and deed, or that they keep in view the defense of the country's borders (Tucci, 1980: 232). Bon at that time was mainly associated with the cult of the divine king included the belief that he was endowed with both magical power and a special magnificence (Lopez, 1997). Bon dominated the community in general and its leaders in particular, above all the king. According to Karmey, this worship of sacred king and his appendage started between 6th and 7th century, which closely connected to the divinity of a special tutelary god of the king, the "body spirit" (sku bla) who protected the king's power, encompassing everything from his body to his political authority to the order of universe.

This tutelary god was mostly mountain gods (Karmay, 1975), these kings did not leave earthy remains when they died, but ascendant bodily by means of 'Mu' luminous rope to heaven. This belief in the divine nature of the king and their gods, especially the gods of mountain, originally formed the nucleus of their belief system (Bansal 1994). One of the primary responsibilities of the royal priests and ministers, who were Bon from Zhang Zhing kingdom, then seems to have been the maintenance of the king's health, for if the king become ill or if the body spirit was determined other to be displeased, the safety of the kingdom and even of the universe was in jeopardy, and epidemics and droughts were interpreted as signs of this displeasure. Then Bon were summoned and performed a range of sacredotal functions in service of the divine king, such as officiating at coronation ceremonies and rites of allegiance to the king (Lopez, 1997).

Process of the Monpas

When we look at broader perspective of space and time, the word Mon appears to have a chequered history and was not confined to a single group of people defined by a definite geographical boundary. Monpa is a broad term in fact, given to various groups living in parts of Arunachal Pradesh, Bhutan and the south of Tibet, but also some groups of Eastern Tibet. The Monpas are one of the Scheduled Tribe in India living in western Arunachal Pradesh. According to Stein even in the earliest text, mention is made of Mon people in the east along the Sino-Tibetan border. In the west, the name is given to other low caste communities in Ladakh, and lastly it is applied to Sikkim and Bhutan. In western Himalaya, Handa (2001) reports, the Mons or the Monpas are known to the Tibetan as the Molan, that is 'the dweller of the valley beyond the Himalayan frontiers' who inhabit in the Lahul and Zanskar areas, to suggest their non-Tibetan origin, Alexander Cunningham is of the opinion that the ancient sub-Himalayan people were the Mons. The Kashmiri historical work the Rajatarangiri of Jonaraja mentions the Kal Mon as the original non-Tibetan inhabitants of Gu ge.

It would appear that as the prehistoric Tibetans moved south and west across the plateau they encountered people of various tribes who came to be known generally as Mon (Tucci, 1949: 6). The main habitat of the Monpas in India locates in the district of Tawang and West Kameng, which is in western side of Arunachal Pradesh. It is separated on the North by province of Khams or Khamsyul of Tibet along the 700 mile long crest of the eastern Himalayas, from the tri-junction of Bhutan, Tibet and India to the tri-junction of India, Tibet and Burma; on the west by Bhutan; and on the south by Assam (Bose, 1997). The term Monpa covers three distinct groups who may be conveniently divided into Northern, Central, and Southern.

Taking each by turn, the Northern Monpa are mainly concentrated along the broad valley of the Tawang Chu north including a pastoral group at Mago. They can also be divided into Major distinguishing features between these groups are the dialects. Tawang area broadly falls into three popular divisions, mainly Cha-chum,Thakpa and Pangchen. Central Monpa lives south of the Se la in the region of Dirang and Southern Monpa is in the further south in Kalaktang area both of which fall into district of West Kameng. Historically Monpas inhabits eastern lower jungle are labelled by the 'civilized' and 'cultured' Buddhist Tibetans as savage and outsiders living in thick forest an untamed environment of which they possess a great knowledge, traditionally subsisting not as farmers but rather hunter-gatherers.

Their milieu and way of life does not appeal to Tibetans since 'savage' nature does not represent an ideal state to the Tibetans mind. It may even be said that part of the aspiration of Tibetan religious ideology is to eliminate wilderness by subjugating it. We often see this scheme that promotes to control nature in the name of civilization, that is, science. Once fierce and uncultivated nature, and that of Bon deities, is included within the sphere of Buddhism and represented Buddhism language, nature and supernatural is tamed.

The process to reach present Buddhist Monpa has been parallel to the process of Tibetanization of original inhabitants of the land. It had distinctive characteristic, which simply cannot subsumed into homogenous sphere of Tibetan Buddhist culture. As the impact of Buddhism was less and low comparative to the main Tibet due to geographical and political distance, this land of Monyul have sustained more liberal in terms of 'un-tamed' life and interaction, which could be cradle of Bon faith.

Bon Medicine Among the Monpas

Cosmology and Etiology: The interplay between the microcosm and the macrocosm configures pre-Buddhist Bon, with multifarious divine manifestations. All other appearances are suffused with religious significance for the people's life (Tucci 1980:177). The entire existence of the Monpas, their knowledge and practice, cognition and construction is suffused and coloured by the experience of the spiritual. In ancient time, the sphere of nature and man was integrated whole. Theg lha (celestial spirits), srin (terrestrial spirits) and klu (subterranean spirits) and humans were not separated, and could exchange conversation, and stones, trees and earth all spoke the language of humans (Belleza, 2001: 36). In those days, cosmos was not stratified; human could commune with nature and that of spirit directly and everyone resided in the same horizon.

In Monyul, this tight bond between human and nature is not yet to a relic, human still can commune through the bonpa's age long inherited art of healing, and also through the Monpa's (Medicine man) dream. It is a gift from the abode to ease the suffering of the people. When menpa is asleep, Phu (Mountain spirit) goes to the menpa's dream, and when menpa wakes up, it returns to its body again. Menpa in Dirang village says, the night before patient comes to him, he sees the dream visited by Phu of Medicine. When he wakes up, there is medicine under the pillow. Or, Phu informs treatment for the coming patient on tomorrow, and instructs the place and time that he can get necessary healing material such as herbs. It is only through dream he can cure, otherwise he is just one of the member of the village. Not only to the side of physician, in the Sarali village of Nafra circle, patient also see the divine dream which foretells the own coming disorder, which often is the capture by don, evil spirit, and dream in red is a sign of illness.

This interrelatedness of the macrocosmos is homologous to the microcosm, the relationship of 'Lu-Lha-Yong'. Lu is aquatic spirit resides and rules the underworld, Lha is generic term of the gods dwells sky, but in this context it indicates the guardian spirit on the head of individual accompanying the whole life. Yong is soul in

Dirang Monpa word. This trinity is so intently united, something bad happen to Lu or Lha, Yong falls ill in response to the offence. For the Lha who resides the top of the head, the body of the host is a shrine. Therefore, when watery area where Lu lives gets polluted, or when Lha defiled by the host's visiting to polluted place, for example, the house just after delivery, Yong fall into the state of grip, defilement.

Usually it manifested swelling some part of body and eye, bad throat. But the ailment can be cured when the Lu or Lha is purified ritually or through retrieval of cleanliness. In the rite, the smoke of juniper reaches to realm of gods and spirits, and the rage appeased by the fragrance of the juniper. This relation expressed by another formula: Lhadhan-Medhan-Ludhan Sum (Lha, Human, Lu, Three) (dhan is suffix for plural). Since all three kinds of being are living together under one roof, if Me, human conducts simultaneously reflects to other two, and human receives the return of what she did.

The hallmark of the Bon supernatural geography overlaps the holistic phenomenology of illness, and the structure of the triad cosmos corresponds to the spiritual arrangement of the therapeutic intervention and expertise of specialists. And the earthly experience of the illness is projected to the cosmological happenings (Tucci, 1980). In the Monpa tradition, cosmos was triad, not the six realms of Buddhism. The world of supernatural forces is divided into three planes of existence: the sky, intermediate or atmospheric space, and the earth and underworld, respectively dominated by the Lha, the Nyan and Lu (Namkhai, 1995). The sky and the subterranean world each have several storey, usually nine above and nine below. This application of number nine is specifically Bonpo concept, the storey are reached by a 'sky door' and an 'earth door' the former being the hole in the roof for the light and smoke, the latter the hearth (Stein, 1962).

To delineate pre-Buddhism Bon etiology, briefly I sketche illness causation of don following to the triad cosmology. In the realm of sky, Lha resides to watch out the human deeds and morals. Any mistreat of the things and waste of the food and resources leads to sickness which attributed to the disrespect to them. For example, Chu lha, god of water feels offended when pairs of socks are washed in water (meant for public usage), or if someone spits or urinates there. He punishes the defilers by causing pain or sore to their feet, mouths or genitals. At the banks of the rivers and ponds, the two-metre filthy stretch of water should be left untouched before using it for consumption.

Nyan, the spirits of the trees and rocks are easily annoyed and send sickness and death by way of retaliation. Nyan is also offended by the chopping down of any trees that may be held sacred locally, by the digging up of the sacred ground, by the smell of burnt food, and by the beams of torches or lamp cast on the tops of hills or mountains consecrated to him (Mukherji, 1995: 150). There are certain places, one have to conduct rite to ask for permission to cut trees. In same fashion, there is rite to unearth stones to prevent from illness by those deeds.

Sadag are spirits of the grounds of any locality to which on many occasions offerings are brought. In general terms, they can become irritated when one 'wounds' soil, their domain, through work, excavation, or building. The grounds, which held the hearth should be dug out and thrown into water, in default make Sadag annoyed and punish the owners or defilers with the disease (Mukherji, 1995: 174). Among Monpa in Dirang circle, Sadag is called 'Lou'. The stone with lou has to be kept clean always. It has synchronic linkage with villagers, for when some one put the fire on the lou, the offender or his/her family members would get burn in his body. It is not healed by applying the medicine, but by a performance of rite.

The land that has been inherited since forefather days, has a lou in particular stone of the land. If the lou is not kept clean, any members of family are subject to fall ill. Bonpo can detect which stones is a lou by pouring goat's milk. If the stone is lou, it gives bad smell, and it absorbs milk as if it drinks. If it is offended by any means even without intention, unknowingly, it causes swelling in the body. In Chug village, one child had swelling at his leg, and it was not getting better against medication. When his parents consulted with bonpo who diagnosed it is due to the stone thrown to the ground, which provoked lou. When it is removed from the ground, he was cured.

In Monpa villages, if villagers do not treat Lu proper way. In other words, if the place like Lu dwells such as stream or spring was polluted by washing socks or dishes, then not only the offender, sometimes entire family fall the ill-state such as sick or fail of crops. In Monpa villages, Lu lives in the dry area. It is much more powerful and readily enraged.

The mountains are regarded both as 'pillars of the sky' and 'pegs of the earth'. From ancient time to the present day, they are 'god of the country' or 'masters of the place'. The summit of any of the sacred mountains was a place of contact between heaven and earth, the two being linked by a sky ladder (Bansal 1994). This concept of connection between heaven and earth is nucleus of the Bon faith, and the mountain was, and is until the present day, the midpoint of two spaces. (Tucci, 1980).

This worship of mountain is the core concept of bonpo practice of healing. It is also observed among the Monpas. The mountains where the ancestor descended or on which he lived acquire special sacredness, and cosmogonic or theogonic accounts or complex philosophical attempts at interpretation become attached to them. Because of their sacred nature such mountains a assure of the country, perpetuity give protection to the men living at their feet. In a sense, they become soul of the country.

In Monpa word, the spirit of the sacred mountain is called 'Phu'. It occupies the most important seat in the Monpa pantheon. The 'father' Phu protects and watches out villager's deeds and thoughts, and governs all aspect of everyday life. This is the deity bonpos contact for their service of healing. It is Phu who instructs the treatment, for he is also a cause of the illness. Particular Phu causes particular illness, which can be healed only through that Phu. Task of bonpo is to detect that enraged Phu by divination and to contact that Phu for propitiation by performing rites. Not all the mountain is worshiped as Phu. The chosen grandiose mountain is venerated at the same time feared by all the communities at his feet. Phu manifests everywhere, in every place, in every object or happening. It is thought that most of the illness in Monpa community is his influence by depriving of the soul or possessing into soul by them. The river in the Phu's mountain is symbolised as his blood where the spirits Lu, Tsang Dut and Rimong resides. If river is polluted by human, naturally, it leads that offender to sick. So does by pollution to all nature where those spirits resides such as water, stone, tree, even hearth.

As we have seen above, each locality has their own Phu in the mountains surrounds the village. It is said that Phu resides on the mountains top. It is believed among Lish villagers that if a helicopter flies over a mountain where the 'Phu' stay, the helicopter will fall or meet with an accident. Phu is the soul of the village, core of the Monpa's everyday life. It protects, watches, and governs the every aspect of living at their feet. Yet, like other deities, the nature of the Phu is also ambivalent and this is a main cause of the peoples illness, too. Each Phu has unique character according to the village context. In the case of Lish villages, there are three Phus. Each Phu affect the man its own way. If any of the Phu possesses a man, the rite has to be performed to that particular Phu which possessed the man.

Although the source is peculiar to the Phu, the attack manifests in common symptom. The main symptom of these possession is madness. It also causes the body pain and shivering. Thus, illness does not merely have a physical origin. One has to distinguish the primary cause (rgyu), which consist of a disturbance of the equilibrium of the three "humours" and contributory cause (rkyen), which is to be sought or in an impurity, a shadow, a defilement (grib) (Tucci, 1980: 173). The malefic power, which represented as 'Don', evil spirits is often provoked by these contributory causes. The impurity or shadow can be of various kinds; it can originate in a sinful action, and also arise through associating with men who emanate a dangerous sacredness, as for example with smiths and armourers. (Tucci, 1980: 173).

Grib is generated by defilement such as at the time of delivery, death, and menstruation. During this period one has to abstain contact with religious settings. It is also caused from eating various impure foods. Thus, food offered by a widow or a murderer brings about a dangerous condition, or burnt food, which offend the phug lha also cause defilement, as does the pouring on the hearth of liquids or substances producing evil smells or smoke, which anger the god of the hearth. An example of this violation of taboo can be observed among religious specialist particularly, as bonpo in Salari village said, when bonpo defiles his body by eating prohibited food such as onion, garlic, and meat, he falls into the grip. This provokes the Phu, which leads bonpos get sick. If one falls into grip, the bla also got affect and exposed to the vulnerable condition.

For people of Tibetan culture, radiation covers every time everywhere. Anytime it may turn negative as 'don'. All sacred nature is continually beset by a whole variety of don, who were presumed to be directly responsible for the ailments and misfortunes. According to the lama in Rama camp village in Dirang circle, there are three hundred thirty kinds of don. He could not enlist them.

As a result of above contributory cause of dregsi (uncleanness), migtsang (impurity) or, more generally, grip Don breaks out. Then the malevolent radiation intrudes into corporeal interiors and brings about in a human a particular state of weakness. That is the moment illness haunts people. On the other hand, it also haunts in the condition of low vital life-forces by other means such as soul loss.

Death by poisoning is a part of black magic, also specializes in powers, which can kill outright, without any physical contact with the person. Poisoning is one of major cause of the not just illness, usually it leads to death. Poisoning is committed by: (1) hand (la doh), (2) eyes (me doh), (3) food (rhe doh). In Tawang, sickness is often attributed to ritual poisoning. But once a person has been poisoned through witchcraft and black magic he can only be cured by the services of another black magic priest. It is also common in Lumla and Zimithang and is practiced mostly by female who are occasionally known and identified. At other times, even ordinary person practices poisoning as a matter of ritual.

According to the Nanda's (1982) report, poisoning a matter of ritual or even habit. In Dakpanang, it is widely acknowledged that poison is not necessarily administered to an enemy. The ladies who believed to poison the people also do it regularly as their macabre profession. As tools should not be allowed to rust, so must a sincere witch sharpen her craft and remain in practice by continuing to poison people at regular intervals. The main motive behind the administration of poison is luck—a desire to obtain the luck and good fortune of the other person (Nanda, 1982). In Tamang in Nepal, which also has bon tradition, it is believed that witches gain control over spirit by promising them food in the form of human sacrifice by poisoning. At that time all the government officer from main India were duly warned that they should eat and drink with these people at their own risk and peril. A Circle Officer of Zimithang would not even allow the villagers to watch him while eating, for fear they would poison him through their eyes.

The withdrawal of the bla from the body and the consequent danger can be the work of dons, which we observed above, because the person is psychologically weak and has no resistance to don. It also is believed for threatening death of the man for whose benefit the ritual is to be performed. The la is especially susceptible during dreams and can be particularly covert the life force of children.

Doctor as Modulator: As the answer or receptor to these ailments in this setting, bonbo takes up the role of modulator between nature and supernatural, and that is role of this form of 'doctor'. To be a bonpo, one has to bear the responsibility of becoming 'public goods', in the sense that he has to be prepared for the house call of the villagers. A bonpo in Lish village said, Like a doctor, if anyone falls sick in the night, early morning or noon or whatever time it may be, and if the bonpos help is sought, and he is obliged to do so. (Interview from Lish bonpo on 27.11.02).

The villagers seek the assistance of bonpo to protect them from the malignant activities of spirit as well as to secure their own health, and service of bonpo is done through the assistance of 'Phu', as a mouthpiece for Phu and to control other subsidiary spirits (Belleza, 2001: 78). When people fall sick, the first resort is be diagnosed and prescribed through Bon lama's oracle and the divination to take next action. This 'health seeking behaviour' is common to the Tamangs in Nepal, the community which is also 'bonpo', is active. Peter reports, "Just as western laymen rely on doctors to diagnose the cause of illness, so the Tamang laymen leave it to the bompo" (Peters, 1998: 72). In a similar bon tradition of Sherpa Yolmo who Desjarlais (1994) met, "bonbo can cure outer illness, but not inner engines. If the inside is broken, the healers cannot cure us, so we go to the hospital".

The outer illnesses to which patients of bonpo refer often involve feelings of malaise due to personal distress and social conflict. For the Bon medicine, these somatic sensibilities borne of the communal exchange of everyday life is the most adept field for healing (Desjarlais, 1994). But these entire adept does not give full play without patient faith. One can do at certain level if the bonpo's spirituality or purity of the mind and body to contact to Phu is high enough. For bonpo's ability to divine the particulars of an illness rests entirely on his relationship with the supernatural. A bonpo in Dirang village says, without prayer, medicine does not work, a bonpo says, and the work of poison is due to power of evil spirit (don), and the work of medicine is due to god (lha). It's not the bonpo who breaks epistemic barriers but rather the gods whom he has the talent for hosting within his body. Through the medium of bonpo's voice, Phu reveals information about the world, knowledge that humans are otherwise incapable of obtaining access to (Desjarlais, 1994). The spokesman for this transaction, a bonpo learns much of what he knows through his relationship with a Phu who teaches and empowers him. The ritual is the forum of this communication, bonpo reaches the Phu who diagnose, and also cures, for the particular Phu is also the cause of the ailment.

However, the purview of the Bonpos among Monpa do not delimit only 'somatic sensibilities', people consult bonpo first for all the kind of illness. In the case of the natural cause, they recommend bed rest or change in diet. In the case of bone fracture bonpo makes fire by iron load and recite the mantras. Then locally available first-aid, such as bandage and herbal paste is applied. They do not perform rites for patients suffering from natural causes. Bonpo in Dirang village said, all rite was done after the diagnosis of the cause such as palpation, palm and pulse reading. On the basis of this examination, bonpo detects if it is due to don or poison or possession or physical cause. If the result tells that it is the intrusion of don, then bonpo goes for divination to fix the ritual to that particular don. For different kind of illness, treatment is also done through different gods. What is physically caused is cured physically, and what is spiritually caused must be spiritually cured (Govt. of India, 1996: 231). However, what is caused physically also ultimately, it was the work of divine providence in the larger cosmological framework. The task of bonpo is to guide most suitable and reasonable way to retrieve normal state of the patient under guidance of divine, the beyond of human intellect.

Bonpo knows the purview of his art. For the case of natural illness with no involvement of witchcraft or dons, he sends the patient to the hospital. For bonpo intuitively knew what he could treat successfully, and what he could not. He frequently acknowledged that doctors are superior at treating cholera and preventing rabies. If it is beyond his control, the death of the patient gives a bad name to him. There are some illnesses (like related to blood) that can be cured by medicines, but the patients those who are harmed by don can not be cured by medicine. The patient Dejarlais (1994: 228) met says, "The doctors in a hospital didn't touch even my pains, but after performing the ceremony, all the pain and nightmares left when bonbo beat me." The ritual healing is not merely exercises in the treatment disturbing emotional states and interpersonal relations, it gives some effect physically by dealing with those sphere of the ailments. To bonpo, patient's aches, pains, weakness, blindness appears as the development of the family conflict, quarrel with neighbour, frustration due to unemployment all these events and relation afflicts patients and it seems that this anxiety laden social situation may have been responsible for the physical symptoms.

Bonpo in Salari tells that without the rite, mad person would remain as such. The greatest success of bon medicine among the Monpas is with illness especially acute, sudden at the onset, yet not incapacitating. According to Bonpo of Salari village, this kind of illness is mostly attack by 'bad air', or don in the form of headache, body ache, eye problem or mental problem. They can distinguish whether the cause is spiritual or physical spiritual by seeing facial expression, shadow, etc. If the illness is ritually or spiritually caused, then it must be treated ritually or spiritually

Nanda (1982) reports her observation on Bon during her tenure of D.C. which is sole written information about then practice of the Bonpo in Tawang area. Bonpo in Hoogla village reads the pulse as well as palm with prayer for clear reading; it should be done in the morning, preferably on an empty stomach and not at night. Bonpo in Hoogla she encounter could predict events of coming future through divination (Nanda, 1982).

At first bonpo palpates the patient at his hands, feet, his forehead and his heart. He then diagnoses the cause such as the kind of intruding spirit and accordingly he prescribes the rite. No rites are performed without through examination. If a rite is performed thorough checking, it is detrimental to the recovery of the patient. In the case of bonpo in Dirang village, firstly he palpates the palms the name and the age of the patients is identified to consult either of brother Phu whose name is 'Dimpu' and 'Bangle' through divination by wheat in water. The divination starts from the recitation of mantras. The mantra bonpos recite consists of special term of Bon. It was common to the rite of bonpos in Dirang circle, the rite itself is conducted to contact particular Phu who is tormenting the patient, but bonpo have to recite the names of all Phu in the area. If he misses the names, it touches the wrath of forgotten Phu. The common tool for calling Phu is Dorje bell. After this, he throws some seeds of wheat in water in the bowl. From there he prescribes the treatment, it would be either ritual or other solution. As like the bonpos in Salari village.

According to Peter (1998: 119) bonpo of Tamang also reads the pulse to diagnose the attack by don or not. For treatment, bonpo blew a mantra at patient's head. This consisted of repeating the magical formula designed to dispatch the don and intermittently slowing on the afflicted area. Bonpo believes that the magical formula he whispers has the effect of a command: i.e., the recitation guarantees the god's obedience (Peter, 1998: 123). A bonpo in Zung village of Lumra circle also examines the planet position through his inherited astrological texts. He examines whether the patient's birth star and the planets are in order and whether the favourable and adverse elements connected with his birth star have come into conflict. For this certain rites have to be performed. The time and place has to be decided by him.

The relevant rituals and magical formulae of pre-Buddhism knowledge have two principal objectives in view; in the first place prosperity, well-being, good fortune (bde legs) in the most material sense, as well as long life (tshe ring), health (nad med), riches (longs spyod), victory over enemies, etc. Then efforts are made to drive out (bzlog) and eliminate of all which stands in the way of this legs, such as poverty, illness and early death (Tucci, 1980: 155). The activity of bonpo thus has an infinitely wide field open before it; in case of drought he can invoke rain, he can banish hail or conjure up inflict vengeance, he can call a halt to epidemics among men and public. In this immense area of ritual techniques for the furtherance of good and defense from evil and the traditional heritage of Monyul can be clearly distinguished.

Bonpos ritual for objective of health is not merely exercises in the treatment of physical/biological illness and diseased organ, but attempts at reorganizing the environmental disunity and imbalance. At the time of communal ceremony such as Phla Festival, the domain of bonpo and the scale of reorganization expanded from individual level to the public level. In everyday life, when one faced with unfortunate events, which approached realization, he/she has available service to improve by option of the numerous types of rites. Broadly, rites are consists of purification (sel) by aromatic plants water or blood, driving out of adverse forces through powerful exorcistic actions (to), and rituals of ransoming (glud). The bla, the soul, can for example be ransomed from danger as in cases of unconsciousness (Tucci, 1980: 175) by soul loss or possession by dons.

As like for doctors there are different medicine for different illness, a bonpo in Sarali village says, for different illness there are different rites, The kind of rites selected thus, according to the kind of 'dons'. By performing the appropriate ritual actions, for example, through an ablution, every stain left by bad actions is cleansed, and the don lose their power over the man so purified. In describing the don it should also be mentioned that they appear in three groups, outer, inner and secret (phyi, nang, sgang).

The juniper tree is a sacred tree of Bonpos.The juniper tree is a sacred tree of Bonpos. To exorcise native forces, the cause of poison viz. grip which weaken positive forces is to be removed. It is done through purifying by fumigation (sang) of juniper and sprinkling of lustrating water called Tsen.

There are a variety of rites for reconciliation with don to repair harm dones by them (Namkhai, 1995: 131). The first task was to evoke the beginning of the world, kind of illnesses. Since the world took form, since it became a mode of being (srid), man has intervened to create the necessary ordering and to give an appropriate form to the habits of his/her life. This process, however, has brought a new situation into existence, which often disturbs or injures those powers that hitherto called particular domains their own. The building of a house, the erecting of a tent on a particular spot, building a bridge over a river, digging in the earth, each of these are intrusions into the domains of other powers which require expiation through appropriate rituals (Tucci, 1980: 142) to reconcile with natural.

This event was the origin of the custom. According to Tucci, the bonpo sources account for these rituals or narrate the origins of particular customs in the appropriate contexts. The treat of these subjects and their narratives not only provide an explanation for the origin of the custom concerned, but also contain the assurance that no harmful effect can arise from it, and that its repetition will evoke once more the primal moment when after an offence had been committed against the divine and demonic powers the sure means to remedy it was found. In short, the effence has taken place. Toward of any consequences of this offence, protection is provided by recitation: 154).

The mdos, yas, lud are devices to extricate one from the threatening dangers of hostile powers. These powers can be of bodily and material or immaterial and invisible nature. It is called curative image (ngar lud). The image of the person afflicted by illness or misfortune, the accompanying shapes of tsamba dough, the little tsamba figures of man and animals all around the main figure these are all transformed in a magical fashion into real things beings able to satisfy the demand of don. Tsamba are used to symbolize gifts for the gods. In the pre-Buddhism context, animals such as horse, sheep, dog were sacrificed communication between the deities and the man to maintain the relationship as the medium of "intercessional prayer".

A bonpo in Salari performs the rite with the white hen and after that the hen is released into the jungle, in initial phase of rite. If the confrontation takes place without success, then recourse is done finally by means of magical compulsion; if it doesn't work one had to commit real sacrifice of animal such as white hen or black sheep.

Interestingly, after visiting of fourteenth Dalai Lama in Dirang for Kala chackra initiation, a number of Bonpo have given up the sacrifice by hearing his speech. This practice has further been given up. Poisoned patients have also been leaded by Bonpo. In the protracted rite, he detects the cause such as bewitchment and its persecutor and venue. Through meditation in front of the patient, and ritual sips from a cup of chang and recitation of mantras, bonpo approached patient and lowering his head, placed his mouth against patient navel. Slowly he sucked the navel and then lifting his head turned and spat into an empty cup, which he had placed nearby. Bonpo repeated this ritual thrice, sucking a curious liquid out of the navel till the cup was almost half-full. Then he lifted the cup, examined the contents and declared. "The poison had been administered to you through a red chillie but now it is out of your system". Needless to say, the patient improved and was soon backing to normal health (Nanda, 1982).

Magical procedures also enable the soul of an enemy to be called by force. For this rite, family summons a bonpo, he divinates how the spirit was lost, where it has wandered, and how best to receive it. He then ritually searches for and attempts to call the lost life-force back into the body of his patient (Dejarlais, 1994: 13). If a person falls sick due to soul loss, there are rites designed to bring the la back into the body, known as "calling the la" (bla'bod). In this connection of the cosmological arrangement, there is clear territorial distinction between Buddhist lama and bonpo in the religious performance for healing. The domain of lama is sickness caused by 'Lha' the gods resides highest part of cosmological hierarchy. Thus, lamas do not deal with Phu, by saying that is too low for them. The strata of Lha are also extended the seat for the Buddhist gods and saints. In Monpa context, the class of Lha and Sange (Buddha) is almost identical.

The difference reflects also to the therapeutic effect. People say in Monpa villages, the rite of bonpo is more 'quick' and 'cost effective' than that of Buddhist lama. The healing rite takes brief time hence cheaper, but needs more repetition. Because in the case of bonpo, it is bargain between Phu and bonpo over the recovery of the clientele. Bonpo demands strongly the return at the cost of offering of Torma (dough made of flour), cloth, ornament, sometimes sacrifice.

According to one villagers description, it is like 'corruption type' bribing the Phu or don to release or leave from the patient soul. But it can also express as 'reciprocal', in the relationship one negotiated in equal basis. On the other hand, lama takes one day fully. It is time taking because lamas go step by step with patience and compassion by reading lengthy texts to implore and convince the spirit to make patient free. According to Nyingma pa village lama

(Buddhist), therefore the result is 'permanent', no repeater. But according to bonpo, villagers come more to bonpo. According to bonpo in Dirang village, after consulting lama, if it is no recovery, patients come to bonpo. Therefore, according to some patients who have been cured, bonpo is more effective.

Conclusion

Faith healing comes from the nature or supernature; it is never of the healer himself. He is a just medium who serve the seats by its purity and pristine of the self and body. Illness is caused by may be some infection or imbalance of the humor, but all that is administrated by supernatural. Therefore, only supernatural can cure and heal the source of illness, through the medium such as bonpo, but it not the deeds of bonpo himself.

This does not impose the own philosophy or framework of doctrine, rigorously remains as the third person that is mere medium. It remains a farmer as same as other lay person, it does not accumulate special attitude to distinguish medical professionals. In this system of thoughtless tends to aggregate a certain view which construct the discourse to specialize particular individual or group and less intentional manipulation for proliferation of own belief exists. The power is not attribute to the particular individual as bonpo, but to the Phu, the almighty power that governs every sphere of the life and word. It is not the bonpo who cures and ails, but it is Phu who does everything. For them, what bonpo announce through divination is not by him, but Phu, and more important relation is with Phu, and bonpo's transparency as medium. In the Monpa context, bonpos are aware their knowledge came from Shenrab, but he does not share the position of absolute supremacy like Buddha in Buddhism, or Shenrab in post-Buddhism Bon. The worship of sacred mountain is the core of Bon in pre-Buddhism version, and the mountain is very pervasive all the main controller of the all power whether it cause illness or heal illness.

Buddhism was founded by one individual and every virtue and merit is attributed and accumulated to that particular human, irrespective of contents of the teaching. That is utilized for the enlargement of the organization by legitimizing it. In this process, the power and legitimacy has to be augmented by subjugating other way of seeing, i.e., knowledge, and it is become the absolute truth to the member of organization, and other knowledge was transmuted dominant version which subservient to the 'truth'. Thus, the knowledge is structured of the composition of hierarchy. However, this movement is not one-sided and top down. It is realized because of the involvement of the subservient into the logic of dominant discourse.

Unknowingly in uncritical manner, one conspires the strength and cogency of the discourse. In this structure there is no victim and no explorer. Everybody is the confederate by ignorance of the position of the self. Through this paper researcher intended to rethink the extant notion of popular medicine not by evaluation through modern medicine framework to promote allopathy, but by placing same line as the expertise which is already existing always and playing a role in its own right. From the viewpoint of different culture, it looks the very 'construction'. The 'bonpo' rite works out and they get relief. For the followers of the faith, it is the most, effective system.

This everyday life of religion system is same to all cognitive structure of knowledge also from the other cultures point of view; it may be seen as fabrication. But in the same way, the common sense knowledge we take its authenticity for granted is based on strong faith. As Burger ascertains these common-sense-knowledge intrinsically has religious structure. In this 'plausibility structure', one of the realities is justified to take for granted by people commonly convinced, as a result it confines the all speculative question. The essence of the plausible everyday life is, in fact, consist of a kind of agreement.

If we wish to make sense of perdurability of non-biomedical knowledge and techniques to some in these places, we need to understand how they thought it rationalized more adequately than its competitors, the frailties of our concrete existence in the world. Human beings act rationally in the sense that their actions are purposive rather than expressive. Even through human action can appear irrational or senseless to an outside observer, according to this perspective, individuals always have reason for acting the way they do. Moreover, these reasons are always contemporary in that they are grounded within structures of meaning which mediate between the environment and the individual's experience of it.

In other words, human action is rational from within the structures of meaning individuals use in order to realize their interests as they perceive them. (Wiling, 1999: 46). They, like ourselves, held that some beliefs and practice were sensible and others foolish. Destructive disease were particularly terrifying deformations of human existence, and the belief, that we have won or are in the process of winning some degree of apparently rational mastery over them counts for a great deal among us. And this system of reasoning is true to all knowledge modality. It may provide a context for understanding not only present medical system but also the possible structures of forms, which have yet to be invented. It can be done by analysing the very nature of popular medicine and religions thought.

References

1. Atkinson Paul, (1995), *Medical Talk and Medical Work*, Sage Publication.
2. Arnold, David, (1988), "Introduction: Disease, Medicine and Empire" *in* David Arnold ed. Imperial Medicine and Indigenous Societies, Manchester University Press, Manchester.
3. Barbara, (1995), *So Close to Heaven*, Alfred. A. Knopf, New York.
4. Bansal B.L. (1994), *Bon: Its Encounter with Buddhism in Tibet*, Eastern Book Linkers, Delhi.
5. Berger P.L. and Lackmann T., (1966), *The Social Construction of Reality*, Penguin, London.
6. Belleza vincent John, (2001), *Antiquities of Northern Tibet*, Adroit Publishers, Delhi.

8

Healing Practices amongst the Gaddi Tribe of Himachal Pradesh

Introduction

Health and illness are two polar words. World Health Organisation (WHO) gave a Utopian definition of Health as a state of complete physical, mental and social well-being and not mere absence of disease or infirmity. "Health is of universal interest and concern." Forest Clements said All human societies not withstanding the scale of development have a concept of what makes a healthy living as well as conception of illness. According to Mukherjee and Nandy (1986: 274), health is not only the result of interaction between an individual's hereditary contribution with his natural and cultural environment but it is largely determined by the biological and cultural adaptation and evolution of the society and the population. Landy (1977) defined a state of health as "the condition of an organism that permits it to adapt to its environmental situation with relative minimal pain and discomfort, achieve at least some physical and psychic gratification and possess a reasonable probability of survival." While on the other hand a state of disease according to Landy "is a condition of the organism that seriously obtrudes against these adaptive requirements and causes or behavioural dysfunction". Whether or not there is a case of illness and whether or not an individual is healthy, every society has to prove this cultural objective.

Tribes are relatively isolated and autonomous groups. They have their own cultural system and medical system is one of the important system of tribal society. The tribal social structure has its own structural and ethnic specificity and the disease that inflict upon the tribals are likewise specific to the attribute of their social structure. The knowledge of disease, their classification and etiology is a part of their cultural system and they develop methods and ways of curing the diseases. In tribal societies, "Health is not an isolated phenomenon, but part of the magico-religious fabric of existence", and of the social, ethical, and cosmic equilibrium. In tribal societies, health, disease and medicine is inextricably linked to the area of social relationships and to the magico-religious world. Physical diseases, psychic disorders and even death are mostly thought of as the result of personal hatred and as having been affected through the intervention of spirits, ghosts, gods or other forces belonging to collective belief. Only a few types of illnesses disturbances and death are viewed as being independent of human responsibility or supernatural agency. "Disease is considered as a disequilibrium in the body as well as in society" (Appiah-Kubi, 1981, pp. 2, 14).

Such diseases are cured by magico religious healers. In tribal societies, system of cure is not only based on magico- religious means but also on plants. Tribal people have a developed pharmacopoeia and some rudimentary knowledge of medical techniques at individual level. Both these techniques, i.e. magico-religious and herbal medicine are used to cure sick either together or separately. People have knowledge about the plants in their surroundings and also attribute cultural beliefs and practices to the plants. Thus, medicine in tribal societies address both supernatural and empirical theories of disease. It includes various systems of medicines—herbal, supernatural, home-remedies and even surgical methods.

Many practices like avoidance of the house in which a death has occurred, distinction of hot and cold food and hiding of bodily waste for fear of their being used by witches and sorcerers, serve hygienic purposes. Therefore social structural practices of tribals put some sort of implications towards the concept of health. It acts as a preventive medicine.

In the contemporary world, tribal are societies are giving way to the outside world and other medical systems. It may not be possible to find a community thriving on its own medical system with no impact of the western bio-medicine. There has been a wider spread of western medical system but at the same time, indigenous system still co-exist with deep rooted belief in curing and giving possible explanation behind the cause of disease and illness. In this paper an attempt has been made to focus upon the disease causation and healing practices of Gaddi tribe of Himachal Pradesh.

The Gaddi: Disease and Cure

The *Gaddi* is the generic term used for all the indigenous population who lives in the Chamla and Kangra district of Himachal

Pradesh. The Gaddi is one of the tribe of Himachal Pradesh and according to 1991 census, their population is 86,511. The largest bulk of the population lives in Bharmour tehsil of Chamba district and few are scattered in Kangra district. The abode of *Gaddi* is popularly known as *Gaderan*— the home of *Gaddis*. They follow Hinduism with special emphasis on *Shiva* and *Shakti*. The land they inhabit is also known as *Shiv-Bhumi*. The language spoken by them is *Bharmauri Gadiali,* which falls under the Indo-Aryan family and its *pahari* sub-family. Their script is known as *tantrik*. Occupationally, Gaddis are agriculturists, it is the primary source of their livelihood. They are also transhumant. Their subsidiary occupation is rearing of goats and sheeps. Some of them large herds.

The Chamba district is situated in the alpine pastoral zone between north latitude of 32°-10' and 33°-13' and east latitude 77°-55'. The whole region is mountainous and remains under snow cover for about 5-6 months. The area has thick and dense forest with low rainfall and low humidity. The community occupies the inaccessible, inhospitable terrain. It is a high altitude area and remains cut off most of the time because of heavy snowfall.

Common Diseases

Such a physical environment poses a severe challenge to the Gaddis and also affect their health. The common disease prevalent among them are: goiter, venereal diseases and all types of leprosy. The staple diet of the people is maize and due to this indigestion and bowel-complaints are common. Symptoms of malnutrition, especially pallegra and night blindness are common due to deficiency of vitamin B and vitamin A, respectively. Eye infections, rheumatic infection and skin diseases, anaemia, diarrhoea, dysentery, small pox cholera are also common. Other diseases are chest diseases such as tuberculosis, pneumonia, etc.

Supernatural Disease Causation and Treatment

When a disease strikes, evergone everywhere goes to a doctor. But the *Gaddi* believe in supernatural cause of illness. Sickness and disease amongst them is thought to be punishment inflicted by deity a form of in some cases and in others, it is seen as a result of an evil consequence. *Gaddi* have profound faith in disease caused by *dayans*, spirits, ghosts etc. To satiate them, offerings and sacrifices are made to respective spirits and deities.

Illness Caused by Spirits, Ghosts and their Treatment

Autars: It is regarded as malignant spirit causing illness but thoughtful enough to warn people in their dreams of any impending disaster. The Gaddis believe in spirits whom they seek to propitiate by sacrifices. They are known as autars (or ancestral spirits), which means spirits raised to the level of local deities. The spirit of a deceased person who died childless is worshipped as autars. To propitiate autars appearing in dreams and threating death; *jemanwala* is performed with offerings made four times at night, of *ghunganian* (four balls), nettle baths and bran bread. The sick person dons clothes which are made for the spirit, with a silver image of the dead and then worships the autars idol, which is always set up near any stream and a he-goat is sacrificed. Autars are also propitiated on *puranmasi* and the *amawas* days. In order to ward of evil eye, the children also wear similar images.

Kailung: Kailu Bir or *kailung* is believed to be a demon causing abortion. Kailung is propitiated in the form of darat (or sickle). To propitiate him, the woman puts 4 copper coins along with her necklace invoking the name of the kailung. Two or three months after the delivery, the mother and the purohit worships and offer sacrifice to the demon by putting up a large stone under a kointh (or walnut).

Gunga: A spirit, which is equally menacing but does not attack humans, is Gunga. It is a disease-spirit of cow and when it attacks, they fall ill. It is believed that it is a very powerful demon. Gunga is propitiated by settling aside a tawa of bread in its name. A piece of iron is made and thus the deity is taken into the cattle shed where it is worshipped by the sacred fire, on Thursday. A he-goat is sacrificed and some drops are sprinkled on the iron. Gunga is worshipped every fourth year. Some cakes and sweets are served to the family members, while the rest are buried.

Super Natural Agencies: There are some other supernatural agencies also Joginis (the rock spirit), Rakshanis, Banasats, Chungu (the demon inhabiting on walnut tree or mulberry tree and under the Karangarh Shrub), Naags, Sidhas, Devis, Birs, respectively in whom Gaddis also believe.

Devo Sanskars: There is a belief amongst Gaddis that spirits of the deal can cause harm. Gaddis are very particular about observing what they call Devo Sanskars (rituals connected with the spirits of the dead), lest they haunt their living relations and can cause illness and other misfortunes to them. To please them, small houses are built on the village outskirts called bangalands, and the spirits are supposed to live there quietly.

Illness Caused by Magicians and their Treatment

Magic: It is believed by Gaddis that human beings are also instigator of disease through magic. According to them dayans (witches), chellas, black-magicinas, who has knowledge of manipulating the power and know the other objects used in causing illness. People take help of them to harm others or they use their magic to harm others. There are four types of magic:

(a) **Vashikaran:** The patient's eyes become as that of an owl's and he cannot speak.

(b) **Maran:** Poison is given to a person through magic for killing him.

(c) **Contagious:** A part of a animal is carried to acquire its characteristics or as a protection against it.

(d) **Others:** To make anybody a leper or a skeleton.

Witchcraft: The *dayan*, according to Gaddis, masquerade in the disguise of women during the day. They leave their abode at night and put their broom-sticks in their place and cast the spell on their family members, so that they may not become aware of the *dayans* departure. The *dayan* rides on *garur*, lion or *mrig* and flies away and assemble in a forest, where they dance and sing throughout the night but return to their home before the people are awake.

If a dayan wants to kill a person, she flies to a *jot* or *dhar* and brings some herb with her. Then, she feeds the herb to the person she wants to harm and the person becomes ill. If such person is not treated in time by a *chella,* he dies of an unknown disease. The *dayans* are considered very dangerous by the community.

To counter their spell, there is a supernatural witch doctor, *gardi chella* possessing powers. He worships almost every God. He cures those patients who are afflicted by black magic or witchery. The *doli* (the patient) gather at his residence for treatment. He begins by playing *dupatara* (a stringed instrument) to the beat of a drum. Meanwhile, he throws a small shell, cowrie towards the *doli* who fall in trance and start dancing. At the end, *chella* discloses the name of the *dayan* who gave him *booti* (herb). Then, *chella* ask patient to dip their palm and feet into a bucket full of water, while his body is dusted by *mor-mutha* (peacock's feathers). As a result, some dust, hair, thread, etc. come out of the patient's body and fall in the bucket of water. This process continues for a week, till the doli recovers his health.

Mani: If a person has an enemy, he goes to a chella and invites illness on him. Illness is brought on by burying some objects— a tuft of hair, *dhoor* (soil) of the dead or an effigy of *satisaryan* (turmeric) over which spell has been cast— in the house of enemy with the help of magician. Due to this, all the family members fall sick. To cast away this evil, a ceremony is held. The *chella* keeps a mani (a wooden pot) in the house. Some neighbours are collected around it and a *Kangana* (red thread) is tied on the wrist of one of them and then the *mani* is put into his *kangana* tied hand. The *chella* chants the mantras and scatter the grains of rice ormah around. The man with *mani* starts moving and fetches the man to that place where spell was cast. This action is performed for three times. The *chella* asks the people to dig the floor, where the *mani* turned down and thus the buried articles are found and dugout. By this procedure the bad spell which has been cast is considered to have been removed.

Magico-Religious Treatment for other Ailments

Stomachache: A patient with stomachache is treated by the *chella*, who gives a thread to the patient after chanting some mantras, for wearing around neck. Purified *dhoor* is also given to the patient.

Fever, Backache and Snake Bite: For fever, backache and snake bite, the *chella* waves the *bhang* plant over the patient with chanting of mantras.

Small Pox: In order to recover from small pox, people pledge *manauti* to Shitla Mata and they offer *akhi* to the goddess after cure. The *chella* waves the *bhang* plant over the head of the patient and a *dhuni* consisting of Harmala, satisaryan and mithi dhup is offered. Prayers are also observed in her praise.

Natural Remedial and Curative Practices: This is also practised amongst Hindus of northern India Gaddis also make use of their knowledge of home remedial practices and surgical treatment to cure diseases.

Conclusion

The Gaddis of Himachal Pradesh believe in disease caused by spirits, dayans, and deities. To propitiate them, they often sacrifice animals for the deities and spirits, and worship these deities. They also use talismans and observe certain taboos to avert the ill-effect of evil-spirits. Besides this, they put nature into use such as medicinal

The Disease and their Homely Treatment

Name of the diseases	*Indigenous Name*	*Treatment*
Cough	*Khang*	The maize cob after removing the grains is reduced to ashes and administered in small doses.
Stomach ache	*Petepeer*	A brew of powdered *ajwain*, sump and common salt is prepared. A pinch of sugar or *bura* is added and given to the patient.
Fever	*Tap*	*Choti ilayachi* and *ajwain* are boiled and given to the patient.
Backache	*Dake peer*	The affected portion is massaged with warm mustard oil. Then a lump of salt heated in the fire is wrapped in some old clothes and the concerned part is fomented with it.
Snake-bite	*Kira dank*	The *lim* is tied tightly with a black woollen string above the bite. Sometimes the effected portion is also cut.
Anaemia	*Lizsa*	*Vaidya* or doctor is consulted.
Eye itching	*Chippad*	*Rasaut* is rubbed into water or milk applied inside the affected eye.
Dyspepsia	*Kabj*	*Summaken, trij, pesori gulab* and *khand* are mixed up and boiled. Thereafter the juice called *duchhandu* or *kadhu* is given to the patients.
Diarrhoea	*Jangal*	*Belgiri* is grinded and given to the patient after mixing up the same with *khand.*
Dysentry	*Marore*	*Dodas* or *happu* (opium) are boiled in water and *kadhu* is prepared. Thereafter, it is given to the patient.
Scorpion sting	*Bichchu Dank*	Iron is touched on the affected portion.
Small pox	*Mata Dhammi*	No Medicine. Only precautions are taken.
Cholera	*Haija*	*Chhoti Ilayachi, soya* and *podina* is mixed up with *khand* and boiled in water. Thereafter it is given to the patient.
V.D.	*Firang*	This disease is rare in this region. However, if anybody falls victim of this disease, he consults the doctor for treatment.

The Surgical Techniques of the Gaddis

What for?	*Techniques*
Bleeding from a wound	*Gudar* (cotton) is burnt into fire and prepared *dhor* from it and is pasted on a wound. Thus the bleeding from a wound is stopped.
To cure a broken bone	The broken bones are kept in joint form and the *plum chaks* (bamboo pieces) are placed around the affected part. There after a *patti* is rolled on it. It is untied after 3rd day, then one week and so on and again tied after examining the limb
To cure a wound	(1) Turmeric is applied over the wound. (2) Sometimes pepers are grinded with mustard oil and applied to effected part.
Eye's operation	No technique. Doctors are consulted.
Teeth removing	Some local dentist, if available, removes the teeth from mouth with help of a *januira* (an instrument).
To operate a boil	When the boil becomes yellow, they operate it with *kard,* a type of knife. Thereafter, some solution is applied to the part.

herbs, roots, etc. for curing purposes. The Gaddis also have good knowledge of surgical treatment. Medical facilities are also made available to them by the government which they accept and utilize with willingness but the presence of these medical facilities does not improve their health because they are very scarce and out of reach.

To avail medical facilities they have to travel long distances, as the area occupied by gaddis is highly undulated. Doctors, nurses and other health providers are not much interested in working in such areas. Besides this, area remains covered with snow for almost 4-5 months which results into meagre transportation and communication, which directly affect the medical facilities provided to them. Thus, the Gaddis of Himachal Pradesh are left with no choice but to rely upon their own indigenous medical system. At the same time, their indigenous medical system is 'hope generating' and the explanation of disease causation given by them falls within their world view.

References

Balgir, R.S., (1995), Environmental constraints. Health and Population Trends among the Muslim Gujjars of Himachal Pradesh, India, J. Human Ecol; 6(3): 191-96.

Bhasin, Veena, M.K. Bhasin and Indera P. Singh, (1991), Ecology, Culture and *Development: Gaddis and Pangwals of Himachal Pradesh,* J, Hum Eco, 12(3): 253-302.

Channa, S.M. (ed.), (2002), Encyclopadia of Religion: Health and the Super Natural Diseases and Cure in Tribal Society, *India: Cosmo Publication,* Vol. 11.

Clement, Forest, (1932), Primitive Concepts of Diseases, *University of California Publications in American Archeology and Ethnology, 32.*

Gupta, S.K., V.P. Sharma and N.K. Sharda (ed). (1998), Tribal Development—Appraisal and Alternatives, *New Delhi: Indus Publishing Company.*

Jerath, Ashok, (1995), The Splendour of Himalaya Art and Culture. *New Delhi:* Indus Publishing Company.

Joshi, P.C. and Anil Mahajan (ed.) (1990), Studies in Medical Anthropology, New Delhi: Reliance Publishing House.

Kakar, D.N., (1977), Folk and Modern Medicine. *New Delhi: New Asian* Publication.

Kayastha, S.L. (1964), The Himalayan Beas-Basun: A Study in Habitat, Economy and Society, Varanasi.

Lamba, Rajni and Shalini Mehta (1995), Priorities in Indian Medicine: A Tribal *Perspective,* Indian Anthropologist, 25: (2)-12.

Landy, David (ed), (1977), Culture, Disease and Healing: Studies is Medical Anthropology, *New York: Macmillan Press Ltd.*

Mandal, Hrisikesh, Sumit Mukherjee and Archana Datta, (2002), Anthropological Survey of India, *New Delhi: Caps Micrographics (P) Ltd.*

Paul, B.D. (ed), (1995), Health, Culture and Community, *New Delhi: Russel* Sage Foundation.

Shashi, S.S., (1977), The Gaddi Tribe of Himachal Pradesh: A Sociological Study, *New Delhi: Sterling Publication (P) Ltd.*

Verma, V. (1996), Gaddis of Dhauladhar: A transhumant tribe of the Himalaya, New Delhi: Indus Publishing Company.

9

Conservation and Regeneration of Endangered Gymnospermic Medicinal Plants in Kumaun Himalaya

Abstract

During recent past in the western countries a growing consensus on the issue of conservation and propagation of rare and endangered plants has attained very high academic value and importance. Unfortunately in India, geographers have not diverted their attention and caliber towards the plant geography with reference to conserving, regenerating the endangered plant wealth simply because of either lack of proper training or ignorance. Keeping in view the real world problems at local and regional levels a programme jointly framed by geographers and botanists in Kumaun University has given a new dimension and direction to plant geography and biotechnology development.

The present research-article has been devoted to conserve, preserve, propagate and regenerate the two most important endangered forest gymnospermic medicinal plants named *Taxus* and *Ginkgo*. Kumaun Himalayas is an abode of innumerable medicinal plants, many of which are on the verge of extinction like *Ginkgo biloba*, *Taxus baccata*, etc., due to heavy human encroachment and exploitation. *Taxus* is commonly known as "Thuner" in Kumauni and as "Talispatra" in Ayurvedic literature whereas *Ginkgo* is known as "Balkuari" in Hindi and "Maidenhair Tree" in English. The former plant *Taxus* produces an important anticancer drug "taxol" whereas the later plant

Ginkgo produces "biloves" a drug highly effective in treatment of cerebral and peripheral vascular disorder in the modern medicinal system. A few patches of *Taxus* trees are growing mixed with deodar forests in Jageshwar area of Almora hills. The condition of Ginkgo, a living fossil, is particularly worst and the plant number can be counted on finger tips. By implementing our technology these two endangered species can be saved from getting extinct. Successful regeneration and propagation of these two plants by cut-shoot technology has been achieved in the present investigation.

Key words: *Taxus baccata, Gingo biloba*, vegetative propagation, endangered gymnospermic medicinal plant

Gymnospermic plants are presently represented by the least number of genera and species in the plant kingdom because majority of them has already become extinct. They have certain limitations of their life cycle such as they grow only as trees, exhibit very slow growth, no accessory means of reproduction under natural habitat except through seeds, anemophylly as the only means of pollination and seed dispersal. The wood is not much economically important and least diverse in habitat occupying only the temperate regions of the world in contrast to the angiospermic plants. In addition to others, these factors have also significantly attributed to their rate of extinction.

Taxus baccata (The Himalayan Yew) and *Ginkgo biloba* (Maidenhair Tree) are the two important medicinal gymnospermic plants, which are already on the records of Red Book Data. The bark and needles of *T. baccata* are the source of a natural product "taxol" a drug which is used for the cure of breast and ovarian cancer during the recent years (Holmes et al. 1991, Runawicz et al. 1993). This plant has also been the source of the Unani system of medicinal drug "Zarnab". Out of nine species of *Taxus* known from the entire world, *T. baccata* is the only species growing exclusively in Kumaun region in Jageshwar forest (north-west Himalaya) and in the hills of Meghalaya and Manipur (north-east Himalaya) at altitudes between 1800-3300 m. Due to indiscriminate exploitation of the Himalayan yew by the local people in connivance with some pharmaceutical companies, the entire *Taxus* population has reached almost to the brink of extinction.

Ginkgo biloba occurred as far back as the Triassic some 2×10^8 years ago. Such remarkable antiquity has captured the imagination of botanists, as Steward remarked "we see Ginkgo biloba: as an emblem of changelessness, a heritage from worlds of an age too remote for our human intelligence to grasp, a tree which has in its keeping the secrets of the immeasurable past". The plant virtually has no its living relatives hence is rightly said to be a "living fossil". Recent studies have shown that the plant extracts have anti-tumor (Itokawa et al. 1987), antistress activity (Rapin et al. 1994) and also cures impotency (McLeod 1993). In India the plant is not known growing in wild state, however, very few individuals are growing in some gardens of U.P., Himalaya and Himachal Pradesh and their number can be counted on fingertips. The present study was, therefore, undertaken for vegetative propagation and conservation of these two endangered plants and the result obtained therefore are presented in this paper. The dwindling populations of *Taxus baccata* and *Ginkgo biloba* will certainly result in their extinction from the surface of the globe, particularly from India, if immediate steps for their conservation and propagation are not taken.

Materials and Methods

Between the end of June and middle of July, young shoot twigs, 10-15 cm long of *Taxus baccata* and 25-50 cm long of *Ginkgo biloba* were collected from healthy plants from Jageshwar forest and Nainital, respectively. The samples were cut under water and stored in polybags. The same day samples of *T. baccata* were treated overnight with a non-hormonal chemical and that of *G. biloba* were treated at cut ends with growth stimulants of auxin group for five minutes and were subsequently planted in polybags containing garden soil, decomposed oak leaves and organic matter (2 : 1 : 1). The plants were then kept in cool shady places. The plants were watered regularly and the soil was not allowed to get dry. The plants were cared and observed regularly.

Results and Discussion

In case of *T. baccata* a well-developed callus formation was observed at the cut ends by the end of December. By the end of February well developed brownish apical and 4 to 6 lateral buds were formed. At the cut ends a prominent and very delicate callus mass was developed along with initiation of a member of adventitious roots. The buds started sprouting by the end of March alongwith the elongation of numerous roots by 3-5 cm long. The buds fully developed into long shoots by the end of September. The initiation of new buds started again in the months of November-December and were fully developed by the end of February. *T. baccata* exhibits single growth during the first year. During this year a bud develops into a 7-10 cm long shoot. The successful growth of the plants was reported in 75-80 per cent of the samples which is significantly high. Since the growth of the *Taxus* plant is very slow and has a long period of seed dormancy and also a very poor seed germination under natural habitat, therefore, it is advisable to propagate the plant vegetatively by cut-shoot method which can meet with the growing taxol supply crisis in the future.

In Europe, *Taxus brevifolia* (the western yew) is the main source of the drug taxol (Wani et al. 1971). The primary source of taxol is the bark and needles of the plant. According to an estimate, the western yew is relatively plentiful, however, the isolation of sufficient taxol to treat 50,000 to 60,000 breast and ovarian cancer patients would eliminate the plant in a few years (Heinstein and Chang 1994). In Indian context, the status of *T. baccata* is very critical and alarming due to its ruthless exploitation by the people for commercial purposes. The efforts are on around the world to regenerate the plants through tissue and embryo culture techniques in laboratory but no significant success has been achieved as yet. Therefore, the regeneration and propagation of *T. baccata* and other species is urgent and inevitable in field plots. After sufficient growth; needles and small twigs could be harvested on a yearly basis without destroying the trees.

In the case of *G. biloba* by the end of February most of the cuttings showed onset of buds and by the second week of March these buds appeared green and sprouted with a few young leaves in clusters in some cases. Some cuttings were removed from the soil to observe root formation, if any, and it was noted that the root had elongated to about 0.5 cm. About 30 per cent of the cuttings showed root rotting and eventually died while the rest 70 per cent cuttings appeared normal in growth and development. By mid April the root system showed further growth and the number reaching to about six; 1-2 cm long and about 1-1.5 mm thick, but mostly without lateral roots formation.

All the plants were then transferred to the earthen pots and kept in full sunlight over a fortnight and frequently watered. This resulted in further sprouting and elongation of shoots. By mid May the buds showed further growth and elongation. Most of them developed into dwarf shoots bearing a small crown of foliage while one or two assumed the form of long shoots. In some cases suckers developed from the base of the cuttings, projecting from the soil surface. These suckers were yellowish green with green tips. By this time a massive root system with extensive lateral root formation had also developed.

Though reproduction of *G. biloba* through suckers is known only in old larger plants, the formation of suckers in young plants as reported here can be helpful in manifold and extensive propagation of this species in India. From the review of literature it is evident that no seed formation takes place in *G. biloba* in India nor any attempt was made for its vegetative propagation. In view of this act and since the species is an endangered one its conservation and propagation by vegetative means needs an urgent attention. Present studies and the results thereof on the vegetative propagation of *G. biloba* are significant on account of high percentage of survival and hitherto unreported development of suckers.

In China, Japan and in some western countries efforts are on for growing *G.biloba* vegetatively (Balabushka 1987, 1990). This aspect becomes more important in view of high medicinal value of the plant. In China most of the larger plants of *G. biloba* are reported to produce suckers and although a number of intact seeds have been observed under the trees but no seedling development was noted (Tredici and Del-Tredici 1992).

Acknowledgement

The authors are thankful to Dr. S.D. Dube, Director, VPKAS (ICAR), Almora (UA), Dr. LMS Palni, Director, GBPIHED, Almora and Dr. SS Mishra, Director, HRDI, Chamoli (UA) for their valuable help in conducting this research work.

References

Balabushka V.K. 1987, Vegetative propagation of introduced woody species with the aid of growth stimulants. *Lesmoe Khozyaistro*, 8: 57-58.

Balabushka V.K. 1990. Results of the trials of growth regulators on summer cuttings of introduced woody plants. *Bull. Glavnogo Botanischeskogo sada*, 156: 65-67.

Heinstein P. F, and Chang C. J. 1994. Taxol. Annual Review of Plant Physiology and Molecular Biology 45 : 663-74.

Holmes F.A., Walters R S and Theriauly R.L. 1991. Phase II trial of taxol an active drug in the treatment of metastatic cancer. *J. Natl. Cancer Instt.* 83: 1795-805.

Itokawa H, Totsuka N, Nakehar K, Takeya K, Lepoittevlin J. P. and Asakawa Y. 1987. Antitumor principles from *Ginkgo biloba L. Chemical and pharmaceutical Bull.* 35(7): 3016-3020.

McLeod D. 1993. The herbal treatment and management of impotence. *Aust. J. Med. Herb.* 5 (2): 4144.

Rapin J. R. Lamproglau I. Drieu K. and DeFeudis F V. 1994. Demonstration of the antistress activity of an extract of Ginkgo biloba (Egb, 761) using a discriminate learning technique. *General Pharmacology* 25 (5): 1009-1016.

Runawicz C. D, Wiernik P.H, Enizing A. L, Goldberg G. L and S. B Horwitz. 1993. Taxol in ovarian cancer. *Cancer* 71; 1591-1596.

Tredici P-del and Del— Tredici P. 992. Where the wild ginkgoes grow. *Arnold Boston.* 52 (4): 2-11.

Wan M. C, Taylor H. L, wall M. E, Cogent P and Mcphal A. T. 1971. Plant antitumor agents. VI. The isolation and structure of taxol, a novel anti-leukemic and anti tumor agent from Taxus brevifolia. *J. American Chem. Soc.* 93: 2325-2327.

10

Medicinal Plants in the Northwestern Himalaya: a Public Involvement Approach Analysis

Abstract

The present study deals with the indigenous uses, status of trading and future prospects of the cultivation of some important medicinal plants of the Kullu valley. Total 57.5-80% households almost utilize more than 20 plant species for domestic uses in their routine. In addition, 40 to 47.6% households were engaged in extraction and trading of 10 plant species from their natural habitats. In general, trading of medicinal herbs from the remote villages was mainly concentrated in Kullu and has been recognized as an important market for export. Medicinal and aromatic plants have contributed considerably in fulfilling the requirements of folk life and improving socio-economic status of indigenous communities in the northwestern Himalaya since time immemorial. The native inhabitants and state forest department receives good economic benefits from trading or permitting the trade of medicinal plants.

Indigenous communities have shown keen interest in cultivation of pharmaceutically important medicinal plants. On an average basis, 56.6% households were willing to start cultivation of medicinal plants. However, to provide technical know-how about agro-technology of medicinal plants, financial support and cost/benefit analysis were the preferred extension services required by the villagers. Currently, the rate of exploitation of several medicinal plants has increased manifolds, whereas existing resources are not adequate to meet ever-increasing commercial demands. Hence, indigenous use, socio-economic values of important medicinal plants of the Kullu valley, and prospects for farmers' involvement in cultivation are mainly discussed in this paper.

Introduction

Northwestern Himalaya is a reservoir of resources for the survival of human beings (Purohit, 1993). It is also among well represented hot spot of plant wealth in the world. This area is abode of distinct socio-cultural practices having economically important plant wealth (Aswal and Mehrotra, 1994, Singh, *et al.*, 1997). The relationship among native communities and plant wealth is strongly revealed by well developed traditional health care practices and a variety of plant uses in ceremonies, routine household uses and trading for economic gain (Farooquee and Saxena 1996, Maikhuri *et al.*, 2000, Singh, 1999). In past few decades medicinal plant wealth of Indian Himalaya has earned a worldwide recognition not only due to it potential but also due to its fast rate of depletion. How to deal with the dwindling status of several important medicinal plants is now a days a foremost concern in the Himalayas (Khoshoo, 1993, Purohit, 1997).

The Himalaya is fortunate that two important anticancerous-drug plants, viz. Himalayan Yew (Taxus baccata) and Himalayan May apple (*Podophyllum hexandrum*) occur in this region. However, instability of ecosystems and vulnerability in the resource potential make northwestern Himalaya ecologically fragile zones (Kala, 2000). Human population explosion, over exploitation of natural resources, imbalances in sharing of resources, poverty, land hazards and erratic weather conditions are major factors for depleting of important resources from this region. The rate of the extraction of natural resources far exceeds the rate of natural regeneration or production (Bhadula *et al.*, 1996).

It has been already accepted that medicinal plants could be the potential resources for socio-economic upliftment of the Himalayan states viz. Jammu and Kashmir, Himachal Pradesh in the northwestern Himalaya states and Uttaranchal in the central Himalaya. Nevertheless, excluding cultivation of *Sassurea lappa* (Kuth) and *Inula racemosa* (Mano) in cold deserts of Lahaul & Spiti, Himachal Pradesh (Kuniyal *et al.*, 1997) age-old cultivation of medicinal herbs with traditional food crops in the vicinity of Nanda Devi Biosphere reserve (NDBR) in Chamoli district of Uttaranchal (Maikhuri *et al.*, 1998) and sparse cultivation (encroachment of natural habitats?) of Rhubarbs (Rheum sp.) in the north-eastern Himalaya, whole pharmaceutical requirements of Himalayan medicinal plants are fulfilled from wild habitats (Bhadula *et al.*, 2000). Excellent findings are reported on developing agro-technology of several important Himalayan medicinal herbs.

Therefore, questions may be arise, why the raw materials for drug industry are not being supplied from the farmers' field? In fact, people's involvement in natural resource management is still least addressed. (Dhar *et al.*, 1999) and needs of conservation education programmes have been stressed for promoting public awareness (Dhar *et al.*, 2002). Environmental conservation in and around biological and recreational hotspots as well as in religious places has also been considered to be carried out through public/tourists involvement. The main idea is to link conservation of natural resources with socio-religious values of the local villagers and outside visitors (Kuniyal *et al.*, 1998). In addition, to recognize and promote the development of low value and less recognized profiles may be worthwhile for scattered natural resources in the mountain (Rawal and Dhar, 2001). Therefore, in case of promoting and adopting cultivation of medicinal plants, this attempt was initiated to find out the problems of indigenous community. Peoples participation in medicinal plant cultivation and its commercialisation could lead to fruitful outcomes, as yet meagre attempts are being made to involve local communities.

Methodology

A questionnaire based socio-economic survey of 100% ouseholds in these villages was conducted for existing indigenous uses and trading of medicinal herbs from this area. Three remote villages, namely, Shapaka (1400 m), Tichi (1850 m) and Zanahl (1900 m) of Dohranala area in the Kulu valley were selected for present study. Crude drug traders in Kulu were interviewed for exact rates of the medicinal plants and part of plants usually traded. Total quantity of medicinal plants exported from Kulu during 1992-93 to 1997-98 and royalty charged by forest department for issuing export permits were obtained from a circle office of state forest department, Kulu.

Results and Discussion

A large proportion of the native population was collecting medicinal and aromatic plants for their routine domestic use as well as for trading (Table 10.1). Average 62.3% households in all the villages were using medicinal and aromatic plants in routine household use whereas 43.1% were also engaged in extracting minor forest produces for trading.

Table 10.1
Collection of the Medicinal Plant from the Natural Habitats of three Villages Dohranala Area of the Kullu Valley

Purpose of collection	*Shapaka (n = 10)*	*Tichi (n =12)*	*Zanahl (n =12)*
Indigenous/household uses	80.0	58.3	57.5
Trading	40.0	41.7	47.6

About 80% households in Shapaka, 58.3%, at Tichi and 57.5 % at Zanahl collect medicinal and aromatic plants from natural habitats for their routine household uses. In addition, 40-47.6% households in the selected villages also collect plants from wild habitats for trading in the nearby market.

Native communities use a total 24 plant species for traditional health care and routine household purpose (Table 10.2). The general illnesses treated with traditional health care practices were wound healing, cold, cough and fever. Plants extensively used by native villagers for indigenous use were *Aconitum heterophyllum*, *Angelica glauca*, *Bunium persicum*, *Dactylorhiza hatageria*, *Dioscorea deltoidea*, *Thymus surphyllum*, *Taxus baccata*, and *Viola odorata*. It is interesting to note that plant species which do not occur in the surrounding of the study villages, are collected from other high altitude areas like alpine regions, or the cold desert environment or purchased from retail sellers in nearby towns. Plants not occurring in the study area, yet used by native communities are marked with asterisk (Table 10.2).

Unfortunately, the bark of *Taxus baccata* was being viewed as a cheap item, whereas undoubtedly it is among the top ranking plant product for clinical uses. Twelve medicinal plants were regularly in trade from this region (Table 10.3). *Aconitum heterophyllum* was top priced raw material for pharmaceutical uses followed by *Dactylorhiza hatageria*, and *Bunium persicum*. Average market rates of other plant produces traded from this region ranged from Rs. 17.00 to 100.00 per kg. However, royalty per quintal (q) charged by the State Forest Department for issuing permits was very attractive. The highest amount of the royalty is charged for export of *Dactylorhiza hatageria* (Rs. 6000.00/q), followed by *Bunium persicum* (Rs. 2000.00/q), *Pistacia integrema* (Rs. 1000.00/q), *Dioscorea*

Table 10.2 Indigenous Use of Some of the Medicinal and Other Plants by the Native Communities of the Kullu Valley

S.No	*Botanical name*	*Local Name*	*Part used*	*Indigenous use*
1.	*Acorus calamus*	Boch	Rhizome	Wound healing, to relieve cold
2.	*Aconitum heterophyllum**		Patis	Tuber Stomach, fever
3.	*Angelica glauca*	Chora	Root	Spice, flavouring agent
4.	*Artemisia tornefortiana*	Seski	Leaf	For worms in digestive tract
5.	*Arnebia euchroma*	Ratanjot	Root	Hair tonic
6.	*Berginia ligulata*	Mandaru	Rhizome	Wound healing
7.	*Betula utilis*	Bhoj	Gall	To relieve stain
8.	*Bunium persicum**	Kala Jira	Seed	In tea, for cold
9.	*Cinnamomum tamala*	Tejpatra	Leaf	To relieve cold, cough
10.	*Dactylorhiza hatageria**	Panja	Tuber	Wound healing, tonic
11.	*Delphinium denudatum* *	Mundal	Seed	Insect repellent
12.	*Dioscorea deltoidea*	Shingli	Root	Soap substitute
13.	*Jurenella macrocephala**	Guggal	Root	Incense
14.	*Mentha longifolia*	Padina	Leaf	Fever
15.	*Picrorhiza kurrooa**	Karu	Root	Fever, coolant
16.	*Rheum webbianum**	Chhuchi	Root	Wound healing
17.	*Rumex hastatus*	Malori	Leaf	Cleaning ornaments
18.	*Sapindus mukurossii*	Doada	Seed coat	Washing woollen cloths
19.	*Saussurea lappa**	Kuth	Root	Cough, joint pain
20.	*Skimmia laweola*	Nair	Leaves	Incense
21.	*Taxus baccata*	Rakhal	Bark	Tea substitute
22.	*Thymus surphyllum*	Banajwain	Seed	To relieve cold
23.	*Valleriana wallichi*	Nihani	Root	Gastric disorders
24.	*Viola odorata*	Banafsa	Leaves	Fever

* Plants marked with asterisk are obtained from outside the selected villages or from the adjacent areas of the Kulu valley.

Table 10.3
Economics of Important Medicinal Plants

SN.	Botanical name	Life form	Plants part in trade	Current Market Rates (Rs/kg)	Royalty Rs/quintals
1.	*Aconitum hyterophyllam*	Herb	Roots	1033.00	1500.00
2.	*Angelica glauca*	Herb	Roots	32.00	125.00
3.	*Bunium persicum*	Herb	Seeds	350.00	2000.00
4.	*Dactylorhiza hatageria*	Herb	Roots	625.00	6000.00
5.	*Dioscorea deltoidea*	Herb	Roots	27.00	900.00
7.	*Picrorhiza kurrooa*	Herb	Roots	94.00	540.00
8.	*Pistacia integrema*	Tree	Galls	100.00	1000.00
9.	*Rheum webbianum*	Herb	Roots	17.00	110.00
11.	*Taxus baccata*	Tree	Bark	10.00	600.00
12.	*Podophyllum hexandrum*	Herb	Roots	44.00	450.00

deltoidea (Rs. 900.00/q) and *Taxus baccata* (Rs. 600.00/q). Export fee for other medicinal plant products ranged from 110.00 to 540.00 rupees/q. Average market rates, royalty charged by the state forest department for issuing export permits of some important medicinal plants is shown in Table 10.3.

In past some decades Kulu town has earned recognition for being an important export market of the Himalayan medicinal herbs. The details of the export of medicinal herbs from Kulu during the year 1992-93 to 1997-98 reveal that there has been a good export of the crude drugs from Kulu. In the year 1992-93 a total 477 quintals of the medicinal herbs enlisted in Table 10.3 were exported from Kulu. Thereafter the quantity of export decreased and in 1997-98 it remained only 152 quintals (Figure 10.1). In subsequent years due to scarcity of raw material in the natural habitats or prohibition on trade of some rare and endangered plant species. The export of these medicinal plants could not remained constant or increasing the export did not increase in volume.

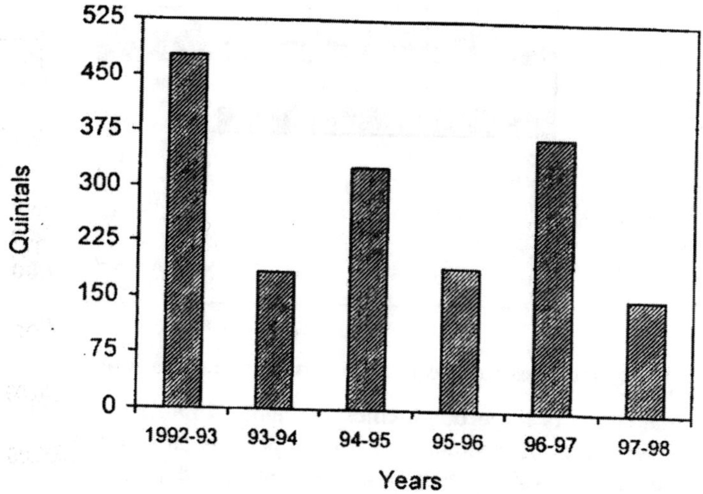

Fig. 10.1. Euport of Medicinal Plants from Kulu.

Peoples Perception for Cultivation

The highest percentage willingness of villagers for medicinal plants cultivation was recorded at Shapaka (i.e., 70%). While only 15.7% households were not found interested to cultivate of medicinal plants (Table 10.4). On an average 56.6% households in the selected villages were interested to cultivate medicinal plants. There was also considerable number of households (28.28%) who could not respond either of the two options

Though traditional use and collection for trade of medicinal plants in the Himalayan region is an age-old practice. However, people have not yet started to cultivate commercially as well as

Table 4. People's Perception for Medicinal Plant Cultivation

Do you want to cultivate medicinal plants?	*Shapaka (n=10)*	*Tichi (n=12)*	*Zanahl (n=21)*
Yes	70.00	33.33	66.64
No	20.00	8.34	28.80
Can't say	10.00	58.33	9.52

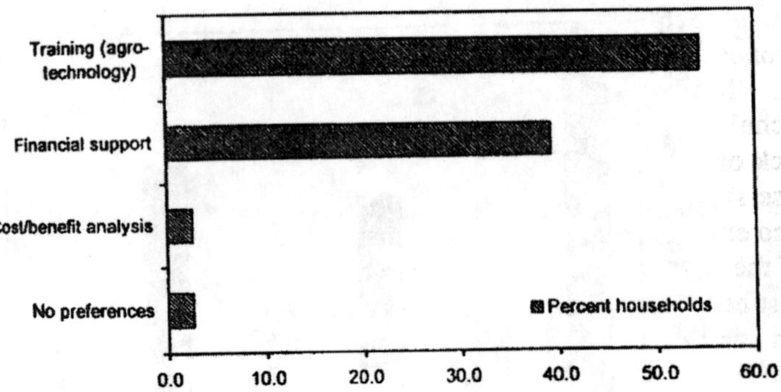

Fig. 10.2. Preferred assistance required by villagers for medical plant cultivations.

pharmaceutically important medicinal plants. Notable factors in this regard were lack of technical know-how, poverty and lack of data for cost/benefit analysis. A very few were interested in assessing first the cost/benefit analysis of the suggested system and just to try (Figure 10.2). A large proportion (54. 44%) of the indigenous population was not aware of the agro-technology of medicinal plants; or what plants they should cultivate. In addition, 39.42% households were seeking financial support for cultivation initiatives.

Discussion

Traditional health care system is based on the plants or plant extracts all over Himalayan region. It has been postulated that around 85% of the traditional health care is based on drugs obtained from plant sources (Kala, 2000). A survey conducted in the remote villages of the Kullu valley reveals that native communities are largely dependent on the plant resources for their routine household needs and economic benefits. In addition, some of the endangered plants are regularly traded from this area. Further, it is also important to note that in a majority of the cases, the belowground parts are dug before seed maturation by the unskilled workers therefore, hampering regeneration chances (Nautiyal, 1986).

For issuing export permits, the state forest department charges an attractive amount of the export fee. In addition, the natives also earn good economic benefits from trading of medicinal herbs. *Aconitum heterophyllum* and *Dactylorhiza hatageria* were among the plants traded on good cost in the nearby Kulu town. Kulu town has been emerged as an important export and inland trading market of the medicinal plants. To provide technical knowledge of the agro-technology and awareness about the medicinal plants occurring in the nearby areas. Farmers can be attracted by telling them about the economic benefits of the medicinal plants.

Majority of the interested populations was willing to have technical support or undergo training of the agro technology. However, lack of extensive research and development programmes have been less supportive in this regard. In addition, poor living conditions also enforce them to seek some financial support. A small proportion of the native population was also aware that they should know the cost/benefit of plants whatever and whenever they are told to cultivate. An approach to develop a medicinal plant based agroforestry model may be advantageous. There is some important plant,which species might be considered for development of the agroforestry model (Table 10.5).

Conclusions

The following important points for the future of medicinal plants was revealed byy the survey conducted in some selected remote villages of Kulu valley :

- Medicinal plants have a central role in a routine household needs as well as in the socio-economy of the native inhabitants.
- Trading of the medicinal plants has always been remained an attractive and thus stands as economically profitable.
- Still the natural habitats are sole sources of extraction and by trading of medicinal plants, therefore, natural stock is facing a sever threat of depletion.
- The native communities were keenly interested in the cultivation of the medicinal herbs; however, lack of technical knowledge and agro-technology, poverty and confusions about the cost/benefit ratio are still the main barriers.

In the light of the aforesaid points the Research and Development Organization should concentrate more on research programmes rather than the research projects. That will help in achieving academic as well as extension goals. These attempts should be further concentrated on the assuring dividends of native inhabitants in the management of dwindling medicinal plant resources.

Mountain agro-ecosystems have been central in the agro-pastoral activities of the native inhabitants. Therefore, in the current scenario medicinal plants may be grown under canopy of the agroforestry trees or under canopy of the orchards. Some of the multipurpose

Table 10.5 Tree Species Considered to be Helpful in Developing Medicinal Plant Based Agro-forestry Models

	Botanical Name	*Local Name*	*Utility*
1.	*Aesculus indica*	Khinaur	Fuel wood, dry leave fodder
2.	*Alnus nitida*	Kosh	Fuel, good N_2 fixing tree
3.	*Cedrus deodara*	Deyar	Timber, oil yielding
4.	*Celtis australis*	Khark	Fodder, fuel
5.	*Cornus macrophylla*	Karchan	Fodder, fuel
6.	*Ficus sp.*	Phagera	Fruits, fuel, fodder
7.	*Grevia oppositifolia*	Beal	Fiber, fodder, fuel wood
8.	*Myrica esculanta*	Kaphal	Fruits, fuel
9.	*Olea ferrn ginea*	Kahoo	Fodder, dye
10.	*Pistacia integrema*	Kakarsinghi	Galls, fuel
11.	*Pyrus pashia*	Shagal	Fruit planting, fuel
12.	*Quercus incana*	Ban	Fodder, fuel
13.	*Robinia pseudoacacia*	Kikkar	Fodder, fuel wood
14.	*Sapindus mukurossii*	Doda	Seed coat, fuel wood
15.	*Robinia pseudoacacia*	Kikkar	Fodder, fuel wood
16.	*Sapindus mukurossii*	Doda	Seed coat, fuel wood

tree species have been enlisted in the Table 10.5 Medicinal plant based agroforestry models will benefit by the development of these plants.

Future Prospects

- Estimation of active components and simultaneously genetic improvement through modern techniques of plant propagation.
- Establishment of small-scale industries for the processing of raw materials.
- Supply of extracts to the pharmaceutical industries or to the international market.

11

Rural Poultry Farming: A Model for Rapid Generation of Rural Income and Employment— In the North East Regions of India

Introduction

The congenial temperate climate and its temperate, vegetation existing in the Himalayas are highly favourable for exotic high producing livestock. Moreover the highlanders in the Himalayas have a traditional pastoral economy which has been handed over from generation to generation with their typical kinds of livestock such as yaks, sheep, goats, pigs, poultry etc. Therefore like the other areas of the world, India has tremendous prospect of livestock raising in its different parts, particularly in the cooler hills of the Himalayas.

Keeping the above discourse in view the present paper is a modest attempt to analyse the present situation of development in the Himalayas and propose a sustainable scheme for the Himalayas which would, not only meet the food requirement of north-east people but also prevent environment from deterioration. Before such a model is proposed, the present Himalayan Environment and farming situation in the Himalayas with special reference to Sikkim Himalayas as it falls in the north east regions of India must lee discussed.

Himalayan Environment

Over the years there has been wide-spread deteroration of the Himalayan environment today, caused by rapid deforestation, over grazing of the natural pasture lands, indiscrimate felling and cultivation of the steep hill slopes and other economic damages caused by the rivers of the Himalayas. The Himalayas exercise a great influence on the environment and economy of the people inhabiting the greater part of northern India constituting mainly the Indo-Gangetic and Bramhaputra plains. These problems are extensively reviewed by (Paljor and Sahu 1995, unpublished) and recommended that the top priority in the Himalayas should be given towards prevention of top soil from erosion as it is the basket of bread of the people inhabiting in the region.

Situation Analysis in Sikkim

Sikkim located in the Eastern Himalayas, joined the mainstream in 1975 as India's 22nd State. Owing to mountainous terrain only, 11 per cent of the total area of 7100 sq kms is under cultivation. Even though the agricultural production is not favourable owing to difficult terrain and high precipitation, yet 75 per cent of Sikkim's. 4.35 lakhs population depend on a subsistance oriented agriculture and animal husbandry farming on small holdings. The present rural livelihood system in Sikkim is presented in Fig 11.1

Rural Livelihood System in Sikkim

Farmer's Families
Silvi Culture
Input System from Production System of Farm
Crop Husbandry
Animal Husbandry Outer System
Environment

Fig 11.1

Source: Schmidt. P. Indo-Swiss Project Sikkim 1994.

The farmers families, cultivate and grow crops and rear livestock (90 per cent of the farmers) the cattle, yaks, goats, sheep, pigs and poultry in small numbers and utilize the forests. As part of their livelihood they also earn cash income from off farm activities. The elements of the farming systems (crop husbandry, animal husbandry and silviculture) are very closely interrelated. From the forest timber, fuel need and a substantial portion of fodder requirements are met. In addition the farmers collect edibles in the forest for themselves and also for their pigs and poultry. Fodder is also cut from the agriculture land and from fodder trees. Further, crop residues like paddy and millet straw, forms an important part of the diet of the livestock. The cattle are the only source of draught power and supply substantial portion of manure. In brief most of the farmers of Sikkim demonstrate excellent land use system, the practices like contour terracing and furrowing, bunding, manuring, mulching and inter cropping adopted by these farmers are never found in other states of India. Thus, the present rural livelihood system is well balanced from an ecological point of view.

However, with the increase in population and the limited availability of land as 70 per cent of the holdings in Sikkim are smaller than 2 hactares, more and more farmers are migrating towards urban areas for off farm activities. In addition Schmidt (1994) has observed that the effect of population growth mainly caused by migration is already causing pressure on land as the area under cultivation is being expanded causing a decline in quantity and quality of forest and pastures; increasing in cropping intensity; staple crops are replaced by cash crops.

These changes in farming scenarios are already causing not only pressure on land but on environment as well, as many farmers are complaining about the change in environment and decline in soil fertility. Similar observation has been made by F.A.O. (1995). Hence, under such situation poultry farming, which require minimal use of land, labour and capital would be an ideal model for development. Before such a model is proposed it would be meaningful to examine its success stories in Nepal Himalayas and in our own country, i.e., India as well.

Country Experience Nepal Himalayas

In Nepal a dramatic growth rate of chicken population is observed for the latter period 1988/89 to 1992/93 which is 2.5 times the earlier annual growth rate. The poultry population in 1984/85 was 8920281 and 10158851 in 1988/89 and the same rose to 13600807 in 1992/93 (Dhakal, 1996). Poultry industry in Nepal is emerging day by day from small scale farmers who have kept 100 to 500 birds to big farmers having 25,000 birds. From the above Nepal studies it is concluded that the poultry farming is mainly suitable for the hills where almost 62 per cent of the poultry population are found and also produce 62 per cent of eggs compared to the mountains and Terai regions. Thus, based on Nepal experience poultry programme would be highly suitable for the north-east regions of India where the climate is almost similar to that of eastern Nepal.

India

In India, the ex-post evaluation studies carried out by the National Bank of Agriculture and Rural Development (NABARD) in Kerala,

Madhya Pradesh and Maharashtra have indicated that the rural poultry projects had made a positive impact on generating rural income and employment (State 1996). The findings are presented in Table 11.1.

Table 11.1

Ex-post Evaluation of Poultry Schemes in India by NABARD

Scheme	*Reference year of study*	*Average Unit size Beneficiary.*	*No. of Units*	*No. of Beneficiaries*	*Unit cost Rs/Bird.R.*	*Net income per Bird. R.*	*Financial rate of return FRR.%*	*Incremental employment generated per year (Man days)*
Broiler Development Kerala	1989-90	800 Per cycle	100	40	43.53	0.80/ bird	50	15956
Poultry (Layer) development Maharashtra	1988-89	539 birds 1029 birds	44 34	20 14	153.58 152.22	14.62 17.62	23.20 25.50	5472 10692
Poultry (Layer) development Madhya Pradesh	1990-91	9492 birds	45	25	145.00	42.76	43.4	251000

Looking at the financial rates of return, net income per bird, etc. under Indian condition, it is concluded that the poultry farming has made a positive impact on generating rural income and employment (Table 11.1) The policy adopted for poultry development by India has comparatively helped to achieve sustained high poultry growth in the last 2-3 decades, mainly under the semi-intensive systems.

Besides Nepal and India the local governments in most of the Asian and African countries also encourage small poultry units through subsidized programmes to serve as source of income, employment and proper nutrition to the village families.

Some like high feed cost, disease, mortality, lack of development of rural markets and seasonal fluctuations in eggs and meat prices are some of the problem these industries face. These problems can be overcome by developing appropriate technology to improve the skills of the farmers through proper training and maximum utilization of environmental feed sources for sustainable village poultry farming. Side by side rural input NGO's or state poultry development corproations should organise markeing outlets where the poultry ownes can be remunerative priece for eggs and meat.

In New Zealand the farmers produce are marketed by the Government/Boards and the farmers are at their liberty to concentrate on production. Similarly in China the marketing and price control is managed by the government/comparatives and the production is in the hands of the farmers (Paljor, 1993). Similar approach should be adopted by the Northeastern governments in India.

Based on the studies of successful viable model for poultry farming in Bangladesh by Jenson (1996), the same model is proposed for adoption in the Northeast regions of India. The model (Fig. 11.2) is a three pronged organization where each prong has its specialized functions. The institutional structure behind the model has to be state/central government through the respective department of Animal Husbandry and Vetrinary Services poultry co-operatives and State Poultry Development Corporations.

Integrated Poultry Production Model Proposed for North East Region

Production	*Supply*	*Services*
Breeders	Parent stock	Village group
Hatcheries	Feed	Training
Chick rearing	Vaccine/ Medicine	Credit/savings
Small holder	Marketing	Extension

Fig. 11.2.

The farmers, as far as possible, should sun the proposed model. In the production line up should run the proposed model there should be breeders to produce quality hatching eggs. These hatching eggs should be hatched in the mini hatcheries and the chicks thus produced must be reared by the expert chick rearers as the chicks require special environmental conditions from the day old till the growers stage. Once these chicks are out of the prooders they must be raised by the small farm holders. Hence, this production line is very important where each farmer has to play their key role and to maintain this discipline and at the same to keep the production line functioning. It should be supported by time strong lines of supply and service.

There should be regular supply of parent lines of good quality and the breed must be supplied either by the poultry development corporations or the state government agencies or by a reputed private firms whose quality of breeds have been tested by the Central Random, Testing Farms. The feed in the villages may be sold by a farmer; it should be purchased from a government agencies or from a reputed firm. In its absence the concern 'farmers should mix the local grinded crop produce with fishifeal, vitamins and mineral mixture. For the vaccines/medicine the state government should either set up a treatment centre in the village or train the local poultry workers to vaccinate the birds. The vaccines must be supplied free of cost by the government and in case of the village which is located in the remote area a cold chain must be maintained to save the vaccines.

Regarding the marketing of eggs a farmer with good accounts background preferably a retired accountants to collect eggs in the villages and maintain proper accounts should be appointed and these eggs should be collected either by the NGOs or the state poultry co-operatives periodically. Finally the service line should have a village level group or 'think tank' to discuss relevant subjects and finalize the selection of new poultry holders in the village. The service line should also be supported by a training institute or a centre run by the government, a well established with sound financial backing to provide of credit facilities to the farmers. It has to be established in the villages and finally the extension centre run by the concern department of AH and VS or the State Corporations should support the villages.

The proposed model of poultry farming at village level is well developed and would function well under the Northeastern regions condition where there is good co-operations in the villages and almost all the households rear and consume poultry birds. There is, however, a doubt on the viability of setting of breeders units and hatcheries at the farmers level as maintenance of parent line would involve high technical or scientific resource base and it would a big financial burden for the farmers. Hence, the hatcheries and the breeders parent line should be run either by The poultry co-operatives or the state government farms should run the hatcheries or breeder parent lines.

Based on the evaluation of the above proposed model, it is concluded that the poultry farming would be highly suitable model and for rapid adoption of this model the following recommendations are made.

1. A Hatchery cum Parent Stock farm for Briler cum Layers have to be established in each of the states to cater for commercial day old chicks both for layer and broilers, preferably under Central Sector Scheme with 100% grant or under State Sector Scheme.

2. Farmers here have to compete with the poultry farmers of punjab and Andhra Pradsh. Therefore farming support which include inputs like day old chicks and grown up pullets, balance feed etc. have to be heavily subsidized in the initial state.
3. In the initial stage the state government agencies have to extend full support for the marketing poultry birds, eggs and meat till it is replaced by village poultry co-operatives and private agencies.
4. To cater to disease control and vaccination, central Avian Diagonestic Research Centre at the State level and Avian Diagnostic and treatment centre at the village level have to be established. The vaccines and medicines along with bio-security measures have to be support free of cost by the State Government.
5. An extension and training institute have to be established in each of the state and it should be supported by planned time bound training schedules for the farmers and unemployed youth. The schedule should also be linked with the commercial banks so that the farmers are allotted poultry units right after the training period.
6. For initial capital inputs like housing, equipments and insurance etc adequate subsidized financial support have to be provided.

References

Agriculture Statistics Division: Department of Agriculture Development, His Majestry's Government of Nepal, 1993.

Dhakal, I.P. Status of Poultry Industry in Nepal, Paper presented at XX World Poultry Congress, organized by the Worlds Poultry Science Association (Indian Branch) New Delhi, 2-5 September 1996.

FAO: Report on Rapid Rural Appraisal (RRA) of Goat and Chicken Production in Phongla and Pamphok Villages, South Sikkim and Aritar and Salgari Village East Sikkim-FAO/TCP/IND/4451. Development of small scale livestock activities Sikkim-India, 1995, p. 92.

Jenson, H.A. Semi/Scavenging model for rural poultry holding. Paper presented at (XX Worlds Poultry Congress New Delhi, India, 2-5, September 1996).

Schmidt, P.A. Synthesis of studies conducted on behalf of Indo-Swiss Project, Sikkim from October 1993 and April 1994, pp. 1-50.

Sathe, B.S. Planning and Implementation of Poultry Projects in Developing Countries, Paper represented at (XX Worlds Poultry Congress, New Delhi, India 2-5 September 1996).

12

Improvement of Rural Hill Economy Through the Eastern Himalayan Flora

The life support system of the hill people depends on forests. In the Himalaya, the people and forests always had, symbiotic relationship. The needs of the hill people are bio-mass based like fuel, fodder timber, medicines etc, which are fulfilled from the reserve forests. These requirements have increased many folds over the years due to the rise in population. This has led to a rapid depletion of the reserve forests. In the Himalaya, degradation of forests has also come about due to over use, beyond the capacity of the forests to regenerate, through too much felling, lopping and grazing.

If we have to save the precious forests in the Himalayas, we must improve the economic conditions of the hill people,The Himalayan people must be made self-reliant in the larger interest of the nation. We must create job opportunities in the villages which will also check the influx of villagers to the Himalayan cities which are already over-crowded. Three plant species are discussed, here which grow in the eastern Himalaya. These plants can bring ecological preservation along with economic prosperity.

Amliesho

Of the three plants one is locally called Amlesho 'Thysonalina agrostis' or 'Amlesho' is one such plant which grows abundantly in Darjeeling and Sikkim from 2,000-6,000 ft. It is of three types— (i) Thulo (Big sized inflorescence). It grows between an altitude of 2,000-3,000 ft, and has a big inflorescence, (ii) Majholey (medium-sized inflorescence)— it grows between an altitude of 3,000-5,000 ft and has medium sized inflorescence, (iii) Purkey (small sized inflorescence)— it grows between an altitude of 5,000-6,000 ft and has a small inflorescence. We have yet to harness the full potential of this plant for various purposes. This plant can bring economic revolution with ecological preservation to the people of this region. It grown well in dry as well as wet places. It also grows well on slopes, degraded lands and wastelands. It is a small plant growing upto the height of 8 to 10 ft. and having a life span of many years. It can be easily cultivated by vegetative propagation. This plant has many environmental advantages. The leaves of this plant are used in religious ceremonies by the local Nepali and Buddhist people. Therefore this plant has aesthetic and religions value also.

Soil Conservation, Erosion Control and Landslide Management

Amlesho can be used for stabilising the soil as it is an extremely good soil binder. The massive roots of this plant bind the soil very well specially on sharp slopes and degraded lands. It should also be used in landslide management. It also acts as a wind break. It increases soil fertility— Amlesho has the ability to grow on very poor and degraded soil, The roots and leaves decay and add nutrients to the soil. It has been observed that it turns poor soil fit for cultivation.

Fuel: It is also used by the local people as fuel though it burns fast and has less calorific value.

Fodder: This plant is drought resistant and is an extremely good for cows and sheeps. This is the only green fodder available in winter

Fencing: This plant has been used for fencing against animals and human beings.

Economics: With Amlesho inflorescence sticks, brooms are made. This is an unorganised industry estimated at 15 to 20 crores. The inflorescence (sticks) comes out in the 2nd or 3rd year, which is used for making brooms. These brooms are made in Siliguri and Jalpaiguri and sent all over the country including Delhi, Mumbai, Chennai, Kolkata and Kanpur etc. The people of this region are being exploited by the 'middle-men' who buy the raw material at a very cheap price— 4 to 8 rupees a kilo. The middle-men sell it in Siliguri and Jalpaiguri at 14 to 18 rupees a kilo. The broom manufacturers sell the broom at 24 to 25 rupees a kilo. If the local people are trained in the broom making and the raw material are not allowed to go to the plains, it could bring economic revolution in the rural areas. One person can easily make 100 brooms in 5 hours.If he/she is paid one rupee per broom, he/she can make Rs.100/– in just 5 hours. One kg raw material is enough to make 5 brooms each broom is sold at Rs.5/ – in Siliguri and at Rs.6 to Rs. 8 in other parts of the country.

The inflorescence come in the 2nd year or 3rd year: from the 7th year the production of 'inflorescence' (locally called sticks) is maximum and it remains the same thereafter.

Amlesho has Medicinal Value

The roots of Amlesho are made into a paste and applied to the 'boil' locally to make it ripe and to cure it. It is a common practice in the villages.

Amlesho Compost: The leaves of Amlesho can also be used for making compost.

Amlesho in Paper Making

The Amlesho stem can be used for making paper in the industry. It could help in saving the precious forest in the Himalayas.

Amlesho can be used for making articles. The Amlesho stems can be used for making articles like tables, chairs, baskets and bins etc.

Amlesho in Gasi firrs

Amlesho stems along with another weed lentana and Banmara which have invaded the Eastern Himalayas, can be used in gasi firrs which can provide electricity to the rural areas.

Amlesho has great potential economically as well as ecologically. It needs to be exploited scientifically.

Rhododendrons

Botanists have always been attracted to the magnificient of Rhododendrons. Rhododendron have always received the attention of Botanists for their magnificent flowers. There are 850 species of Rhododendrons in the world. India has 86 species of which over 70 are found in the Eastern Himalayas. Rhododendrons are very poorly represented in the Western Himalaya (only 9 species).

Rhododendrons appear as trees from 5,000 to 8,000 ft. As the altitude increases from 8,000 ft to 12,000 ft. Rhododendrons exhibit luxuriant growth and it is the ideal zone for the growth of Rhododendrons and has the maximum numbers. Rhododendrons are normally propagated through seeds and cuttings.

The local people use Rhododendrons for various purposes by the local people. The make wine from it, they make squashes and they use them for medicinal purposes. The leaves of Rhododendrons anthopogon ('Palu' as it is called locally) are used to make an incense that has been used in Buddhist Monasteries for centuries. Rhododendrons arboreum (Lali Guras) flowers are used to prepare a wine locally called (Raxi). This wine has medicinal properties. It in also an antidote for high altitude sickness. The wine is brewed in Meghma, Tonglu and Sandakpu area of Darjeeling District. It is used to check diarrhoea and dehydration of body fluids. The local people collect the flowers, with them for 24 hours and then squeeze the juice out from the flowers. The flower juice is placed in wooden barrels, molasses are added to it and then it is fermented with yeast for about a month and finally distilled into wine.

They prepare "Rhododendron Squash" from the flowers of Rhododendron arboreum: they collect the flowers, boil them in water and the extract is filtered and then boiled in sugar and made into squash which also has medicinal properties. Both of these are commercial proposition and can be exploited commercially to improve the economic lot of the people.

If some one has a headache the leaves of Rhododendrons arboreum are used to relieve it. A paste is made of leaves and applied to the forehead to relieve the pain. The flowers of Rhododendrons arboreum are eaten by the local people when a fish bone gets stuck up in the throat. Probably, the flowers produce chemicals which dissolve the bone. The leaves of Rhododendrons Campanulatum (locally Milo chimal) are mixed with Tobacco and used as snuff. Khukuri handles and gift boxes are also made from Rhododendron.

There has been a tremendous destruction of the Rhododendron habitat in the past few years. This is quite evident in Lava forest in Kalimpong and Tonglu range in Darjeeling. This is largely due to development activities and the local needs for fuel-wood and charcoal. The Environment Protection Society submitted a proposal to the Darjeeling Gorkha Hill Council that Rhododendrons should be cultivated in an organised manner and it could boost local economy if the medicinal properties of Rhododendrons are commercially exploited. It is now almost certain that the Rhododendron flowers contain chemicals which lower the blood pressure and keep the heart healthy. Mr. D. Chakravarti, Principal Secretary, DGHC, invited a team of scientific experts from the Central Drug Research Institute, Lucknow, who are now thoroughly investigating the medicinal properties of Rhododendrons. If the rich medicinal properties of Rhododendrons are established and the locals grow Rhododendrons it will bring ecological preservation along with economic prosperity in this region.

Banmara

"Eupatorium Adenophorum" (EUPATORIUM ADENOPHORUM) locally called 'Banmara' is a dangerous weed which has infested huge areas of forests, agricultural and wasteland in the Eastern Himalayas and the U.P. Hills. Banmara is an erect herb belonging to the family Asteraceae, which grows up to a height of one metre. Banmara grows abundantly from 1,000 metres to 2,000 metres. The plant is not eaten by animals and is spreading like wild fire in the Eastern Himalayas. It provides no fodder, no fuel and suppresses the growth of other plants. It is very much like the 'Lantana Camara' of the U.P. Hills.

The only use is that the local people use it as an antiseptic and anti-bleeding agent. The leaves and tender stems of this plant are crushed to extract the juice, which is applied to cuts to stop bleeding and the cut is protected. This is very effective but is not marketed and no further research has been done in this direction.

Banmara has been a bane to farmers, tea gardens and foresters in the Eastern Himalayas as it does not allow other crops to grow. Scientists have been doing research work on it but unfortunately they have only been able to use it for composting which is hardly an achievement.

I have been working on this plant for the past many years. Later on Swapan Sen, a paper technologist, joined me and we have been able to turn this ecological manace into a resource which can be used for economic upliftment of rural folks, employment generation and eco-friendly industrial development of the Eastern Himalayas and the UP Hills (in the UP Himalayas, Euptorium is replacing the dominant weed Lentana Camara).

Hand made paper of very high grade and quality has been developed by me from Banmara. This has tremendous employment generation potential in the Eastern Himalayas, particularly in Sikkim and Darjeeling. A large number of people can be gainfully employed in the villages and a large number of cottage industries can be developed. A month's training programme is enough to train the village folks in hand paper making and the accessories for this cottage industry are minimum. This hand-made paper has tremendous export potential.

We have also been able to extract a green dye from Banmara which is rare. There has been a tremendous demand of vegetable dyes as the synthetic dyes are carcinogenic and they react with the human skin. The dye extracted from Banmara has been able to fix itself to fabric and it has fastness properties and is resistant to the action of water. The jute fabric does not have the thermal comfort but when the jute fabric dyes are simply dipped in Banmara solution, the jute fabric develops good texture and thermal comfort. This has very high export potential, particularly to countries like China, Nepal, Thailand, Bangladesh, etc. We have also made a herbal after shave from the juice of Banmara.

Banmara can also be used to make quality compost. A new technique has been developed to convert this weed into a resource. In this techniques, Banmara is collected, chopped into small bits and then dumped into specially designed compost rooms. These rooms have a fibre glass roof to crap heat and perforated pipes are inserted from all directions. The chopped, weeds are tightly packed into the compost rooms and sufficiently moistened with water. Microorganisms convert this weed into compost. After the compost is ready, it is taken to the drying pit for drying and then stored in godowns. This Eupatorium Compost is very light and is excellent for nursery raising. It has been proved that it takes less time to raise seedlings by using Eupatorium Compost. This compost is also excellent for vegetables and the yield may go up many folds.

This technique is very fast takes 25 days in summer and 35-40 days in winter, eco-friendly and can help in sustainable agriculture, horticulture, floriculture and Nursery raising in the hills.

13

The Eastern Himalaya: Environmentalism and Economic Development

Abstract

The peculiar environmental and strategic conditions applying in the Eastern Himalaya have so far limited the options for economic development. These is are doubt in the mind of any planner that there is an over whelming economic potential in the area. However, the agenda for preserving the environment need not per se be inimical to development, if the direction of economic growth can be brought to balance with nature. The makings of a new and imaginative development strategy for the region is suggested which focuses on the quality of its natural and human resources, which if implemented can restore the options that had earlier been foregone.

The Eastern Himalaya

The Eastern Himalaya is considered among the principal hotspots for biodiversity. Himalayan region extends from Sikkim and North Bengal to Arunachal Pradesh, and including the other North East states of Assam, Meghalaya, Mizoram, Nagaland, Tripura and Manipur. The region is repository to a richness of flora and fauna unrivalled on the face of the planet. Ironically however, it also happens to be economically the poorest region within the country. The unique microclimate of the region which ranges from the tropical to the alpine over varied ecosystems combines with fine human resources that are aptly suited to the rugged mountain area, and in fact have great economic potential. What is currently lacking therefore is the foresight and political will required to take hard decisions.

A good deal of time and resources are expended today in imposing developmental programmes, many of which possess no relevance for the region. Thus, in spite of years of vigorous planning and the rich natural resource endowments of the region, it continues to languish in all fields. For stability to be assured to this otherwise vulnerable part of India, the path of economic development can be the only answer, since neither will guns ever bring peace, nor can money buy gratitude. In such circumstances, conversion of the rich regional biodiversity into sustainable economic growth, which is adapted both to the environment and culturally rich people of the area, becomes imperative. Therefore planning in the Eastern Himalayan region should ideally be on terms with the potential of the region.

Economic Activity

The principal economic activities therefore on which the region should concentrate are the '3Ts' i.e., tea, timber and tourism, besides the generation of hydel power and development of horticulture, floriculture and pharmaceuticals based on medicinal herbs along with the handicrafts industries.

The tea industry itself is eco-friendly, has soil stabilising characteristics and highly labour intensive. It is indigenously found in the Northeast Himalaya. The region is well known both for the quality and quantity of the tea it produces for the world market. There is need for the industry to make a rapid breakthrough along the lines achieved in Sri Lanka, East Africa and nearby Bangladesh. Involvement of the people of Eastern Himalaya, both as tea workers at all echelons and as owners too becomes the need of the hour. Co-operative growing for the supply of green leaves, selection of clonal materials suited to particular subregions, rejuvenation of old and moribund tea gardens and a consistent marketing strategy are areas where urgent attention is called for. It may be remembered in this connection that it was the colonial rulers of the country who established tea in the region.

It is a good 150 years now since the event. There is no reason therefore why after generations of workers have toiled in the gardens, their present successors should not have larger say in the industry. This would in fact bring forth the greater dedication so vital for the health and productivity of the industry. Management by remote control cannot be the answer anymore. There is also the need to prevent existing gardens from falling into ruin the Peshoke way. There must be will to find just solutions no matter how hard and costly these may be. It is heartening in this respect that the nontraditional tea areas in the region are making such a breakthrough. Beginnings have been made in Sikkim, Arunachal Pradesh, Manipur, and Nagaland, etc. Since the cause of watershed management is today being championed in the region, the growing of tea should be very much encouraged as a part of this strategy.

Potential for Farm Forestry

Nent comes replantation of forests. Trees are a renewable resource. The demand for wood continues to grow with the rise in living standards. Paper is indispensable. The Himalayan region is the largest repository of tree species that suit all microclimates and needs. Prudence thus rest on the advocacy and implementation of tree farming programmes on marginal agricultural lands and wastelands to encourage farmers to adopt these trees as cash crops. Co-operative tree farming well supported by financial institutions would go a long way in this direction. There are in fact few other activities in a Himalayan context where employment generation can be as colossal as is possible through tree farming. Land preparation, planting, tending, harvesting, processing and marketing, and repetition of this cycle on a sustainable basis can create a myriad of economic avenues suited to all sections of the community.

The example exists of New Zealand where one insignificant tree species from the US West Coast (i.e., *Pinus radiata*) has proved the single most important species for farm forestry. New Zealand today is not only self sufficient in timber, paper, etc., but also exports a substantial quantity of these as major export commodities. All the tree plantations have come up on small private holdings. Inspite of being relative newcomers to professional forestry, the farm foresters have made up for lost time and their expertise at growing and managing trees as a commercial crop is second to none. Farm forestry has made New Zealand one of the richest countries in the world in per capita terms, and has put wealth into the hands of people whose only assets are land and time. Introduction and planning of this form of cultivation into the Himalayan region is urgently called for. It has been observed that Pinus patula which was introduced from Central Mexico to the Darjeeling hills in Sixties has distinct possibilities.

Alder (*Alnus nepalensis*), birch (*Betula sps.*), teak (*Tectona grandis*), poplar (*Populus ciliata*) can be grown on a 10-20 year rotation on higher reaches of Himalayas. These are some indigenous species. for higher reaches and (*Populus gamblei* for subtropical areas) and so on. Inclusion of these in a well coordinated farm forestry programme would not only solve many present ills but would also generate employment and economic growth. Importantly, the demand of wood based products both in India and in its neighbouring countries with the rise of middle class affluence has risen remarkably. A large number of fast growing nitrogen-fixing tees species serve the dual purpose of fertilising the soil while also producing quality wood. *Acacia mangium* from Australia and *Leucana leucocephala* from the Philippines are among them. What would be required is an immediate trial run with proven provenance in a large number of potential sites to prove their suitability. Most of the objections that the arena of forestry is facing today from various quarters in India are targeted to faulty planning and tardy implementation of forestry schemes. One cannot but agree.

However, just because the reckless felling of trees raises the hackles of environmentalists, this does not mean that responsible forestry should be shunned. We could consider the case of *Cryptomeria japonica* from the Darjeeling hills. Although an exotic, the species has proved to be a fine fastgrowing species, well suited to several elevations. A well-managed *Cryptomeria* plantation on a 20 year rotation would adequately meet local demands for wood, since each acre of the plantation would have a likely yield of around 5000 cft of timber. At present value, this would be worth Rs. 10 lakhs @ 50,000 per acre per annum. Few other crops, whether tea or oranges, could match this. Therefore to discard *Cryptomeria* as being ecologically unfriendly would be great mistake. It is not necessary that the usage of land has to be perfectly ecofriendly over every inch. A judicious compromise from the point of human needs is equally important. Monoculture with coniferous species is an important forestry operationin many developed countries form US to scandanaera.

Agroforestry is an important area of stress along with tree farming. The larger cardamom (*Amomum subulatum*), which grows in the region is a perfect example of a crop that can grow under almost 80 per cent green cover. Judicious management of the plantation will produce both cardamom and quality wood. Sikkim's total production of over 4000 MT of cardamom on a sown area of less than 7500 sq. km has positioned it as the largest grower in the world. The plantations are all on smalholdings using the time tested methodology envolved by the people of the area. This example, which offers substantive evidence of the importance of agroforestry, has also helped Sikkim to greatly increase commercial output from its forests over recent decades.

People's Involvement

Nagaland has received funding of Rs.1000 crore from the Canadian International Development Agency [CIDA] through the India-Canada Environmental Facilities [ICEF] endeavour. Though it is continuously being ravaged by insurgency, it has launched an agroforestry project. The project which involves government and people's participation is the brainchild of the Nagaland Chiel Secretary A.M. Gokhale. Perhaps the most significant feature of the project is that it does not seek to eliminate *jhum* cultivation which has been both a timetested agro practice as well as a way of life for the region ranging from the Indian North East through to Laos and Vietnam, but aims at making it more stable and profitable. Village womenfolk have been given a prominent role in its implementation.

The Nagaland Chief Secretary comments "if money for this project can be generated from some viable sources, it will mark the end of insurgency because everybody will be busy making money." This should in fact be the correct approach and the Governments of India and Nagaland and international funding agencies should collaborate further in multiplying its success. There are reasons to believe that the economy of the State would completely change with the implementation of the project, as the microclimatic region there resembles that of contiguous Myanmar where valuable tree species like teak, etc. show excellent growth.

A well and imaginatively developed cultural tourism package would greatly boost tourism in the region, besides helping to preserve this rich heritage. For tourism, one of the largest industries in the world today, the Eastern Himalayas hold many attractive features. The stress however should be on culture, adventure and nature–oriented tourism. The diverse ethnic communities resident in the region, with their distinctive cultural heritage reflected in their dress, handicrafts, music and dance, and folklore, as well as "their architectural and farming styles, and food habits, hold tremendous appeal to the tourist. Eco- or nature-oriented tourism also has tremendous potential. The wealth of alpine flowers found in Sikkim and Arunachal Pradesh, and of orchids all over the region is already well-known.

However, the richness of the rhododendron species found in the region is second only to Yunnan in China, and the primula and *Meconopsis* (blue poppy) collections are equally diverse. Moreover, trees of great dendrological interest are found here, along with rich bird life and colourful butterflies, which all have special appeal for tourists. For the tourism potential to materialise, the requirements are methodical planning and well-organised tours conducted by persons having special competence in each field. Birdwatchers and rhododendron fanciers are high-bracket tourists. As such, meticulous conservation of the Eastern Himalayan habitats by duly involving the people who residing in their immediate vicinity becomes vitally important. It should be remembered that such prized habitats can easily be destroyed if they are flooded with mediocre and disinterested visitors.

Examples from Bhutan and Arunachal Pradesh may be cited in this respect, where the steps taken to promote tourism have so far been cautious but in the right direction. The daily spending requirement per international tourist of $250 per diem in Bhutan and $150 per diem in Arunachal Pradesh has not deterred visitors from being in the queue. A similar policy can spread the economic benefits of tourism over the entire region. Arunachal Pradesh is perhaps the last inaccessible bastion of some of the finest floral and faunal reserves, to which visitors from all over the world have been eagerly waiting to rush in, particularly after the Eastern Tibetan ranges in the vicinity of Namche Barwa and Yunnan have been thrown open. A well-conceived ecotourism programme that revives the nature-trails followed by Hooker, Kingdom-Ward, Ludlow and Sherriff will not only bring greater economic prosperity to this region but also help to conserve this natural heritage. Local people can wecome the qreatest conservationists one they realise that nature reserves offer tourism products that bring prosperity to their door.

Other Economic Avenues

The environment and economic potential of the Eastern Himalaya apart, the hydroelectric power potential of the region cannot be ignored. The capacity in fact is great enough to meet the entire regional power demand. However, an integrated regional approach has to be invoked where the power-generating states, power-using states and countries, and international funding and investment agencies mould themselves into the form of a consortium. This would help to bring in the best technologies on offer in the world, and would also offer regional transparency in all deals. The issue of the economic prosperity to be derived from the generation of hydel power is in fact one area where responsible citizens of the region must close their ears to the howls of the mob, and stand

and fight for their economic rights. With hydel projects coming on stream in series across the region, this will require that all catchments be well protected and well managed. Properly-managed watersheds along all river systems are not only absolutely basic to biodiversity conservation, but can also make a tremendous contribution to controlling the floods which commonly menace the entire region including Bangladesh. Imports of technology which enabled Scotland and certain Latin American countries to lift water from downstream locations to supply water to upstream towns by day and to generate power by night can also mitigate the acute shortages of water felt in some of our prime hill stations. It is in such areas, that international development agencies can be put to work. For this very purpose only international agencies were formed.

For economic activity to flourish in the true sense of the word, a need for the development of basic infrastructure exists in the Eastern Himalaya. For this, infrastructural authorities such as the North East Infrastructure Development Corporation must play a constructive part. Reopening of border trade with China, Myanmar and Bangladesh may also be purposefully pursued by associating state governments in the region, which know the ground realities. Many of the issues which presently appear vexed will solve themselves in their own time if today the focus returns to the advance of trade and commerce. Beginning have already been made at the country's western frontier. This time New Delhi should look eastwards. What is also important is to respect the distinct identity of each state in the region. By their nature, the people of the Eastern Himalaya are gentle and law abiding. It would not be in the national interest to betray their trust. Thus the protections and privileges which for historical reasons have been assured to then through various articles of the Constitution should be preserved and respected and dilution prevented.

Thus, the people of the region have to rise above petty issues and stand on their own feet. To look upon Delhi for doles all the time cannot help in this. It is likewise necessary that the political leadership should shun populist programmes and adopt the path of economic growth. For this, they have to recognize that democracy is not about pleasing all the people all of the time, and rapid economic development alone can provide the political stability which gives substance to the power that all parties crave. All this may seem a tall order but commencement has to be made.

Industrial Development in the Uttarakhand Himalaya

The paper studies regional disparity in industrial development in Uttarakhand identifying five levels of high, moderately high, moderate, moderately low and low development. Significant disparities are brought out in the block levels of industrial development attained in Uttarakhand, which would have to be overcome for integrated development of the area. Pragmatic measures are suggested for developing industrially-backward areas of the Himalaya.

Industrialisation and Development

The study region comprising the 12 districts of the Uttarakhand Himalaya does not generally suit the setting up of large industrial plants, because of limitations like rugged topography, steep slopes and deep valleys, inhospitable climate and lack of infrastructure. A few large and medium-sized industrial establishments are however located in the southern region which is favoured by gently sloping lands, and better transport and banking facilities.

The degree of industrialisation attained by an economy is often considered an important indicator of development. Industrialisation at the small scale is vital to the development process in several ways, the greatest advantage being the provision of employment in a native setting which helps the development of inherent talents and aptitudes of the people in occupations congenial to them.

The region still lags behind in industrial development. A number of programmes and schemes have since been formulated by the Government of India, the state Department of Industries and Handlooms and other State agencies to attract industrial investment into Uttarakhand. Presently, 6821 SSI units exist which are widely distributed across Uttarakhand at the rate of 149 SSI units per lakh population engaging 1.13 per cent of the total workforce on the average. Keeping in view the limitations of the area, more small-scale industries based on available raw materials are being encouraged.

The Study Area

The region of Uttarakhand, also popularly known as Uttaranchal or the UP Hills, forms part of the Central Himalaya in Uttar Pradesh, extending geographically from 28°52′ N to 31°23′ N latitude and 77°56′ E to 81°5′ E longitude (Map 13.1). This region of about

51125 sq km collectively covers Garhwal and Kumaun divisions and constitutes 17.36 per cent of the total area of Uttar Pradesh. Extending from the *terai* or *bhabhar* belt at the Himalayan foothills to the south to the snowclad peaks of the Himadri which demarcate the Indo-Tibetan border to the north, the region is separated from Nepal to the east by the Tons-Yamuna and the Kali-Sharda rivers. The 12 districts of Uttarakhand, namely Uttarkashi, Chamoli, Dehradun, Tehri, and Pauri Garhwal, Rudraprayag, Pithoragarh, Almora, Champawat, bageshwar, Nainital and Udham Singh Nagar include 39 tehsils, 89 blocks, 633 nyaya panchayats and 6257 gram sabhas. Total rural population in the study area is 4,333,714 or about 76.23 per cent of the total population of Uttarakhand.

Purposes of Study

The present study investigates relative levels of industrial development in Uttarakhand and various other features that relate to this. Two hypotheses to be tested against the regional experience are that:

(a) natural environments are not conducive to industrialisation in mountain regions; and

(b) welfare from the industrialisation measures initiated by government and voluntary organizations is not reaching the people of the region.

Many attempts have been made at measuring the industrialization and development potentials of various regions within the country. The studies conducted. have suggested ways and means for achieving development of backward areas. Not many scholars have analysed the level of development in economically backward region of Uttarakhand. Even these studies confine themselves to certain districts. No geographical study has been undertaken of Uttarakhand at micro-level in which comparative levels of industrialisation have been analysed. The present study makes a modest attempt in this direction.

Industrialisation Indicators

A number of indicators of industrial development at micro and macro levels have been studied in Prakash (1977), Dubey (1981), Gosal and Krishan (1984), Singh (1987), Ramchandra and Raghu (1987), Singh (1991), and Kantawala (1992). Two such indicators selected to measure the levels of industrial development in the present study are the number of SSI units per lakh of population, and the percentage of workers engaged by SSI units as a proportion of total workforce. Selection of these indicators is based on the availability of data, and the importance, accuracy and suitability of the indicator to the contexts of the study region.

Statistical abstracts, publications, and records maintained at district, tehsil, and block headquarters, etc., for the period 1992-94 were great help though these were scattered all over uttarkhand right to block level. The concentration index method has then been used for measuring levels of industrial development. Two stages are involved in the calculation:

Table 13.1 Levels of Industrial Development

Level of industrial concentration	*Index Range*	*Number of block*	*Percentage of total block*
High	[CID>124.0]	21	23.6
Moderately High	[86.4 < CID< 124.0]	13	14.6
Moderate	[48.8, CID < 86.4]	22	24.7
Moderately Low	[11.2 <CID <48.8]	31	34.9
Low	[CID < 11.2]	2	2.2

(i) index values for each indicator are first computed at block level.

(ii) computed index values of each indicator are then combined and averaged over the number of indicators to find out the value of the composite index.

Indexed indicator values at block level are calculated with the help of following formula.

$$CD_d = \frac{V_{ae}}{V_{ar}} \times 100 \text{ where } CD_d = \text{indexed value of indicator } a$$

V_{ae} = Value of a at block – Level

V_{ar} = Average regional value of a

The composite index is then defined over different indicators for each block by

$$CID = \frac{CD_{a1} + CD_{a2} + CD_{a3} + \dots\dots\dots\dots + CD_{an}}{N} \text{ where}$$

CID = Composite Index of development

N = Number of Indicators

After grouping the Uttarakhand blocks by the levels of industrial development described under the five listed categories, the block categories are then mapped and analysed.

Observations and Analysis

The highest composite index (552.2) is observed for Bheemtal block in Nainital district, and the lowest (4.4) is for Berinaug block in Pithoragarh district. The difference between these values shows that there is wide variation in levels of industrial development at block level, (see Table 13.1 & Map 13.2). Thus, Index values for all industrial development indicators are combined and averaged for each block to obtain the composite index value for industrial development.

(i) High Concentration [CID>124.0], 21 Uttarakhand blocks (23.6 per cent of the total) fall into the category of high industrial development. These are widely distributed over the region. Higher presence of SSI units and higher percentage of industrial worker categories because of these units are the main reason why the blocks fall under the high category.

(ii) Moderately High Concentration [86.4 < CID < 124.0] 13 Uttarakhand blocks (14.6 per cent of the total) fall into the category of moderately high industrial development. These blocks are scattered in patches but mostly cluster in the central and western parts of the region. Blocks in the category show moderately high to high presence of SSI units and industrial workers within the population.

(iii) Moderate Concentration [48.8 < CID < 86.41]. 22 Uttarakhand blocks (24.7 per cent of the total) reveal moderate indices of industrial development. These are highly concentrated in the central part of the region. The moderate value of the index results basically from moderate to moderately high presence of SSI units and moderate percentages of industrial workers.

(iv) Moderately Low Concentration [11.2 < CID < 48.8]. The highest number of 31 blocks (34.9 per cent of the total) have moderately low indexes of industrial development. These blocks are located in the eastern and central part of the region. They come under this category because of moderate to low presence of SSI units per lakh of population and of industrial workers within the population.

(v) Low Concentration [CID< 11.2]. Only 2 blocks (about 2.2 per cent of the total), namely Berinaug and Jakholi in Pithoragarh and Tehri districts respectively, fall under this category. Low percentages of industrial workers and low presence of SSI units are the main reasons for the low indexes attributed to these blocks.

General Conclusions

The study has shown that 38.2 per cent of the Uttarakhand blocks reveal moderately high to high distributions of SSI units per lakh population and percentages of industrial workers respectively.

It also shows that 37.1 per cent of the blocks have witnessed moderately low to low levels of industrial development, mainly due to inhospitable environmental conditions and lack of infrastructural facilities, etc. Uttarakhand nevertheless has good potential for development of forest-based industries. Hence, industrialisation programmes for the region should be drawn on the basis of locally-available raw materials and infrastructure, and local demands for different products. Further, the programmes should suggest appropriate locations for new industrial units.

Forests are the principal resource of Uttarakhand. Forest cover in the region has dwindled considerably due to reckless felling of trees by the local people to fulfill present needs. Judicious planning is needed not only to maintain existing forest cover but to enhance the area under forest. Social forestry and other afforestation programmes should hence be given top priority. It is also necessary that the climatically suitable, drought-resistant and fast-growing species selected for afforesting new areas should have commercial and industrial importance also.

Table 13.2
Comparative Levels of Industrial Development in Uttarakhand

Block		*Composite index*
Number	*Name*	*Value*
High Industrial Development		
1.	Bhimtal	552.2
2.	Rudrapur	469.3
3.	Kashipur	408.6
4.	Dasholi	341.3
5.	Doiwala	327.8
6.	Karanprayag	280.3
7.	Hawal Baug	264.9
8.	Haldwani	261.0
9.	Purola	250.5
10.	Pakhera	242.8
11.	Bhatwari	223.0
12.	Duggadda	221.0
13.	Joshimath	204.8
14.	Raipur	166.1
15.	Thorali	163.7
16.	Terikhat	154.2
17.	Ramnagar	146.8

Block *Number Name*		*Composite index* *Value*
18.	Vikasnagar	143.0
19.	Naugaon	130.8
20.	Dewal	127.0
21.	Pauri	124.6
22.	Khirsu	121.5
23.	Dhari	116.6
24.	Dunda	116.5
25.	Gauri	115.8
26.	Chakrata	111.2
27.	Chaukutiya	110.5
28.	Okhal Kanda	110.2
29.	Bageshwar	102.6
30.	Dhangoo	99.3
31.	Kota Baug	92.0
32.	Dawara Haat	89.0
33.	Chinyali	88.3
34.	Sahaspur	88.2
35.	Baital Ghat	85.9
36.	Bhiklyasein	78.0
37.	Ghat	77.5
38.	Rikrelal	76.9
39.	Ukheemath	75.7
40.	Chand Kote	74.3
41.	Kalsi	74.0
42.	Ramgarh	72.6
43.	Lagadda	71.1
44.	Nainidada	67.7
45.	Dhauladevi	67.6
46.	Augustmuni	66.0
47.	Narayanbagad	65.9
48.	Borokhal	65.7
49.	Bheinsiyachhana	63.9
50.	Narayanpokhri	62.5
51.	Sayalde	55.2
52.	Panwo	54.8
53.	Leinsdowne	54.1
54.	Bajpur	53.8

Block Number Name	Composite index Value
55. Garud	50.8
56. Jaspur	48.9
57. Gairsein	48.7
58. Taluka	46.6
59. Suit	46.4
60. Sitarganj	46.3
61. Chamba	45.7
62. Gadarpur	44.1
63. Pithoragarh	42.2
64. Kote	38.3
65. Kupkote	37.4
66. Thailesan	37.1
67. Kaljikhal	35.5
68. Thaudhar	34.1
69. Champawat	31.5
70. Devprayag	30.4
71. Barakot	27.8
72. Pratapnagar	27.3
73. Narendranagar	26.9
74. Jakhdedhar	26.8
75. Kirtinagar	22.7
76. Khateema	22.1
77. Bhillangna	21.9
78. Prem Keshwar	21.6
79. Munsiari	19.9
80. Jaunpur	19.6
81. Moona Kote	18.6
82. Patee	17.7
83. Lohaghat	17.4
84. Kanali Chheena	16.0
85. Dee Dee Haat	15.2
86. Dharchula	14.2
87. Gangolihat	13.8
Low Industrial Development	
88. Jakhali	10.9
89. Berinaug	4.4

References

1. *Census of India*, 1991.
2. K.N. Dubey [1981]: *Regional Disparities in Levels of Socioeconomic Development in Uttar Pradesh*, unpublished Ph.D. thesis, Punjab University, p. 108.
3. G.S. Gosal, G. Krishnan [1984]: *Regional Disparities in Levels of Socioeconomic Development in Punjab*, Vishal, Kurukshetra, p. 63.
4. B.S. Kantawala [1992]: 'Sectoral Development in India: An *Interstate Analysis', Indian Journal of Regional* Science, 24 (1): 27-36.
5. R. Ramchandra, B.V.Raghu [1987]: 'Regional Disparities in Chittoor District, Andhra Pradesh', *Indian Geographical Journal*, December 62 (2): 79-90.
6. Shri Prakash [1971]: 'Regional inequalities and Economic Development with Special Reference to Infrastructural Facillties in India', *Indian Journal of Regional science*, 9 (2): 180.
7. L.R. Singh [1987]: *Planning Atlas of Uttar Pradesh*, Planning Department Government of Uttar Pradesh, Lucknow, explanatrory note.
8. Neema Singh [1991]: 'Industrial Development in Haryana: An Appraisall', *Indian Geographical Journal*, July 13 (2): 149-167.

14
The March of Commercial Forestry

It is strictly forbidden for us to go into the [state] forests to cut lumber or firewood, but those who have money are free to exploit the biggest forests.

The rapid growth in forest industries, in consonance with the greatly expanded nature of industrialization since Independence, has necessitated an increased cut from the Himalayan forests. To facilitate increased extraction the building of roads into hitherto inaccessible forests became necessary. The relative isolation of many hill areas was ended as major highways and all-weather roads were built to transport timber and other forest produce to urban markets. Along with the communications network came the ubiquitous contractor whose job was to transport the produce to be processed by large-scale industries in the private sector.[1]

In official circles the need was long felt for better communications, the lack of which was an impediment to greater exploitation of the hill forests. Though a rail line to the Alakananda valley, planned as early as 1920,[2] did not materialize, since 1947 road building in the hills has occurred at a rapid pace, especially after the creation of three new border districts in 1962. A Rs 56 million World Bank project was started in 1972 for the construction of 1330 kilometres of new roads and 16 new bridges, and the renovation of 620 kilometres of existing roads in the UP Himalaya. This project was initiated on the grounds that past road construction represented but a 'nominal fraction of the total requirements for the full exploitation and proper development of these [hill] forests'.[3] The building of roads into interior areas was viewed with satisfaction as a development, which would enable the sale of hitherto untapped oak forest.[4] Now, the clear felling of oak and its replacement with planted conifers was being envisaged.

Table 14.1
Outturn of Selected Species in Uttarakhand
(cu. m. sawn wood)

Year	*Deodar*	*Fair and spruce*	*Kali*	*Chir*
1930-31	2917	–	14191	31885
1934-35	4333	–	–	30299
1948-49	7561	4616	595	59041
1950-51	9542	10987	5135	87415
1955-56	9316	14923	–	99761
1960-61	9571	39502	5380	107435
1965-66	10531	20010	4727	134587
1970-71	11612	39766	5166	200030
1971-72	67379	29722	8362	159930
1972-73	48623	60106	5162	206645
1973-74	10830	28926	8983	230787
1974-75	15464	37463	9742	186114
1975-76	29971	71493	10896	295745
1976-77	14712	37980	5632	267458
1977-78	8863	67682	5077	264509
1978-79	7965	84954	6023	319081

Source: UP Forest Statistics, 1978-79 (Lucknow, n.d.)

However, road building, by opening up virgin forests for use as industrial raw material elsewhere, has failed to materially help the hill economy. The net benefits to the hill people have been 'starvation' wages as forest labour, while the fragile mountain ecosystem has deteriorated further through imperfect alignment and hasty construction of roads.[5] In addition, improved communications have made penetration by urban pleasure-seekers possible; and with the Himalaya 'being sold as a Mecca for climbers, adventurers and tourists', deforestation and allied ecological degradation to meet their needs for firewood has proceeded apace.[6]

Table 14.1 gives some details of the increasesd pressure on the forest department. The dramatic expansion of resin-tapping operations was a further burden, not reflected in the table. In the Alakananda and Bhageerathi valleys, this was greatly helped by road-building operations. Resin outturn after reaching a peak of 4.18 lakh quintals in 1974-75 (valued at Rs 74.8 million) averaged 1.30 quintals in 1978-79.[7] Over harvesting was taking its toll.

These pressures of rising commercial and industrial demand called for a significant intensification of commercial forest operations. Important modifications introduced in forest working were the reduction in the diameter at which resin tapping was commenced, and the lowering of the age at which chir trees were cut. Incentives such as the awarding of bonus to resin mates who exceeded their targeted yield were also suggested.[8] Meanwhile, the sale of chir wood was given a considerable fillip when laboratory trials of the Forest Research Institute (FRI) revealed that the utilization of chir waste (i.e. material left after the conversion of chir to sleepers) for paper making was a viable proposition.[9] With a view to selling the waste and utilizing the considerable areas of chir affected by twist (and hence unsuitable for sleepers) the forest department entered into a contract with Star Paper Mills of Saharanpur, owned by the Bajoria family. Under the terms of this contract, effective from 1 October 1961 to 30 September 1981, the mill would be sold waste timber and twisted chir trees at ridiculously low prices.[10] Approximately 15 to 20 thousand tonnes of pulp-wood were supplied annually to the mill.[11] Further research at the FRI established that ash and hornbeam could be used in the manufacture of sports goods. This by-product was sold to a sports goods company.[12]

The state became commercial-minded. Senior officers started using timber for their own work, i.e. they started poaching, thus helping timber thieves. They put a restriction on villages for using forest wood. The high rates at which forest produce was sold to the surrounding population (as compared to the rates existing before 1947) and the takeover of disputed land by the department were also the subject of complaint. The department was widely believed to be in connivance with timber thieves.[13] In a bid to tighten control, the government had given the department extensive powers in the management of forest panchayats. Under the new rules, panchayats could only fell trees marked by the department. Local sale of slates and stones (used for housing) and export of resin were only allowed with the permission of specified senior forest officials who also directed the quantum of extraction and its destination. Finally, panchayats could retain only a fixed share (40 per cent) of any royalty on the sale of produce from their forests.[14]

More crucial, however, was the wilful neglect of the local population in the extraction and processing of forest produce. No SSI were set up. Initial hopes that road building would lead to industrialization and generation of local employment were belied by government policy, which consistently favoured the export of raw materials to be processed by large industry in the plains. A sizeable proportion of the resin extracted—estimated at 85-90 per cent of the total output—was dispatched to the Indian Turpentine and Resin Co. (ITR) near Bareilly, in which government had the majority shareholding. Of the remainder, some was allotted to local co-operative societies and the rest sold by open auction. Initially, ITR and the co-operatives were sold resin at the same rates. This policy was changed in the 1970s, with ITR being supplied at the earlier (subsidized) rates, while local units had to buy resin at open auctions.

In any case, these units were often allotted inaccessible forests where tapping was not economically feasible. As a result of such neglect, they rarely operated at more than 50 per cent capacity.[15] Requests to lower prices by Rs 15 per quintal to meet the costs of transporting processed resin to railheads were also not acceded to.[16] Discrimination against small units by the government was matched by its refusal to end the contractor system of forest working. While policy documents recognized the need to do away with the intermediaries who, it was admitted, exploited both their labour and the forests, in practice the system continued to be patronized.[17] Under the initiative of Sarvodaya workers, forest labour co-operatives (FLCs) were started in different parts of Garhwal and Kumaun. Repeated pleas to the government to allot them blocks of forest at concessional rates went unheeded.[18]

In fact, the chief conservator of forests had himself suggested at one stage that the department actively promote the working of FLCs in the hills. He was, however, tersely informed by the governor that 'since the forest department is a sort of commercial department, it cannot be expected to extend concession in the transaction of its business, even to co-operative societies.' The official was referred to the experience of Bombay state, where such a scheme had cost the government 'quite dearly and considerable amounts were lost to the exchequer'.[19] Apparently, the role played by contractors (almost all of whom belonged to the plains) as political patrons stood in the way of the implementation of stated policy objectives.

Several features testify to the marked degree of continuity between colonial and post-colonial forest policies. While the pressure of industrial and commercial classes may have replaced strategic imperial needs as the cornerstone of state forestry practices, in both periods 'successful' implementation of policy has been at the expense of the hill peasantry and their life support systems. The use of silvicultural and other strategies of manipulation and control, designed to limit and carefully regulate the access of the surrounding population to the forest, has been remarkably invariant throughout this time span. Finally, the forest department, assigned the role of a revenue generating organ by both the colonial state and the Tehri durbar, has continued to be a veritable money-spinner for the government of Uttar Pradesh. Between 1967-68 and 1978-89 forest revenue from the hill region increased from Rs 962 to 2020 lakh.[20]

Ecological Change and the Money-Order Economy

It had argued that in the period before commercial forestry, hill peasants were able quite comfortably to meet their subsistence requirements and have, occasionally, a surplus of grain for export. The egalitarian structure of the village community, the abundance of forests and other natural resources, and its insulation from the political instability of the Indo-Gangetic plain all contributed to the autonomy and relative prosperity of hill society. This depiction found verification from the numerous accounts of European travellers and officials, which repeatedly contrasted the fine, upstanding hill peasantry of the nineteenth century with poverty-stricken villagers in other parts of India and even in Europe.

It is considerably at variance with the situation as it exists today. An element of continuity, no doubt, is provided by the continued dependence on agriculture. While population pressure has led to the fragmentation of holdings, there exists little opportunity for the emergence of a class of capitalist farmers. Thus, in terms of the indices of 'modernization', for example, the use of improved seeds, irrigation, commercial crops, etc., hill agriculture fares poorly.[21]

Table 14.2 presents data on the occupational structure of six exclusively hill districts in 1971, or just prior to the Chipko movement. The overwhelming importance of agriculture obscures one crucial fact: that while farming systems in the Himalaya continue to be subsistence-oriented, cumulative social and environmental changes have undermined the hill Society's capacity to feed itself. Foodgrain output is no longer adequate for subsistence. Whereas for most families it was a point of pride not to purchase food from the market, declining yields and an increased population have forced a majority of peasant families to buy a significant portion of their grain requirements.[22]

Table 14.2
Percentage Distribution of Work-force, 1971

District	*Cultivators*	*Agricultural labourers*	*Animal husbandry/forestry*	*Agriculture as percentage of total population*
Pithoragarh	78.01	1.30	1.62	80.93
Almora	80.51	1.99	1.02	83.52
Uttarkashi	85.90	1.00	1.55	88.45
Pauri	82.97	1.03	0.73	84.73
Tehri-Garhwal	90.96	0.55	0.68	92.19
Chamoli	86.52	0.49	0.19	87.15

Source: Computed from 1971 census, in G.C. Tewari, *An Economic Profile of the Hill Region of Uttar Pradesh*, Occasional Paper No. 10, G. B. Pant Social Science Institute, Allahabad, 1982.

The substantial deficit between production and consumption—estimated at around 160 kgs of grain per person per annum—can only be met through purchase in the market.[23] In order to keep pace with rising population, hill peasants have adopted two adaptive strategies. First, they have increased their holdings of livestock. The density of livestock has increased from an earlier estimate of 342 animals/km^2 to 474 animals/km^2 in 1980. This is because animal manure is the key input for arresting the decline in yields. Peasants have also colonized new lands. However, while the population has increased by 119 per cent in the last eighty years, cultivated area

Table 14.3
Estimated Yields of Agricultural Crops in Uttarakhand (kg/ha)

Crop	*1896*	*1979*	*Percentage of gross cropped area (1979)*
Rice	1120	1133	17.6
Wheat	898	538	25.4
Barley	NA	362	5.7
Mandua	1120	924	24.6
Jhangora	1100	924	13.4

Source: William Whittaker, 'Migration and Agrarian Change in Garhwal District, Uttar Pradesh', in T.P. Bayliss-Smith and Sudhir Wanmali (eds), *Understanding Green Revolutions: Agrarian Change and Development Planning in South Asia* (Cambridge, 1984).

has increased only by 54 per cent, and cropping intensity has barely crept up by 14 per cent. At the same time, as Table 14.3 suggests, the yields of major agricultural crops have actually fallen.[24]

The degradation of hill forests and deterioration of the ecosystem can be directly attributed to the decline of agricultural productivity. Recent satellite data shows that of the 34,042 square kilometres of land declared as forests in Uttarakhand, good tree cover exists only on 6.6 per cent of the forest land, while another 22.5 and 13.8 per cent can be classified as medium and poor forests, respectively. According to satellite imagery, therefore, over half the land officially classified as forest has no tree cover at all: even allowing for the areas above the tree line and snowy peaks, this is an alarming figure.[25] There is a direct and reciprocal relationship between the loss and degradation of forests and the decline of hill agriculture. On a healthy vegetative slope a dynamic balance exists between the rate of erosion and soil formation. As the expansion of cultivable land in the hills can only take place at the expense of forests or on excessively steep slopes, this in itself increases the rate of soil erosion. Meanwhile, the increasing transfer of leaf manure to farms to maintain soil fertility for human consumption impairs the forests' regenerative capacity. Simultaneously, commercial forestry is radically altering the ecology of natural forests.

The removal of large volumes of timber without the replenishments of nutrients— normally ac-complished through the decay of wood and litter—also increases soil loss, especially in the monsoon season. These cumulative pressures lead to the impoverishment of the ecosystem, and hill agriculture enters a downward spiral from which there is, seemingly no escape.[26] Neither intensification nor expansion of agriculture, therefore, offers a viable solution to the growth of human population and the loss of control over forest resources. Faced with multiple environmental hazards, Uttarakhand society is in a 'state of continuing economic deterioration'.[27] A second and more widespread adaptive strategy is to look for alternative sources of employment. As these do not exist within the Himalaya, Uttarakhand peasants have no option but to emulate their counterparts from Nepal and 'follow their soils down the slopes'.[28] While this process was set in motion during the colonial period, male migration out of the hills has greatly increased since 1947.

These migrants work mostly in the armed forces, the police, and as clerical workers and menial servants in the towns and cities of northern India. Village studies have reported that over half of the adult male population does not reside in the village for most of the year, being forced to seek employment elsewhere. On my visits to hill villages I observed a preponderance of children, women and old men, testifying to the absence of able-bodied males. In some parts more than 60 per cent of the family income is generated outside by male migrants who remit a major portion of their earnings (by money order') to the village.[29] Uttara-khand now has, therefore, a dual economy—based partially on remittances and partially on the eroding basis of subsistence agriculture.[30] In the absence of alternative energy sources, deforestation and the money economy have placed an additional strain on the women, left in the village to pick up the pieces of farm life. The customary tasks of fuel and fodder collection now require far more time and effort than they did earlier. Increasingly charged, too, with agricultural tasks, the woman's lot is a miserable one, poignantly captured in the writings of local activists.[31]

Yet the malaise of hill society is by no means restricted to one section of its population. The processes of environmental change that came in the wake of commercial forestry have had a devastating impact on the social fabric of Uttarakhand: fragmentation of the family, erosion of local authority structures and co-operating institutions, and a crisis of confidence resulting from the decline and fall of a once prosperous system of agrarian production. As the commercial sector of the plains begins to cast a covetous eye on other natural resources of the hills (e.g., water and minerals), we begin to see a strong parallel with the exploitation of mountain peoples in other parts of the globe.

Kai Erikson's description of Appalachia serves in its essentials, if not in fine detail, in capturing the economic and ecological exploitation of the Himalayan villagers: The men and women of Appalachia are among the most truly exploited people to be found anywhere. In the beginning, they had rights to good land. It was covered with timber; rich seams of coal ran under its crust. It had soil fertile enough for the modest uses to which it was put and its forests were alive with fish and game. In the course of a few decades, however, dating from the last years of the nineteenth century, almost all of these valuable resources were cut or scraped or gouged away [by outsiders]; and when the land lay bruised and exhausted from the punishment it had received, the people of the region had virtually nothing to show for it.[32]

Fragments of a Pristine Consciousness: 'Community' Management

When reservation of hill forests was done, villagers were not given due weightage settlement officers put their foot down. They believed though erroneously that the management of the forests not reserved would be made over to the villages, restricted their rights in many cases.[33] In anticipation of protest, villagers were in fact told that while the reserved forests would be in the strict control of the forest department, 'they would be given complete freedom of operation in the remaining areas.'[34] Although proposals were mooted at various times, there was no concerted attempt to establish village forests on land not vested with government. In British Kumaun, after the forest movement of 1921, the Grievances Committee did consider the establishment of village forests on land taken away from the forest department. An official sent to Madras to examine the system of communal management there strongly recommended the creation of similar reserves, to be controlled by villagers, in Kumaun.

In face of the active opposition of forest officials, who argued quite falsely that village management of forests reflected a lack of concern for the needs of future generations,[35] these proposals were implemented only in piecemeal fashion. Despite official apathy, foresters, in both the colonial and post-colonial periods, have admitted that the panchayat forests in Garhwal, though small in extent as a consequence of government policy, were often well maintained,[36] with many having done 'exemplary work in connection with forest protection and development'.[37] Where ownership was still vested in the community, forests continued to be well looked after—such as the twenty-mile stretch between Rudraprayag and Karanprayag in the Alakananda valley where the government had explicitly made over the forests to the neighbouring villages.[38] In Tehri Garhwal, too, informal management practices continued to prevail over forests not taken over by the durbar. A recent survey concluded that while some panchayat forests there are in better condition than the reserved forests in the area, they are uniformly better maintained than forests under the jurisdiction of the civil administration.[39]

During fieldwork in the valley of Badyar, a tributary of the Alakananda, I came across a panchayat forest containing both banj and chir, with profuse regeneration of the two species coming up side by side. A village school teacher explained how extraction was carefully regulated, with monetary fines being levied on offenders. Exceptions were made only in the case of religious festivals, or when the timber was required for community purposes such as the construction of the panchayat *ghar* or a school. In Uttarakhand the age-old panchayat system had been accustomed to handling diverse issues of which forest matters, though undoubtedly very significant, were only one aspect.[40] The partial breakdown of traditional mechanisms of allocation and control has been a consequence of the commercial penetration of hill economy and society that followed in the wake of state forestry. Yet cases continued to be reported of the lath panchayat of the village (an institution not recognized by law) managing small blocks of forest for the common welfare of the village community as a whole.[41] More rarely, it was individuals rather than the community that took the lead, a notable example being Vishveshwar Dutt Saklani, brother of the peasant leader Nagendra Saklani (martyred in the 1948 movement), who has over a period of forty years planted and raised to maturity thousands of broad-leaved trees in the Saklana area of Tehri Garhwal.

As forest officials were constrained to admit when oak forests were entrusted to nearby villages who appointed their own chaukidars, lopping was done systematically and the trees well protected.[42] And in Kumaun numerous instances were reported of panchayat land being closed to grazing by common consent, the copious regeneration in these forests presenting a 'striking contrast' to the heavily browsed reserved forests.[43] A recent study of the Aglar valley in Tehri Garhwal reports the existence of a large community grassland used equitably and without friction by the inhabitants of as many as seventeen villages.[44] In Ranikhet subdivision of Almora district, a civilian reported in the 1960s that there were a 'large number of successful forest panchayats'; and in certain localities the only forests that existed belonged to them.[45]

Admittedly, there are variations. In Kumaun, where commercialization had penetrated earlier, the experience of forest panchayats is far more mixed. Yet, whether judged on its own terms or against the manifest failures of state forestry, the fine performance of van panchayats in parts of Garhwals and Kumaun is instructive. This situation has prevailed where cohesive and largely egalitarian village communities have retained some control over their forest habitat. It was left to the Chipko movement to awaken and crystallize this fund of local knowledge in the hill peasantry's latest and most sustained challenge to the march of commercial forestry. It also testifies to a reservoir of local ecological knowledge that has managed to persist amidst a century of alienation and protest.

References

1. Cf. Sunderlal Bahuguna, *Uttarakhand mein Ek Sau Bis Din* (Dehradun, 1974).

2. Cf. R.N. Brahmawar, *WP for the Garhwal For. Div., 1930-31 to 1939-40* (Allahabad, 1938).
3. Uttar Pradesh Forest Department, 'Forest Development Project, Uttar Pradesh, India', mimeo, n.d. (1971), pp. 117-21.
4. Introduction by B.P. Srivastava in V.P. Singh, WP for the West Almora For Div., Kumaun Circle, 1966-67 to 1975-76 (Nainital, 1967).
5. Madhav Gadgil, 'Towards an Indian Conservation Strategy', paper presented at the Workshop on a New Forest Policy, Indian Social Institute, New Delhi, 12-14 April 1982, p. 26.
6. G.D. Berreman, *Himachal: Science, People and 'Progress'*, IWGIA document no. 36 (Copenhagen, 1979), p. 19f.
7. See *Uttar Pradesh forest Statistics 1978-79* (Lucknow, n.d.), for details.
8. See, for example, N. K. Agarwala, 'WP for the Kedarnath For. Div., Garhwal Circle, 1972-73 to 1981-82', mimeo (Nainital, 1973), pp. 168, 339-40.
9. S.R.D. Guha, 'Chemical Pulps and Writing and Printing Papers from *Chir (Pinus longifolia Roxb)', Indian Forester*, Vol. 84 (1958), pp. 235-40.
10. For details, see N.K. Agarwala.
11. Estimated from figures given in different working plans; 1 tonne of paper requires 2 tonnes of pulp wood.
12. Agarwala, 'Kedarnath WP', pp. 78-9.
13. See *Yugvani* (YV), issues of 17 July i960, 21 July and 18 December 1966, 4 October and 18 October 1970, and 18 April 1971.
14. Agarwala, 'Kedarnath WP', pp. 28-30.
15. V.P.S. Verma, WP for the Tehri For. Div., Garhwal Circle, 1973-74 to 1982-83', mimeo (Nainital, 1973), pp. 44, 55; National Council of Applied Economic Research, *Growth Centres and Their Industrial Potential: Chamoli* (Delhi, 1975)-Interview with C. P. Bhatt, May 1981.
16. See YV, 17 February 1974.
17. Cf. Ramachandra Guha, 'Forestry in British and Post-British India: A Historical Analysis', *Economic and Political Weekly* (in two parts), 29 October 1983 and 5 November 1983.
18. YV, issues of 30 October 1960 and 14 June 1970.
19. GO no. VOB 289/XIV-378-56, 23 July 1960, from assistant secretary, UP government, to chief conservator of forests, UP (office of the conservator of forests, Tehri circle, Dehradun).

20. See UP Forest Statistics, 1978-79 (Lucknow, n.d.).
21. Cf. Waheeduddin Khan and R.N. Tripathy, Plan for Integrated Rural Development in Pauri Garhwal (Hyderabad, 1976).
22. Marcus Moench, 'Resource Utilization and Degradation: An Integrated Analysis of Biomass Utilization Patterns in a Garhwal Hill Village, Northern Uttar Pradesh, India', MS thesis, University of California, Berkeley, 1985, p. 22.
23. S.C. Joshi, D.R. Joshi and D.D. Dani, Kumaun Himalaya (Nainital, 1983), p. 233.
24. W. Whittaker, 'Migration and Agrarian Change in Garhwal District, Uttar Pradesh,' in T.P. Bayliss-Smith and Sudhir Wanmali (eds), *Understanding Green Revolutions: Agrarian Change and Development Planning in South Asia* (Cambridge, 1984), p. 125.
25. N. C. Saxena, 'Social Forestry in the U.P. Himalayas', mimeo, ICIMOD (Kathmandu, 1987), p. 7.
26. Whittaker, 'Migration and Agrarian Change', pp. 114-17.
27. P. H. Gross, Birth, Death and Migration in the Himalayas (Delhi, 1982), p. 184.
28. Cf. Eric Eckholm, Losing Ground (New York, 1976).
29. See 'Report of the Task Force for the Study of Eco-Development in the Himalayan Region', mimeo, Planning Commission (New Delhi, March 1982).
30. Cf. Whittaker, 'Migration and Agrarian Change', p. 129.
31. See, *inter alia*, Bahuguna, 'Uttarakhand'; Sarala Devi, 'A Blueprint for Survival of the Hills', supplement to Himalaya: Man and Mature, Vol. 4, No. 6, November 1980; and for a treatment in fiction, C.P. Bhatt, Pratikar ke Ankur (Gopeshwar, 1979).
32. Kai Erikson, *Everything in Its Path: Destruction of Community in the Buffalo Creek Flood* (New York, 1976), p. 68.
33. No. 3681/XXVI-2, 4 May 1915 from comm., KD, to chief secy, UP, in FD file 83/1909, UPSA.
34. See note by J.R.W. Bennett, 26 August 1919, in ibid.
35. Cf. A. E. Osmaston, 'Panchayat Forests in Kumaun', if Vol. 58 (1932), pp. 603.
36. G.M. Johri, WP for the Garhwal For. Div. (Allahabad, 1947), p. 20; D.N. Lohani, *WP for the North and South Garhwal Divisions*, UP, 1958-59 to 1972-73 (Allahabad, 1962), p. 35.

37. *Report of Kumaun Forest Fact Findings Committee* (Lucknow, 1960), p. 37.
38. Note by D. Joshi in FD file no. 83/1909, UPSA.
39. Personal communication from Madhav Gadgil, 25 July 1981.
40. Cf. *Garhwali*, 14 February 1920.
41. Census of India 1961, Vol. XV, Part VI, Village Survey Monograph, no. 5, *Village Thapli, Tehsil Pauri, District Garhwal*, p. 2.
42. Uttarkashi Working Plan, quoted in Sunderlal Bahuguna, '*The Himalaya: Towards a Programme of Reconstruction*', in K.M. Gupta and Desh Bandhu (eds), *Man and Forest* (Delhi, 1979).
43. V. P. Singh, *WP for the West Almora For Div., Kumaun Circle*, 1966-67 to 1975-76 (Nainital 1967), pp. 109-10.
44. Cf. Moench, 'Resource Utilization', pp. 106-07.
45. Prakash Kishan, *The Broad Spectrum* (Delhi, 1973), p. 58.

15
Industry and Minerals: Uttarakhand

Industry

During old days trade and industry in Uttarakhand hill region were limited to sale and purchase of Borax, Shilajeet, Wool, Ghee, Carpets, Honey, Herbs, Woollen clothes and products of hill/tribal handloom industries such as Thulma, Blanket, Pankhi, Pasmina and Chutka, etc. At present there is a scope to establish cottage as well as small scale industries throughout the hill region of Uttarakhand. The traditional occupation like Goldsmiths, Coppersmiths and Blacksmiths can be modernised. Even though the Shilpkars (Craftsmen) have left their traditional trade as a result of modern industries, there is still scope to revive the traditional handicrafts of the hill region to augment the efforts of national handicraft industry so that craftsmen can increase their income and earn foreign exchange for the country.

Efforts are being made to establish locally available resources based village and cottage industries, pollution free foot lose industries for which main thrust is on the following programme:

1. Adequate infrastructure and industrial nucleus suitable to hill region.
2. To develop entrepreneurial skill through training programme consultancies and technical know-how.
3. To provide incentives in the form of assistance, raw material, credit and marketing facilities etc.
4. To promote investment in public as well as joint sector venture through various state corporations.
5. To develop growth centres by providing package of services at focal points.
6. The main thrust is on village and cottage industries based on local resources viz. agro and forestwaste based, mineral

and wool based industries for which incentives and promotional measures are being intensified.

The existing state of industries in Uttarakhand hill region and scope for future development is given in the following paragraphs.

Village and Small Scale Industries

Small Scale Industries: It is the responsibility of Department of Small scale Industries or Corporation give necessary assistance in the form of loan, subsidy, hire purchase, marketing, capital participation to establish few protected small scale industries such as potteries etc. Similarly Leather Development Corporation helps in design, training of rural artisan, procurement and marketing assistance. Director of industries provides necessary technical assistance, statistical and documentation cell. Managerial assistance, share capital and special societies for weaker section are formed by Industrial Corporations. Testing and development facilities are provided in testing laboratories, quality control and marking.

District Industries Centre: Assistance in the form of loan, interest subsidy, consultancy, subsidy and margin money loan through growth centres is given by District Industries Centre. Assistance to small scale Industries is given in the form of power subsidy, interest subsidy, consultancy subsidy, state capital subsidy on generating sets and stamps duty subsidy. Development of industries is also dependent on industrial potentiality, market survey and entrepreneurial development programme. Research and development is undertaken through various Nursery sheds, Engineering College, Technical Institutes, National Productivity Council (NPC) and Rural Industries Centre. Special programmes are also included for hill and tribal areas.

Handicrafts: The Handicraft corporation provides necessary share capital, showroom and marketing facilities, incentive, awards, carpet complexes, advance Chikan training, development of wood carving and seasoning, hosiery training-cum-production centre, loan to Artisans. Brassware Corporation is engaged in development of brassware by providing raw material, technical, financial and marketing facilities to artisans and entrepreneurs engaged in production of brassware. Training is provided to willing candidates through various production centres as Master craftsman.

Khadi and Village Industries: Khadi and Village industries sector is engaged in promoting the production of wood based industries and other industries in villages.

Handloom: Handloom sector is responsible to provide necessary financial, technical, marketing and training facilities to individuals as well as co-operatives engaged in weaving of cotton or silk products including dying.

Sericulture: Sericulture involves establishment of model Chowki rearing and demonstration farms and Oak Tassar development schemes in the hills. Silk production farm have since been opened and people are being trained to establish their own farms. Silk production Nurseries and farms have been established in the three border districts of Chamoli, Pithoragarh and Uttarkashi.

Medium and Large Industries

Garhwal and Kumaun Mandal Vikas Nigam for the Garhwal and Kumaun Division respectively have taken up schemes for the establishment of medium and large industries this was the system being followed till now. This is likely to be reviewed by the new state of Uttaranchal. U.P. Co-operative Ltd., are engaged in the establishment, modernisation and expansion of Sugar Industry including by product utilisation schemes.

State Government is proding loans shae capital to both Kumaun and Garhwal Mandal Development Corporations and their subsidiaries (*Scheduled Tribes Development Corporation*, State Mineral Development Corporation, State Cement Corporation, State Electronics Corporation, Textile Corporation and Sugar Factories Federation Government for projects established in the hills and for promoting resources based pollution free industries. The main activities/work of these corporation are as follows:

Promotional as well as commercial activities to augment industrial development are being taken up by these corporations. Establishment of industries, promoting tourism by conducting package tours, construction of rest houses, tent colonies and other facilites for tourists, marketing of fruits, herbs etc. are also being taken up by these Corporations. In addition to the existing industries, possibilities of establishing new projects are being explored. These new projects/ units include Paper pulp unit. G.I. Wire Plant, Raw material deposits, Coal Depot, Ropeway, Binocular manufacturing unit, Electronic units, Flush Door Factory etc. Kumaun Mandal Development Corporation had planned to work with Indian Pharmaceutical Corporation Ltd. and establish a unit for processing of herbs and preparation of Ayurvedic drugs. A similar pharmaceutical unit at a suitable site in one of the zero industries districts of Garhwal Division has also been planned.

Efforts are being made by Kumaun and Garhwal Mandal Scheduled Tribes Development Corporation to establish more production-cum-training centres, sale centres and raw material depots to promote business in tribal handicrafts.

Electronics Corporation has proposed following industrial units for the hill region.

1. Low cost Transistor Receiver Units at Kotdwara, Dehradun, Lansdowne and Bhimtal.
2. Unit for manufacture of T.V. Cabinets with modern techniques.
3. Electronics watch manufacturing units.
4. Electronics test and development centres.
5. Electronics Industrial Estates for setting up Electronics complexes at Dehradun and Almora.
6. Unit for manufacture of general purpose components Transistors and Capacitators etc.

State Industrial Development Corporation is developing industrial estate at selected site for establishment of small scale industrial units. A watch assembly unit at Bhowali has been established by this corporation in collaboration with HMT. State Cement Corporation has proposed a medium cement plant of 2000 TPD capacity at Dehradun with an estimated cost of about Rs. 59.6 crore. Besides two mini cement plants of 200 TPD capacity in Pithoragarh District with an estimated cost of Rs. 5.25 crore have been established. Other mini plants in Nainital (Khairana) and Dehradun district are also being processed.

A new sugar mill with an estimated cost of about Rs. 8.00 crores is being established at Sitarganj by the Sugar Factories Federation and expansion of Bazpur Distillary has also been taken up. Expansion of Kashipur Spinning Mill is being undertaken by Textile Corporation, from 25,000 spindles to 50,000 spindles. Besides one new spinning mill of 50,000 spindles at an estimated cost of about Rs. 17 crore is also proposed to be established at Jaspur.

Forest Based Industries

With the vast forest wealth of Uttarakhand, one can easily estimate the bright prospects for the establishment of forest based industries. It is interesting to note that till recently several types of timber based industries like Shuttles, Bobbins and Pencil making were using specific species of imported wood in the form of cut-to-size selected and well seasoned blocks worth Rs. 38 lakh were imported every year. The import of this timber has been stopped and thus, industries were facing difficulties in switching over to indigenous substitutes for timber. Very good species of timber is available as substitutes from the higher region of Uttarakhand (Uttarkashi and Karanprayag). For example, Weft-fir, Deodar and Cypress for pencil are available provided they can be made available to the manufacturing units in the form of blocks and slats. Therefore, there is a scope for the establishment of forest based industries and some of them are explained in the succeeding paragraphs.

Integrated Half Wrought Making Unit: These units can be established close to forests where timber is available and where it can be converted into blocks before despatching to various manufacturing units of pencil slats, Bobbin and Shuttles. Such units will be able to save on extra transportation of timber of thicker size intended for further conversion and supply the required type of timber blocks at reasonable rates to the consumer industries. Bourang, Kharpat, Jheegam, Dhak, Chir, Otteesh, Gular, Gojeena, Kochula, Akhrot, Firm Sod, Tun, Kans, Phaldu and Kanj are suitable for pencil industry. Haldu and Chamkharik are used in the Bobbin industry. The first Shuttle and Bobbin factory at a cost of six lakh rupees was established at Gyansu about three kilometres away from Uttarkashi.

Match Box Industry: The required timber of various kinds of trees is freely available in Uttarakhand hill region. Trees of Semul, Gutel and Ailanthus are available for making match boxes.

Plywood Industry: Another important forest based industry is the plywood industry. The common timbers in the manufacture of plywood are Kanju, Tun, Bourang, Kharpet, Jhingam, Bahera and Mango. Trees of Jheengam, Kajjoo, Kharpet, Godala, Dhak and Phaldu are the raw material for the production of plywood. These trees are also available in plenty and provide a suitable base for the establishment of a plywood industry. The only plywood factory, 'Kumaun Plywood' installed with a capacity of 1,23,000 sq metres produces an average of 17,300 sq metres of plywood yearly.

Wood Bull Sport Equipment Industry: Timber, Chir, Haldu, Pools, Gojeena, Gutel, Mulberry, Phaldu, Kanjo, Ais, Akhrot and Mepil is suitable for wood bull and the sports equipment industry. Mulberry is used for Hockey sticks, Tennis and Badminton rackets. 'Ais' is used for Badminton, Tennis rackets, Cricket bats and Cricket stumps. Teak and Shisham could be utilised for Gymnastic and agility apparatus and Tun for Hockey sticks and Badminton rackets.

Resin Processing Factories: Large quantities of Resin are available from the forest of Uttarakhand and necessary processing plants can be established to produce Varnish, Turpentine, Vasline and Charcoal etc. There are several co-operative resin factories in the hills. The Kumaon Development Corporation has also started a factory at Champawat.

Dairy Farming: Small scale dairy farms can be opened in the hills of Uttarakhand. Suitable pasturages are available at altitudes of 1200-1500 m. Establishment of such dairy farms will be in the interest of the region as they would be able to meet the ever increasing demand for dairy products like milk, Ghee and cheese.

Handicraft Industry: Handicraft industry has also a great scope for development in Uttarakhand. Raw materials are available out of San, Bamboo, Ringal, Rambans and Bheol for making Chairs, Baskets, Toys, Door mats, Chicks, Hand fans and Bags. Presently, a handicraft production centre and ladies woollen shawl centre are functioning at Srinagar and Pauri respectively with financial and technical assistance from Khadi and Village industries Board.

Paper Industry: The paper and paper board are mainly classified in three categories namely (1) Writing and printing paper such as maplitho, etc. The major raw material required for writing and printing paper are Eucalyptus, soft wood, hard wood, Bamboo and mixed grasses, (2) Industrial paper such as wrapping and packing paper, paper boards etc. The major raw material required for such industry would be Eucalyptus, soft wood, Fir, Spruce and Bamboo. Apart from this, various other cellulosic material like waste cotton, hemp, hessian waste can be utilised for the production of this paper, (3) Special paper includes as carbonising tissue paper, filter paper, cigarettee paper and insulating paper. Raw material for this is obtained from soft wood, Eucalyptus, Fir and Spruce. Paper and pulp industry can be established in the region by utilising Sal wood. At present, of the total annual production of 20,000 tonnes of Sal, approximately three fourth is being used by the packing industry. Similarly about one lakh cubic metres of Fir and Spruce wood grown, mainly in the catchment area of Yamuna, offers scope for setting up at least two pulp factories. A decision has since been taken by the government to open a newsprint plant at Lalkuan in the Terai region of Kumaun.

Packing Case Industry: With the development of horticulture and variety of fruits being produced in the hills, the necessity for establishing a packing industry has also been appreciated. Large quantities of wooden packing cases are required for the transportation of fruits to various parts of the country. The timber used for packing includes Utish, Chir, Dhak, Gular, Peepal, Kharpat, Jhingan, Phaldu etc. The technology for the utilisation of Chir pine needles in the manufacture of packing material has also been developed. Proposals are under consideration to set up one such unit each in Kumaun and Garhwal region of Uttarakhand. A factory for making packing material for fruits has been established at Haldwani in Nainital district.

Rope Making Cottage Industry: Trees like, San, Malu and Bheool or Bhemal are locally available are traditionally used for making ropes. Large scale production of these ropes for commercial purpose could further speed up economic progress of the region.

Rayon Grade Pulp: The major raw materials required for Rayon grade pulp are Eucalyptus, pine wood and hard wood. There is no unit of such type in the State of Uttar Pradesh. However, a unit can be established in the Terai region based on above raw material with an installed capacity of 15 to 20 thousand tonnes per annum of Rayon grade pulps.

Sal Seeds: Sal seed oil is mainly used in the manufacture of soaps. It can also be used as a substitute in cocoa, butter for chocolate and confectionery etc. The Sal deoiled cake can also be used in cattle and poultry feeds. At present, there is only one factory at Kashipur utilising Sal seeds in the region. The annual requirement of this unit is of the order of 800 tonnes and this is available from the western circle where the availability of Sal needs is around 14,300 tonnes per year. The production of Sal seeds is seasonal and varies from year to year. According to the information, the oil content in Sal seed varies from 14% to 80% depending upon the region. The oil content in Sal seed, unlike other seeds of cotton, ground nut etc. can only be extracted by solvent extraction method. The availability of Sal seed during the months of June and July is limited and therefore, the other seeds of Mahua, Kusum and Kanji can be taken up for the production of oil along with Sal seed.

Pine Needle Leaf: Pine needle leaves is a forest waste material available from cutting, felling of pine trees and natural felling from living trees. At present there is no utilisation of this material and existence of this material in the forest causes extensive damage to the forest wealth by way of fire. Lot of money is being utilised by the forest department to remove these waste material from forests to avoid damages. The following industries can be considered in the hill areas where availability of this material is in abundant.

1. **Fresh pine needle leaf:** Fresh leaves, which can be obtained after cutting the trees by forest contractor and from living trees, contain essential oil and resin, which can be further used after

proper extraction in various chemical and pharmaceutical industries. The major products which can be obtained by the solvent extraction method of fresh leaf are pine needle oil, resin, pine wad etc. These products can find wide applications in the manufacture of various perfumery compounds, pharmaceutical preparations etc. The availability of fresh pine leaf from the hills will be seasonal. Therefore, the unit for processing green pine needle leaf may be linked up with a unit for producing essential oil based on aromatic plants.

2. **Dry pine leaf:** The major utilisation of these dry leaf can be suggested for the manufacture of pine-wood, which has got extensive application in packing industry. It can also be used in the manufacture of fibre-board for sound proofing in auditoriums, packing material, corrugating medium, rubberised mattresses etc. At the initial stage, depending upon the availability of raw material, industries having an annual capacity of processing 500 tonnes pine leaf can be planned.

Industries Based on Medicinal Plant

The hill region of Garhwal and Kumaun provides favourable conditions to establish industries based on medicinal plants. The climate of this region is suitable for cultivation of various medicinal plants. These plants according to their climatic requirement can be cultivated in different areas of this region and industrial units can be set up to isolate the active ingredients of the medicinal plants. A broad classification of important medicinal plants of this region are given below:

1. **Berberies:** There is wild growth of Berberie, locally called 'Kingor', at high altitude in abundance. At present the roots of this plant are being exported out of this zone. The roots are used for the preparation of drug known as berbertue hydrochloride used in remedies for eye trouble and dysentry.The complete technical know-how of the manufacturing process is available from National Research and Development Corporation (NRDC) of New Delhi.
2. **Dioscorea deltoidia (Yam):** This is natural occuring medicinal plant found in the form of a creeper at places of medium high altitude. It is suitable for cultivation and used for the preparation of drug disogenin which is used for carticosteroids, sex harmones and oral contraceptives.The complete technical know-how for manufacturing process is available from N.R.D.C., New Delhi.

3. **Costus:** The costus plant (Saussuera lappa), locally known as 'Kuth', grows abundantly in the north-west Himalayan regions of India including Garhwal and Kumaun Hills. In Jammu and Kashmir, about 300 quintals of roots are collected annually by the Forest Department while in Himachal Pradesh, it is cultivated mostly in the upper regions of the Kulu valley, and about 1000 quintals of its roots are collected annually. The roots of this plant contains valuable costus oil. This oil finds use in high grade perfumery and has a great demand in cosmetic and perfume industry in India and abroad. However, commercial use of this plant has yet to be made in India. At present entire quantity or roots produced is exported through the State Trading Corporation of India. Costus oil is generally produced by subjecting the crushed costus roots to prolonged hydro-distillation or steam distillation and extracting the aqueous distillate with a solvent. Another method for producing the oil is by first preparing resinolds by solvent extraction and then recovering in solvent, followed by high vaccum distillation of the resulting resinolds. The oil obtained by the steam distillation method finds favour with the perfume industry and fetches high price.
4. **Jatamansi:** This plant is found in abundance in high altitude area of this region. It is an exportable item. Cultivation of this plant can be undertaken for commercial purpose.
5. **Rauvolfia serpentina:** Locally known as 'Sarpgandha'. This plant has a wild growth at lower altitude of this region. The plant is used for preparation of medicines and commercial cultivation of this plant can also be taken up.
6. **Heracleum candicans:** The plant grows wild in this region. The roots of this plant is used for extraction of Xanthotoxin which is a established remedy treatment of leuecoderma. It is used extensively in suntam lotionas in European countries. A process for preparation of Xanthotoxin from Heracleum candicans roots has been developed by N.R.D.C. New Delhi and can be acquired for commercial exploitation. The raw material required besides the roots of Heracleum Candicans are the common solvents which are indigenously available. Major item of plant and machinery like disintegrator, extractor, stainless steel, reaction vessel, pressure filling vacuum, drying oven etc. can be fabricated in the country. The laboratory suggest a 40 kg per annum of the final product as an optimum capacity of the plant.

Other medicinal plants like Timru and Vajardanti also grow in this region which is used for tooth paste manufacturing. Medicinal plants like Samoy and Vanaspa are used extensively to treat cough and cold. The production of these medicinal plants can be increased by organised cultivation, thereby contributing to the income of the local people.

Fruit Canning Centre

Horticulture and fruits are gaining importance. Establishment of suitable small scale co-operative canning centres will go a long way in the overall development of horticulture in the hills of Uttarakhand. A factory is functioning at Ramgarh in Nainital district for processing fruits and vegetables. Another canning factory is being established at Kosi in Almora district.

Wool Industry

Bhotias of upper reaches of Uttranchal have been dealing wool science ages. In Pithoragarh, it is their monopoly. The government has taken a number of steps to give a boost to this traditional industry. Many production units are being run at Munsiari, Dharchula, Didihat and Champawat where woollen carpets, Thulmas, Shawls and Chutkas are produced. 'Kumaun Tweed' which is equal in standard to that produced in Scotland is being marketed. The production is, however, limited as against increasing demand.

Agro-Based Industries

A soyabean unit with a capacity to produce 4 tonnes of oil and 19 tonnes of oil cakes is proposed to be set up at Katarmal near Almora. There is also proposal to set up a plant for making cattle feed by utilising the husk which is likely to cost much less than other feeds. Later auxiliary units are to be set up and sixty-five service co-operatives will be linked with the project in matters of production, marketing and storage.

Mineral Development

Directorate of Geology and Mining is responsible to carry Geological investigation of minerals in the state. Exploration of minerals in undertaken and feasibility report are prepared for exploration of minerals on commercial basis. The execution of the minerals exploration programme is done through State Mineral Development Corporation Ltd.

Mineral Deposits

Minerals have played a leading role in the evolution of civilisation. Long before man discovered or invented agriculture, he had discovered minerals, and for centuries these had been his mainstay. Our stone age ancestors were called so because they carved their tools out of stone. This was the first mineral that man had put to use. Rocks consist of minerals, which are inorganic substances, and contain one or more elements. Both rocks and minerals are derived from the crust of the earth. Then came the discovery of metals like copper and iron. Accordingly, we refer to various periods of history as Copper Age, Iron Age, Bronze Age and so on. The process of discovery went on and today we have 2000 different types of minerals. Metals and alloys in use, like many other natural resources, play a very important role in industrialisation and economic development of the country, State or the region. It is common belief that Himalaya as a whole are rich in mineral wealth. Old mines for various metal ores especially copper, lead, iron ore have been in existence in the Uttarakhand hill region. Nevertheless, whether rich or not so rich, the traditional miners also extracted the metals locally to complete the process of utilisation to the best of their abilities.

During the last ninety years or so, a number of geoscientists have been carrying out surveys and prospecting work in different parts of Garhwal and Kumaun to locate deposits of copper, lead, zinc, silver, gold, iron ore etc. A number of new minerals of utility have been located. But the actual processing and the utilisation of these minerals shrank to the minimum because of the cheaper production of ores and finished materials elsewhere. Therefore, the Himalayan region relatively became non-existent in this field. This widening gap between the presence of minerals at a place and their local non-utilisation due to various reasons is the greatest problem in developing the mineral industry in Garhwal and Kumaun hills. However, this will largely depend upon to what extent we are able to survey the mineral deposits and how fast we are able to exploit them for commercial purposes.During 1978, the Mineral Development Corporation of India had discovered a rare mineral belt with eight per cent of copper with zinc and cobalt in the area of Askote in Pithoragarh district. The minerals of this areas are believed to be rare and similar to those found in Bolivia in South America.

The mineral deposits in India bear only 2.5 per cent of the rare minerals, which are mostly used in industries. A recent survey have revealed the existence of large scale mineral deposits throughout the hills of Uttarakhand. Important minerals available for exploitation in the region are limestone, marble, magnesite scap stone, gypsum, dolomite, rock phosphate and sulphur etc. Besides these, small amount of esbestes, graphite, copper and lead etc. are also said to be available. While some work has been done to locate and estimate minerals deposits, the quantification for most deposits has not been done so far. In absence of the quantificative data the economic viability of these deposits can not be checked and as such only industrial units, which can be assured of the raw material, are suggested to be set up in the region. The research scholars claim much more mineral deposits than estimated by the Geological Survey of India. The state of mineral deposits in the hills of Uttarakhand is given in the succeeding paragraphs.

Limestone: Official lime however is slightly different. Lime-stone deposits are in existence at Chakrata, Lansdowne, Srinagar. Narendranagar and Nainital. Lime is produced out of lime-stones which is used for the manufacture of cement and in all construction work. The large quantities of lime-stone being used comes from various lime quarries around Mussoorie hills.

Dolomite: Deposits of Dolomite are in existence in Dehradun, Nainital and Tehri. Dolomite is double carborate of calcium and magnesium and is mainly used in iron and steel production. It is also used in refractory and glass industries.

Magnesite: Magnesite is inter bedded with Dolomite and is gaining importance because of the development of iron and steel industries. This mineral has been found in existence in Alaknanda valley and between Sarju valley and Kosi river. Magnesite is also available in Almora and Pithoragarh where the deposits have been estimated to be about 3.5 million tonnes. A factory has since been established at Jhirauli in Almora district to produce 30 tonnes of magnesite per day. The high quality yield of magnesite is considered to be the second highest in the country after the State of Tamil Nadu.

Copper: Copper is the oldest metal discovered, and today, it is considered to be of great economic importance. In addition to small scale industries, copper is mainly used by the electrical industries for the manufacture of power lines. Copper deposits have been noticed in Pokhari and Dhampur area of Chamoli district and at many places in Almora, Nainital and Tehri districts.

Gypsum: Gypsum is a dehydrated sulphate of calcium. It is widely distributed non-metallic mineral and is mainly consumed by fertiliser and cement industries. Calcived gypsum is used in plaster and in the manufacture of 'Plaster of Paris'. This mineral is normally found associated with lime stone. The deposits of Gypsum are available in Dehradun, Tehri and Nainital Districts. According to some research scholars, the reserves of Gypsum have been estimated to be 2 lac tonnes in the whole hills region of Uttarakhand.

Sulphur and Graphite: Sulphur is used in chemical, acid, paper, petrol and colour manufacturing industries. Sulphur and Graphite has been found in areas around Nandprayag in Chamoli district and along the Beri river in Chamoli district. Graphite deposits have also been located in two places in Almora and Karanprayag in Chamoli district.

Iron ore: Chandpur and Nagpur in Chamoli district and in Nainital and Almora districts are the areas rich with rion deposits. In fact about hundred years ago, the Britishers had established the Kumaon Iron Company, and furnaces were built, though it had to be closed due to higher cost of production as compared to then existing market price of iron.

Coal: Hard coal has been found near Laldhang in Pauri district.

Uranium: According to Geologist working with the minerals division of the Atomic Energy Commission, there are indications of uranium in the Chamyala region of the Balaganga valley of Tehri district.

Rock Phosphates: The Pyrites Phosphates and Chemicals Limited, a Government of India Undertaking, has discovered six major zones around Mussoorie hills having large deposits of Rock phosphates. Jalikhal Bhusti, Masrana, Chamsadi and Chipaldih have been declared as phosphate bearing area and can produce 1.5 lac tonnes of rock phosphates per annum. The PPCL was presently supplying rock phosphate fertiliser to all States. Bihar, Assam and Kerala have become its major consumers. Further, field investigations have indicated that Mussoorie phosphates have great economic significance. It has been indicated that further analysis and prospecting of these rocks might lead to the discovery of Molybdinum and Uranium-bearing deposits in this area.

Gold deposits: In September 1981, a large deposits of commercially viable gold ore were found in the hilly areas of Pauri and Nainital districts. Along upper Shivalik hill reaches in the Kalachur region of Pauri, a 60 km. long and 2-5 km wide seam of gold deposits has been found. The seam of 'placer' gold which is in the west begins near 'Kalagarh', ends in the east near Kosi river in Ramnagar. The belt stretches through the Corbett National Park, Pauri and Nainital districts.

In an earlier survey, a 9 km long and 2-4 km wide seam of gold had been found in upper Shivalik reaches between Khara and Cheela in Pauri district. The tests have revealed the ore has a recovery of 0.4 gram per ton. The viability of finds is being assessed for commercial exploration.

In addition to important minerals that have been explained in the preceding paragraphs, there are many other minerals like Marble, Glass Sand, Pyrites, Audatusite, Phosphosite, Slate, Shilajeet, Mercury, Alum and Sapphire available at various places in Uttarakhand. In fact traces of Gold and Silver have also been noticed in Almora district. It can be seen that Uttarakhand is rich in mineral and their exploitation could help in future economic development of the region concentrated measures are being taken by the government in this regard.

Mineral Based Industries

Almora Magnesite Limited: Almora Magnesite, which is located about 50 km from Almora is a joint Undertaking of the State Government, Belpahar Refractories Limited and Hindustan Steel Limited and it is the first big industrial unit of the region. It has about 550 workers and more than 96 per cent workers are locals. The unit is progressing fast and had earned a net profit of Rs. 48.88 lac during the year 1977-78. The production of raw and dead burnt Magnesite was 51,740 and 19,820 tonnes respectively, recording an increase of 78% and 49% respectively, as compared to the previous year. The productivity of mines increased from 0.98 tonnes per man shift to 1.26 per man shift. Production in factory increased from 8.54 to 11.7 tonnes per man per month and percentage utilisation of installed capacity increased from 44% to 66%. The turnover during the year 1977-78 was 235.33 lac as compared to 140.04 lac in 1976-77. Steps are being taken to further mechanise mining operation of the project. A planning research cell has been set up to explore the possibility of setting up ancillary industries.

Cement Plant: A Cement plant is proposed to be set up near Mussoorie in Dehradun district. The plant is likely to cost Rs. 31crore.

Calcium Carbide Unit : A Calcium Carbide project is proposed to be set up to Bajour in Dehradun district. The project is estimated to cost Rs. 8 crore and is likely to produce and estimated 16,500 tonnes of calcium carbide within a period of two years. The project is likely to provide direct employment to 260 persons. Four medium scale units will also be set up in that area in the future.

Himalayan Magnesite Ltd. Pithoragarh: First Magnesite calcination plant for the manufacture of dead burnt magnesite was commissioned at Pithoragarh in 1980. The plant is located at the hight of 1600 metres. The project is jointly financed by the Pradeshik Industrial and Investment Corporation, State Bank of India. The composition of dead burnt Magnesite manufactured by this plant gives 'Low Silica' a property not available anywhere in India.

Future Prospects

The State Geology and Mining Directorate are carrying out intensive geophysical and geochemical investigations in the region and the State Mineral Development Corporation is undertaking commercial exploitation of minerals of proved deposits. Under the continuing schemes of Geology and Mining, 17 mineral investigation programmes, which include 6 investigations of non-metallic minerals, 8 metallic investigations and 3 regional geochemical surveys will be continued. It is proposed that besides detailed investigations on non-metallic mineral deposits such as, cement grade limestone for mini cement plants, high grade dolomite, magnesite and soapstone and investigations on newly discovered mineralisation of tungsten and placer gold, would be expedited. An area of 2000 sq km. would be covered in geological mapping and preliminary prospecting in Almora and Chamoli districts to delineate interesting areas of tungston mineralisation.

A regional study based on photo geological interpretation is proposed to be conducted in the Himalayan foothills, covering areas between Kotdwar in Pauri district and Haldwani in Nainital district. The proving of cement grade limestone for proposed mini cement plants would also be intensified. The new investigations proposed include regional geochemical surveys in Gori Ganga Valley Pithoragarh district and preliminary search for basement in parts of Dehra Dun and Uttarkashi districts. These surveys would be taken up with a view to extend the search of metallic minerals to geologically potential new areas which have hitherto been unexplored.

Industrial Units and Workers

The factual details of industries given in Table 15.1 and 15.2 below do not appear to be correct due to big gap between figures pertaining to 1993 and 1985. According to Uttar Pradesh, 1999, the

Table 15.1
Industry (Number of Small/Heavy Industries and Workers) (1984-85)

District (original)	*Small Scale Industries*	*Medium and Heavy Industries*	*Total No. of Workers*	*Total No. of Industries*
1. Nainital	52	20	12,707	72
2. Almora	8	2	679	10
3. Pithoragarh	2	2	400	4
4. Tehri Garhwal	4	1	186	5
5. Uttarkashi	-	-	-	-
6. Chamoli	-	-	-	-
7. Pauri Garhwal	8	1	290	9
8. Dehradun	81	18	9,892	99
Total Hill region	**155**	**44**	**24,154**	**199**

Source: Statistical Diary, Uttar Pradesh, 1987.

Table 15.2
Industrial Units in Uttarakhand Hill Region (1993)

	Industry	*No. of Unit*
1.	Khadi	3,662
2.	Khadi Board aided	11,206
3.	Engineering	2,145
4.	Chemical	524
5.	Mining	3,380
6.	Handloom	2,840
7.	Handicraft	5,856
8.	Silk Based Industries	61
9.	Others	3,652
	Total	33;326
1.	Industrial Estate	9
2.	Small Scale Industries	28,471
3.	Medium or heavy industries	158
4.	Total No. of persons employed in various industries	1,15,480

Source: Hamara Uttarakhand, Dr. K.C. Purohit, 1997.

number of person employed in industrial establishments was 655 per 1 lac of population in Uttarakhand which works to 39300 only. Here again the datas given by various agencies are full of contradictions. The actual position will be known only after the datas are made available by the new state of Uttaranchal. Industrialisation through small scale and cottage industry may be possible in the region provided it is planned and based on forest, horticulture and handicrafts. The traditional cottage industry which included even metal works, house building material and furniture making needs to be revived alongwith handicraft for tourist. Medium and heavy industries in the field of electronics and allied sector is unlikely to pay dividends due to tough competition industries which are well established in other parts of the country.

Communication and Tourism Industry

Communication

General

Transport and communication helps greatly in the movement of population, cultural contacts and exchange of information with outside world which is necessary for the development of the society as a whole. Road and bridges are constructed as per requirement of National highways, roads of Inter-state importance, strategic roads, roads under sensitive border areas, state highways, district and other roads and rural roads both under minimum need programme (MNP) or other than MNP. Necessary survey and investigation including planning and research is also undertaken for the development of the roads. At places roads are constructed as part of railway safety work. Roads are also constructed due to economic importance of the particular region.

Transportation is looked after by the Transport Corporation of the State Government. In addition private operators and companies are allowed to cover transport by roadways. Transport is also co-ordinated alongwith the development of railways. In addition ropeways may be introduced in the hilly area. Inland water transport is also introduced wherever possible. Air services have started giving tough competition in the movement of men and materials.

Construction of Roads

Indo-china war 1962 rangalarm bells. While chinese had constructed a network of roads right upto their border with India, form side to border roads were almost non-existent. After 1962 Indo-China war, the Government of India took appropriate action to develop network of roads in Uttarakhand hill region. Lack of road communication did affect speedy development but helped the people to preserve their culture and heritage. The socio-economic life of the people in the hilly region of Uttarakhand is dependent on proper footpaths and mule tracks. Footpath are commonly used by the people for their day to day work including by school going children, for medical assistance and evacuation of casualities and collection of goods from the road heads. Foot bridges over the rivers are also equally important for faster communication particularly when the rivers are in spate during rainy season.

Today construction of a network of road is a necessity for industrial and faster economic development as well as promotion of tourism and pilgrimage. Considering the high construction cost of roads and geological consideration, the strategy of road development has been modified. Stress is on light vehicle roads where traffic is likely to be less and the formation width of the road to 3.6 metres in straight reaches so that hill cuttings may be kept to the minimum. Instead of only motor roads a mix or motor roads, bridle paths and foot bridges, is now being taken up for implementation.

There is a proposal to give construction of rural roads, missing links, bridle roads and bridges, roads in tribal areas and connecting potential areas, viz. growth centres, tourists spots, horticulture belts and other inaccessible areas the top priority. Keeping in view scattered settlement pattern of hills, the norms under MNP for rural roads has been modified as compared to the national norms viz. coverage of 100 per cent of cluster of villages having a population of 500 and above and 50 per cent coverage of villages with population between 250 and 500 is envisaged for hill areas. On the basis of recommendation of the report of Task Force for the study of eco-development in the Himalayan region, certain corrective measures are proposed to be applied to arrest erosion due to road construction and other factors which are causing ecological degradation in hills.

The British had made only a few roads which they thought were sufficient for administration of the hilly area. These were Rishikesh-Narendranagar, Dehradun-Mussoorie, Kotdwara-Lansdowne, Haldwani-Nainital-Almora-Ranikhet. Now there is wide network of roads in the whole hilly region of Uttarakhand. According to one report, the present length of roads constructed by PWD was 3621 km. Kuchha hilly road, 13 km. multi track, 5530 km. water bound cement concrete road and 6405 km pucca cement concrete road in the hill region of Uttarakhand. For details see Table 15.3 below:

Table 15.3

Length of Roads in Uttarakhand

	District	*Kuchha hilly Road*	*Mule Track*	*Water Bound Cement Concrete*	*Pucca Cement Concrete Road*
1.	Uttarakashi	455	-	318	324
2.	Chamoli	718	-	591	544
3.	Tehri Garhwal	295	-	784	425
4.	Dehradun	96	-	545	243
5.	Pauri Garhwal	581	-	1335	784
6.	Pithoragarh	1000	-	504	507
7.	Almora	393	-	924	947
8.	Nainital	313	-	529	1971
	Total	**3621**	**13**	**5530**	**6405**

Source: Hamara Uttarakhand, Dr. K.C. Purohit, 1997.

Some other agencies have constructed roads which includes 3979 km. kuchha hilly road, 1469 km water bound cement concrete road and 1395 km. pucca cement concrete road. According to Uttar Pradesh, 1999, average length of roads in 1995-96 was 250.70 km for every one thousand square km of land area in Uttarakhand. This may be nearly thousand square km of the land area of Uttarakhand. This may be nearly correct if only water bound cement concrete and pucca cement concrete road are taken into consideration.

Road communication in Uttarakhand region mainly depends on Buses, Trucks, Taxies, Jeep and Cars. The main agencies operating road transport are State Transport Corporation, Garhwal Motor Owners Union Ltd. (GOMU), Tehri Garhwal Motor Owner Union Ltd. (TGMOU), Kumaun Motor Owners Union Ltd. (K.MOU), Seemant Sahakari Sangh, Garhwal Mandal Vikas Nigam (KMVM). State Transport Corporation has limited Buses but Garhwal Motors Owners Union in considered to be the biggest company in Asia.

Railways

Railway communication is presently available up to the railheads of Dehradun, Rishikesh, Hardwar, Kotdwar, Ramnagar, Kathgodam and Tanakpur for the state of Uttaranchal. Direct trains are available up to all important towns in the state of Uttar Pradesh as well as Delhi, Kolkata, Mumbai and Amritsar. No worthwhile efforts have been made to construct railway line beyond the foothills of Uttarakhand hill region, similar to one existing from Kalka to Shimla in Himachal Pradesh, Siliguri to Darjeeling in West Bengal or Mettupalayam to Ooty in Tamil Nadu. In 1921, survey was conducted to construct Railway line from Rishikesh to Karanprayag but no further progress could be made on this project till date. Many experts are of the view that a ring Railway line can be constructed from Rishikesh to Karanprayag-Gairsain-Ramnagar which could totally change the socio-economic life of the people and future of tourism in this part of the country. It is necessary the railway authority survey the area and prepare a feasibility report on this.

Airways

At present landing ground for Aircraft are available at Pithoragarh, Chinyali Shain in Uttarkashi district, Jolly Grant (near Dehradun) and one more is proposed to be at Gauchar in Rudraprayag district. However, it is long way to go before the Air service is fully exploited to promote-tourism and pilgrimage in the hill region of Uttarakhand. A feasibility study of this area for passenger and Cargo services should be undertaken by the Civil Aviation authorities.

Ropeways

Ropeways can be very useful in hilly areas both for quick transportation to hill tops of tourist attraction or for adventure sports like skiing. At present Ropeways are operational at Nainital and Mussoorie mainly for tourist attraction. Another Ropeway has since been installed at 'Auli' near Joshimath which has become an important centre for winter sports in this part of the country.

Post and Telegraph

Postal and telegraph facilities are equally important in this age of fast developing communication system both within the country and outside world. Details of Postal and Telegraph facilities in the hill region of Uttarakhand are given in Table 15.4 below :

According to Uttar Pradesh, 1999 and Table 15.4 above, during the year 1994-95 the average number of Post Office and Telegraph Office for every one lac of population in Uttarakhand was 41.7 and 7.45 respectively as compare to the average number of 135 Post Office and 4.4 Telegraph Office for every one lac of population in the plains of Uttar Pradesh.

Table 15.4
Post and Telegraph Facilities in Uttarakhand

	District	*No. of Post Office*	*No. of Telegraph Office*	*No. of PCO's*
1.	Uttarkashi	124	15	12
2.	Chamoli	334	11	130
3.	Tehri Garhwal	263	64	64
4.	Dehradun	247	45	148
5.	Pauri Garhwal	422	59	66
6.	Pithoragarh	386	9	130
7.	Almora	452	122	162
8.	Nainital	274	132	187
	Total	**2502**	**447**	**929**

Tourism Industry

The importance of tourism has also been realised in India though slowly. In recent years, tourism has become an important industry the world over. Presently the department of tourism in the Ministry of Tourism and Civil Aviation is responsible for organising and promoting international tourism throughout the country. However, the state government have also set up Tourism Departments and Corporations primarily to organise and promote tourism within the states. In the meantime, India's tourism Development Corporation, a Public Sector Undertaking, has been made exclusively responsible for management of hotels, motels and restaurants. The development of existing hill stations/towns could be attributed to either being a centre of administrative offices, religious importance or educational establishments supported by trade and business. But there is unlimited untapped potential to develop tourism in this part of the country. If concerted efforts are made by concerned authorities, there is a vast of scope to develop tourism in this region.

The hills of Uttarakhand have a great potential to turn it into a tourist and pilgrims paradise. Already lakhs of pilgrims from all over the country are visiting the holy shrines of Badrinath, Baijnath, Gangotri, Haridwar, Kedarnath, Rishikesh and Yamnotri every year. Uttarakhand is known as the abode of Hindu God and goddess where people have been coming on pilgrimage to wash their sins and for salvation. Uttarakhand was well known even during the period of '*Ramayana*' and '*Mahabharat*'. Similarly, every year thousands of tourists are visiting the beautiful summer resorts and some of the finest hill stations like Almora, Chakrata, Kausani, Lansdowne, Mussoorie, Nainital and Ranikhet. There are places like Kalsi, Lakha-mandal and Srinagar of great historical importance. The mystery lake of 'Roop Kund' is also located here. 'Nanda Devi Raj Jat Yatra' which takes place only once in 12 years is a unique religious event of this region.

Besides world famous valley of flowers, mountain peaks, glaciers, mountain ranges, big or small rivers are available for adventure sports. Wild-life sanctuaries, including the Corbett National Park are also located here. Lastly, Uttarakhand is becoming a popular playground for mountaineers, trekkers and sportsmen interested in river rafting and skiing. So far 57 religious centres, 72 places of historical importance, 11 wild-life sanctuaries, 16 places for adventure sports have been identified in Uttarakhand. Auli has since become an important centre for winter sports in Asia. It is interesting to note that our great leaders have also appreciated the hills of Garhwal and Kumaun. Mahatma Gandhi said, "In these hills Nature's hospitality eclipses all men can do. The enchanting beauty of the Himalaya, their bracing climate and soothing green that envelops you, leaves nothing to be desired.

I wonder whether the scenery of these hills and climate can be surpassed or equalled by any of the beauty spots of the world. After having been nearly for three weeks in Kumaun hills, I am more than ever amazed why our people need go to Europe in search of health". Jawahar Lal Nehru said, "I wish more of our people living in plains below would visit the Himalayas They can have their fill of flowers there and noble trees and primeval forests. They can breath the free untaimed air which invigorates and they can return strengthened in body, mind and spirit". Development and promotion of Tourism is undertaken alongwith the Transport and communication system in the state. This may involve introduction of Tourist Transport service both in private and public sector.

Tourism can be developed by identifying tourist spot and places of attraction for tourist, development of tourist spots, tourist accommodation in the form of tourist bungalows or Yatri Niwas, way side amenities with good guide and reception centres along the tourist and pilgrim routes. Tourism could also be promoted keeping in view traditional fairs and festivals in the hill region of Uttarakhand. Efforts are being made to develop tourism as an industry. During successive Five Year Plans emphasis is being laid to provide necessary infrastructure and other facilities for which programmes in the shape of suitable accommodation, wayside amenities, transport and communication, training in hotel management and catering, development of important tourist resorts and pilgrim places are being taken up. Besides, programmes of publicity through films, fairs and festivals and package tours are also being intensified for attracting tourists to small tourists complexes.

For promotion of tourism in the private sector, a special loan scheme has been launched under which subsidy is available to local people for construction of accommodation, transport, restaurants, catering and other allied tourist activities. To encourage off season tourism, schemes for mountaineering, trekking, winter sports, development of wild-life sanctuaries are being implemented. Tourism and pilgrimage to all Bigger and smaller shrines in Garhwal and Kumaun Hills has good scope for economic development as well as for generating employment opportunities. All this requires necessary training and guidance to enable local population and the unemployed youth to take up job in tourism, trekking and mountaineering. Construction of Railway lines as close as possible upto Himalayas and Air service can bring about revolutionary changes to develop tourism in this part of the country. The existing facilities for tourist and number of tourist and pilgrims who visited Uttarakhand are given in Table 15.5 and 15.6.

Table 15.5
Existing Facilities for Tourism (1993)

	District	*Tourist Bungalows*	*Beds available*
1.	Uttarkashi	13	560
2.	Chamoli	28	965
3.	Tehri Garhwal	8	300
4.	Dehradun	4	316
5.	Pauri Garhwal	10	409
6.	Pithoragarh	10	236
7.	Almora	12	410
8.	Nainital	17	596
	Total Hill Region	**102**	**3792**

Notes: Besides Tourist Bungalows, tourist make use of Private hotels and Dharamshalas available in all towns in Uttarakhand. Indian tourist are visiting generally in April-May or October-November and foreign tourist are visiting Mussooriee and Auli during winter months also.

Table 15.4
No. of Tourist Who Visited Uttarakhand

(In lac)

	Place	*1991*	*1993*
1.	Nainital	9.70	11.73
2.	Kathgodam	0.46	0.42
3.	Corbett National Park	0.39	0.33
4.	Almora	7.40	8.95
5.	Ranikhet	4.20	5.73
6.	Kausani	0.52	0.47
7.	Pithoragarh	6.50	7.87
8.	Purnagiri (Champawat)	6.10	6.11
9.	Dehradun	12.68	26.96
10.	Mussoorie	15.00	14.07
11.	Rishikesh	47.00	31.42
12.	Gangotri	1.13	1.12
13.	Yamnotri	1.05	1.04
14.	Uttarkashi	1.59	4.02
15.	Joshimath	0.70	0.46
16.	Badrinath	3.50	4.77
17.	Kedarnath	1.19	1.19
18.	Hardwar	53.56	-
19.	Valley of flowers	0.63	0.15

Source: Government of India, Publications.

Note- For detailed information on all places of tourist attraction, pilgrimage, wild life, trekking, mountaineering and other adventure sports see following Part III of this book.

PART III

TOURISM TREKKING AND ADVENTURE SPORTS

General Information

What to Expect

According to Hindu scriptures, pilgrimage to holy places is necessary for the realisation of God, and salvation. There are many holy places for pilgrims throughout the length and breadth of the country. However, according to Hindu scriptures, the four holy shrines in Uttarakhand must be visited by every Hindu for complete salvation. These shrines of Badrinath, Kedarnath, Gangotri and Yamnotri are situated at height ranging from 3050 m to 3966 m amidst scenic surroundings. Shankaracharya established Badrinath as one of the 'four Dham' (sacred shrines) in Uttarakhand. Millions of people of all shades and faith have been visiting these holy places for thousand years.

During old days the pilgrims used to cover the distance on foot from various parts of the country whereas today it is an experience by itself to travel along metalled zig-zag and well maintained roads through the valleys and along fast flowing rivers like Alaknanda, Bhagirathi and Mandakini. The region in known for its rich flora, fauna and numerous herbs and other vegetation used for Ayurvedic medicines.

The hills of Uttarakhand unfold montage of age old forests, orchards, aquamarine water cupped in valleys of lush green and gentle village folk. Amid the lowering mountains there are many holiday resorts like Almora, Chakrata, Lansdowne, Mussoorie, Nainital, Narendra Nagar, Pauri, Pithoragarh and Ranikhet where facilities are available for fishing, trekking and sailing. The riot of colour, music and dance fill the country side from summer to autumn. It is the natural surrounding in these hills which attracted the renowned musician Udai Shankar to open a dance school at Almora. Villagers from all over throng to the towns for festivals like Nanda Devi and Makar Sankranti, where the hills reverberate with the rhythm of Hurka drum and Dholak. Sacrifices are offered to the patron goddesses on various occasions.

16
Traditional Methods of Water Management in the Central Himalayan Agriculture

Water is life line in plains as well as in rivers. In the central Himalayan mountains a rich heritage of traditional methods for water conservation exists. A whole range of indigenous methods is in practice to store and use water for irrigation and other household purposes. These methods are cost-effective and involve the use of locally available material and human skill to construct the water harvesting structures. People follow some traditional norms with regard to the quantity of irrigation water and schedule-frequency of irrigation for the crops they grow. In all the above practices, there is strong community participation for the construction, repair and maintenance of water harvesting structures and rules for sharing the water.

Maintenance of crop field bunds, ploughing methods, relay cropping, mulching, putting weeds and crop remains to fire etc. are some of the methods of in-situ moisture conservation and soil fertility improvement practiced by the farmers. Use of household wastewater and rooftop water harvesting to supplement moisture for kitchen garden and household demands, and disposal of excess water from the crop fields is also in practice traditionally. However, these practices are now degenerating slowly as a consequence of reduction in water resources and apathy of the people for participatory programmes. There is a need to analyze these practices from scientific and socio-economic standpoint to popularize them for cost-effective and environment-friendly management of water resources. The practices have been in vogue for centuries. By modern techniques these can be upgraded.

Keywords: Traditional water conservation methods, Irrigation ponds, Rooftop water harvesting, Rainfall-runoff water harvesting, In-situ soil moisture conservation.

The Central Himalayan mountains in India, varying in elevation from 300 to over 7000 m asl, encompass an area of about 51,000 km^2, from 29° 30' to 31°30' N lat, and from 77° to 81° E long. Human settlement in this region has concentrated between 1000 and 2000 m asl, and agrisylvi-pastoral mode is the predominant way of livelihood. About 15% geographical area of the region is under agriculture and only 10% of it is irrigated. On an average, only 0.8 ha land is available per household of 5-6 family members, which may be distributed in as many as 30 tiny terraces varying in size from 0.01 to 0.058 ha.

This situation limits the use of productive inputs and it has been found that the present form and size of agriculture is insufficient to support the food grain demand of the local people. These constraints have triggered abandonment of marginal crop fields in this region. This region receives about two-thirds of the annual rainfall (150-250 cm) during monsoon season (mid-June to mid-September), and regarded as the storehouse of snow and ice reservoirs making headwaters of many important rivers of northern India. In the recent decades a reduction in rainfall and discharge from these water sources has been witnessed. Many perennial water sources have become seasonal and some of them have dried up. People have also noticed a decline in soil fertility and crop yields. In some places the once irrigated fields producing plenty of food grain have either been abandoned or support growth of coarse grains (drought resistant crops). Once strong community management practices for the use of water resources for irrigation are hardly in practice now. Social institutions, such as water councils (*pani panchayats*) are also being formed. In the face of scarcity of water resources many adaptive strategies are coming up.

This study was carried out to document the various indigenous water conservation (IWC) methods practiced by the farming communities in the rural areas of the central Himalayan mountains. Information on IWC methods was obtained from personal queries with a number of community people including elderly persons and ladies. Sometimes group discussions with the rural people were also held to ascertain the reason behind a given IWC method. Many visits in the rural area of the region were paid to collect the information and verification of these practices was done at the farmer's field level.

A. Irrigation Water Management

1. Canal Irrigation

As elsewhere, in this region also irrigation is mostly done through mud-lined canals (locally called as *kuhl* or *gul*) carved out of the hill slopes along the gradient of gravity. To draw water in these canals stream water is diverted placing big boulders across the stream width and the water leakage is sealed with mud and grass. Sometimes thorny bushes or branches of trees are put beneath the boulders, which trap sealing material flowing with the water and also provide shear strength to the diversion structure.

In case the crop fields are above the stream water level, the streambed is raised (up to 5 m high) by putting big boulders in the foundation and large stone all across the rim of the diversion structure. Sand and other material brought about by the stream gradually gets deposited upstream and the streambed is suitably raised to divert the water flow to the adjoining canal. Use of strong wooden poles by fixing them vertically and horizontally across the stream width to provide shear strength to the diversion structure is also known as a rare practice of water management. The main irrigation canal is distributed into several sister canals joining each of the fields in its command area. A sister canal passing through one peasant's field conveys water to the following fields belonging to another peasant.

Maintenance of canal damaged during ploughing and other agricultural operations and choked due to weeds etc. is the responsibility of the respective field owner. This network of canals is maintained generations after generations and protects the irrigation interests of the farming community. It is noteworthy to see that a network of fine canals, although not legalized, yet works wonderfully well only due to the social cohesion and dependence on each other for irrigation.

In the rainfed crop fields, rainfall is the only source to replenish the soil moisture. Here, peasants practice conservation measures such as, reduced tillage (frequency and depth), and cultivation of drought-resistant crops (e.g., barley, millets, oilseeds and pulses etc.) to cope up with the problem of soil moisture. In normal conditions of rainfall and soil moisture rainfed crop fields are tilled twice and irrigated crop fields thrice for seed sowing. Vegetable fields are tilled / harrowed several time a year depending upon the cropping intensity. Some vegetables require limited harrowing and some require frequent harrowing. However, in case of low soil moisture and drought, tilling is done only once in rainfed crop fields, and tilling depth is reduced by half (<10 cm). People mostly grow local drought-resistant varieties of food crops, which they have selected from long periods of trial-and-error for rainfed conditions.

2. Schedule/Frequency of Irrigation

In the community run canals the community elders fix schedule of irrigation depending upon the crops, season and availability of water. Priority is given to vegetable crops for irrigation. If the water discharge is low, irrigation is done from tail to head of the canal. Each field owner waits for his turn for irrigation. It may come any time during day or night. When plenty of water is available irrigation depends upon the choice of the farm owner and there is no fixed rotation. In this situation water is diverted for irrigation at many points across the canal. Sometimes, when the flow is very low the main canal is blocked and water is allowed to fill in through the canal length. Once it is filled up, the blockade is removed suddenly to use the force of water to travel the desired canal distance rapidly. Sometime more than one peasant shares the water thus stored at one time.

3. Pond Irrigation

This is a common method to store water discharge from minor water sources for irrigation. Ponds are constructed on small seasonal/ perennial streams involving whole stakeholder community for construction of water ponding structures and mud-lined canals, and their repair and maintenance. Everyone abides by the rules of operation fixed by the community. People bring necessary equipments and a mud-and stone structure is built across the stream to block the water flow. Such blockades are usually 5-15 m wide and 1-2 m high. Big boulders are placed at the foundation followed by smaller ones and grass and mud on the top. A hole with blocking arrangement is left at the bottom of the pond and kept close for water impounding. When the reservoir is filled the hole left at the bottom is opened and water is discharged forcefully in the canal for irrigation. The next community member now blocks the hole and uses the ponding water for irrigation subsequently. One such pond is sufficient to irrigate 0.1-0.25 ha crop fields and command area of such ponds is generally 1-2 ha. Sometimes several smaller ponds are created along a stream to irrigate < 1 ha area and may be shared by a few community members.

4. Quantity of Irrigation Water

Peasants irrigate crops based on traditional knowledge. In paddy, irrigation is done 7-8 times throughout the growing period when normal water supply is available. Irrigation is preferred either early morning or late evening to escape the warming up of irrigation water due to sunshine, which is considered harmful for the crop. Sometimes when plenty of water is available, small stream of water flowing is left for most of the growing period (July-August) in the rice fields and an outlet from the corner of the fields for the overflow water is left. This continuous supply of fresh water is considered even more beneficial for paddy. For wheat, irrigation is given at 20-25 days interval and altogether 5 irrigations are preferred for the wheat crop. Light irrigation during winter is allowed and water flow is guided to spread over the field uniformly to avoid excessive wetting, which makes the soil cold, and retards tillering and growth of wheat. For tuberous crops such as, potato, onion, radish, turmeric, ginger etc. irrigation at 20 days interval during winter and at 7-8 days interval during summer is practiced.

5. Micro-irrigation

Crops, particularly chillies are transplanted in small circular pits during summer when water scarcity is acute. Transplantation of chilli seedlings is done at dawn so that the tender seedlings acclimatize to dry hot soils overnight and withstand the drying sunlight of the following day. Life saving micro-irrigation is given to the seedlings @ about 200 ml per plant in the morning and evening daily for the initial one week. To make sure that each seedling gets equal water a container measuring about 200 ml is used and filled with water every time after watering a seedling manually from a larger water container kept nearby. In addition, leafy twigs of nearby available bushes are inserted around the pit to provide shade to the tender seedlings for initial 2-3 days for adaptation in the hostile conditions. Similar practice is done for cauliflower, eggplant, and a number of climber vegetables (e.g., bottle gourd, bitter gourd, ridge gourd, snake gourd, pumpkin, etc.).

6. Rainfall-runoff Harvesting Ponds (*khals*)

In this age-old practice found in some low rainfall areas of this region natural depressions at the hilltops are used to harvest the rainfall-runoff water. A mud and stone embankment towards sloping end of the hill is created for water impounding. Sometimes, channels are also created to convey water from the uphill catchment area to these ponds. This water store is mainly meant for use by the cattle during grazing and camping, and percolation of water also benefits the water discharge in downstream sources. Most of these *khals* are now silted up due to lack of maintenance and people's participation.

B. In-situ IWC Methods in Crop Fields

1. Crop Field Bunds

As elsewhere raising crop field bunds and leveling crop fields is an age-old practice for IWC in this region. In irrigated fields bunds of different height/width are maintained. Bunds are maintained at every cropping season and particularly at the time of irrigation of crops. Usually they are 20 cm high, where regular flood irrigation is available and soil is fine, so that the risk of water stagnation and collapse of terrace riser is avoided. Fields having gravelly soil has 20-30 cm high bunds to store more water, as chances of water percolation are high.

Sometimes a large terrace is divided into two-three smaller ones for ease of leveling and to ensure spread of irrigation water uniformly. In the rainfed crop field bunds are not intensively maintained and the fields are also not well leveled. A bund (stone/mud) is raised only when rainwater is expected to collect in the field or move the soil from the sloping end. However, in place of bunds strong root system of local grass develops and it anchors the edge of the fields tightly and soil creep/erosion under rain is arrested. This grass is seasonally cut and used as fodder for stall-feeding the cattle.

2. Ploughing Methods

The local people follow a number of practices through ploughing to conserve soil moisture, such as the following:

— Soon after winter rains, crop fields are ploughed and compressed leveling is done using a heavy wooden plate. This is done to bury the soil moisture in deeper soil layers to obtain good seed germination.

— Sometimes ploughing is done soon after crop harvest at the end of rainy season. In this way weeds and soil moisture are buried in deeper soil layers. The weed decomposition increases both soil moisture and soil fertility and favours the germination and growth of the following crop.

— During autumn when the fields are under current fallow, some people saturate fields with water to avoid competition for water during the period of high demand for seedbed preparation for *rabi* crop.

— In some places seed sowing is done in a circular fashion to raise paddy nursery. This method is water conserving as compared to broadcast sowing and line sowing of paddy seeds to raise nursery. Water flow left at the entry point of outer ring spreads across the whole field in a circular way. Seedling excavation for transplantation is also easier in this method.

— Geometry of ploughing—first and second ploughing is done perpendicular to each other to make sure that no soil is left unploughed. Ploughing is always started from the sloppy end of the crop field to achieve leveling and reduce soil erosion.

3. Mulching

Crop residue of wheat and dry fodder grass refused by the cattle is used as mulch for in-situ moisture conservation and soil fertility improvement. Mulching seedbeds of vegetable crops such as cauliflower, onion, chilli, eggplant, etc. is a common practice during winter to avoid frost killing, moisture evaporation and to provide warmth and protection to the tender vegetable seedlings. Mulch is also applied to tuberous crops such as turmeric, ginger and colocasia when they are sown during summer to protect soil moisture from evaporation and to increase soil fertility through decomposition of mulch material in the following rainy season.

4. Relay Cropping

Relay cropping is another traditional way of utilizing moisture and shade under taller plants of some crops to achieve better germination and growth of a subsidiary crop. Sowing lentil about one week prior to harvest of paddy crop and sowing radish in between the rows of mature maize crop are some of the examples of relay cropping.

5. Soil Fertility Management and In-situ Moisture Conservation

There are a number of location-specific indigenous methods for soil fertility restoration and in-situ soil moisture conservation found in this region. Some of the methods are summarized in Table 16.1.

C. Indigenous Management Practices to Dispose-off Excess Water

Very often some croplands at the base of the hills are marshy due to seepage from the uplands. Crop cultivation in such land becomes difficult due to excess moisture. Therefore, only some varieties of paddy rice, which tolerate water stagnation, are cultivated on such land. Deep digging of such land is done during spring and the soil is

Table 16.1 Some Indigenous Methods of Soil Fertility Management and In-situ Moisture Conservation in the Central Himalayan Mountains

	Method	*Advantages (SWC)*
1.	Collection of pine leaves from the nearby forests, spreading them over the crop fields and putting them to fire at the time of sowing paddy rice (summer).	The inflammable pine needles burn rapidly and consume the weeds and their seed/root stock at the soil surface. The ash is considered to increase soil fertility. Reduced severity of forest fire due to the use of pine needles is another advantage of this practice.
2.	Weeds and minor crop remains are gathered, allowed to dry and put to fire on the crop fields.	Ash is believed to enhance soil fertility and weed infestation is controlled due to burning of rootstock and seeds.
3.	Vegetal remains/refuse of stall-fed fodder to the livestock is transported to the nearby crop fields and put to fire.	This otherwise slow decomposing woody material associated with stall-fed fodder is turned into ashes to fertilize the soil.
4.	Use of first floodwater for irrigation by some innovative farmers.	The first seasonal floodwater is believed to bring organic matter and humus along with it and deposits fine silt on the field and increases soil fertility. This practice is mostly done in paddy fields.
5.	In-situ manuring in the crop fields	This practice involves camping of cattle in the crop fields overnight for some days after the *kharif* crop harvest. When dung and urine deposition on the fields is considered adequate the camp shifts to other fields. In this practice loss of nutrients and transport labour for FYM from cattle-shed to the fields is saved.
6.	Sowing paddy seeds pre-soaked overnight for nursery preparation	Good germination of these pre-soaked paddy seeds is achieved and irrigation demand for germination is minimized.
7.	Wet soil mixed with seeds of rye (*Brassica nigra*) is placed inside the holes left between the stones of terrace risers	Minimization of water need for germination and use of the unused space of terrace riser for vegetable cultivation.

allowed to sundry. Few more rounds of digging take place at suitable intervals depending upon the soil moisture left. Deep channels (about 1 m) are dug out towards the edge of the terraces, and sometimes in between the larger fields. The sub-surface water seeps into these channels and safely runs away from the cropland. Often more than one peasant owns such land and they all coordinate to make channels for the safe disposal of water away from the marshy land.

D. Roof Top Water Harvesting

In this region rooftops are made up of slates. During rainfall water drips from the rooftop and is collected putting containers beneath on the courtyard. Usually this water is used for cattle (drinking and washing), cleaning clothes, utensils and house premises, toilet cleaning, and rarely for drinking (only when the water is sufficiently clean). Traditionally, there is no special structure on the roof to guide the overflowing rainwater at a fixed location. Therefore, most of the water just flows down through the courtyard and finds its way through holes kept for the outlet of this water, which open in adjoining kitchen garden and serve the purpose of minor irrigation. However, of late, people have also started to fix tin / rubber plastic gutters along this water to fall at one corner of the courtyard and also use big polytanks / drums / permanenetly built small cement-lined tanks to store this water for further use. Sometimes a canal-like carving in the wooden log is permanently kept beneath the roof at the backyard to store rooftop water and for use by cattle.

E. Use of Wastewater

(i) The small courtyard of step well (a stone-lined about 1-2 m deep structure to recover seepage water for drinking) is encircled by a stonewall of about 1 m high, so that trespassing cattle do not make the water dirty. Instead an outlet at the base of the wall is left through which the overflowing water from the step well finds its way to an outside pond, which collects water for use by the visiting cattle.

(ii) Wastewater/leakage arising from community taps is also stored in earthen tanks dug nearby. Neighbouring innovative farmers use the wastewater stored for irrigating kitchen garden crops. In some villages this water is conveyed to the kitchen gardens by canals/pipes and used alternatively by the neighbour.

(iii) Wastewater generated from the houses is also channeled to kitchen gardens and the ash used for cleaning utensils is considered to have fertilizing effect.

Discussion and Conclusion

Every region has knowledge and traditional adaptation. These include experiences on fundamental understanding of processes of ecological change, slope dynamics and biological conservation. Improvement from one generation to another generation takes place in the traditional practices considering previous experiences (good or bad). Indigenous management of water resources is considered to have built-in eco-friendly system of conservation, preservation and utilization of natural resources also in north-eastern region of India. It has been emphasized that local people, especially where irrigation already exists, have an intimate knowledge of local conditions. Farmers with irrigation experience develop a wealth of knowledge about irrigation requirements for local soils and crops. They often have practical design and experience, which should be essentially incorporated at the time of designing an irrigation scheme.

Departmental methods are based on the application of standard rules and criteria, and do not always satisfy farmer's practical needs, whereas farmers' attitudes are more flexible and more innovative. A variety of indigenous soil and water conservation (ISWC) practices in many places in Africa consist of all kinds of stone lines and ridge systems to conserve soil and to make the best use of limited rainfall. Concern has now been shown at various levels for this dying wisdom of rich heritage on water management through community participation. Water management practices forwarded by the modern technology often do not prove cost-effective and face difficulties to withstand the dynamic nature of the mountain environment. The social acceptance of such technology is also a constraint sometimes. However, people continue to upgrade the indigenous practices with the modern technological advances only when they find them cost effective and feasible in the bio-physical environment in which they operate.

17

Man and Forests in the Darjeeling Himalaya: Reviewing Settlement-Fuelwood Equations

Abstract

Because of peculiarities of land-use, the Darjeeling region experiences a forest crisis of unusual dimensions. The paper examines the history of forest policy as it evolved in the Darjeeling Himalaya, before modelling settlement pressure on fuelwood and forest reserves both theoretically and in the light of the demographic experience. Estimating the degree to which present fuelwood needs are unmet by recorded extractions, useful suggestions are put forward towards a regional energy plan.

Man versus Forests

Estimated rates of tropical deforestation on the world scale are at around 100,000 sq km per year, with unique ecosystems having been almost completely effaced, e.g., 98 percent of old-growth forests on the North American continent (excluding Canada), or a similar percentage of the Brazilian coastal rain forest of which less than 2 per cent remains today. Because of the quality of habitat provided by forest ecosystems, the species-loss that is consequent upon their destruction can range between 80-200 species/ha. Thus, the leading cause of species extinctions in the world today is habitat destruction, particularly in tropical rain forests. Since this destruction takes place overwhelmingly through human agency and at least in part because of the struggle of the human species to survive, the phenomenon has considerable bearing on forests in the Himalaya which constitute one of the most unique biodiversity reserves in the world. The present paper examines core conflicts between human needs and forests in India and its mountain regions with case study then being made of the Darjeeling Himalaya. Depletion of forests, therefore is a focal area in the sustainability and conservation debates.

India's Forest Policy: Historical Antecedents

In the renaissance period European experts had started taking in the study of forests. It was only sporadic. No sustained efforts were made to study forestry. The practice of scientific forestry was commenced by foresters such as Hartig and Cotta in Europe, leading eventually to the establishment of schools for forestry in Germany and France around 1825. The British being comparative late-starters in the field, their colonial policy initially looked at forests as wastelands, incapable of yielding revenue unless cleared. Over the decade of the 1860s after assumption of direct rule of India by the Crown following the 1857 struggle and the demise of the East India Company, British colonial and mercantile interests began to look seriously at the diversion of lands to alternative land use in the Crown territories, a practice that had achieved considerable success in Australia, Canada and other British colonies. This had its consequences on the Darjeeling hill areas and the Duars region in the 1860s when investment in India was opened to the British public and successful experimentation with tea led to a land-lease boom with rapid conversion of large tracts of non-revenue wasteland (i.e. forests) in British Sikkim and the Bengal Duars into plantations under tea. Inflows of British public investment into India until the 1920s had been mostly into railway and tea stocks.

Eventually, with the leasing out of wastelands, the seeds of British forestry policy in India evolved under the consultancy of the German forester Dietrich Brandis who had a British wife and whose services had been requisitioned by the British Government initially for the commercial cultivation of teak in the Pegu forests of Burma, and then as the first inspector general of forests to the Government of India. The work of Brandis, which introduced the principles of German production forestry into India culminated in Indian Forest Act of 1865 later comprehensively amended under the Indian Forest Law Act of 1878. After that the first school of forestry was established at Dehradun.

On the eve of the enunciation of the new Forest (Conservation) Act of 1988 [FCA88], India had 747.2 thousand sq km of notified forests amounting to forest cover of around 22.8 per cent, of which

397.8 thousand sq km (12.1 per cent) were reserved forests, 216.5 thousand sq km (6.6 per cent) were protected, 86.7 thousand sq km (2.6 per cent) were unclassed forests and 46.2 thousand sq km (1.4 per cent) were classed as other forests. Forest policy in India since the 1870s had traditionally laid precedence on permanent cultivation has precedence over forestry, on satisfaction of local needs prior to revenue forestry, and only after that on maximization of revenues from forests. However as forestry policy evolved along ecological lines in independent India between 1952 and 1988, a mild energy-cum-biomass emphasis entered the forestry equation with emphasis on increased supplies of timber to the rural sector for implements, fodder and to release cattle dung for manure, alongwith on to indiscriminate extension of agriculture at the of forests, and to an eventual ban on monoculture. The rate of diversion of forest lands to agriculture been around 1.5 thousand sq km per annum light down to 55 sq km p.a. in 1989, following of FCA88.

Forest Conservation Focus

Principal statutory guidelines that govern forest plans since, stress that working plans should belly updated to stress conservation. A disiciplinary approach should be followed in any working plans, and clear-felling by artificial regeneration should be avoided as far as possible. Clear-felling blocks in any case should 10 ha. in hill forests and 25 ha. in the plains, and telling should be stopped for a few years in areas over altitude to allow them to recover. To relieve fuelwood on forests, the guidelines envisage the provision alternative fuel on priority basis to townships any of forests which have populations of 5000 or more at the gravity of the current fuel equations in the light be appreciated from the mid-Eighties estimate country wide fuelwood requirements at around 13.3. tonnes per annum, against which fuelwood supply is tonnes p.a. and recorded production is only tonnes.

Priodiversity Conservation Focus

Intensity has been added to man-forest conflicts growing stress on nature conservation. Protection for the living denizens of the forests in India through a long tortuous debate involving hunters is men who were later more appropriately and by conservationists of different schools. Total conservation of the wilds in selected biospheric reserves become central to the strategy for biodiversity conservation on under the Wildlife Protection Act of 1972 which was the precursor to FCA88. Sanctuaries and National parks many of which have been carved out of reserve forests now cover 141.4 thousand sq km per cent) of India's landmass with their core areas approximately 32.9 thousand sq km (1 per cent). Earlier, the present Government forests were mainly for revenue and strategic reasons in the century. Appropriation of forest wealth which suspension of the common property rights of peoples was accomplished through game laws that used preservation of shooting stocks of wild game to the sporting needs of colonial hunters and by banning tribal/local entry even for livelihood.

However considerations of ecosystemic balance of conservation strategy took a considerably time of come into focus, during which the of predators like tigers and leopards was under State rules. It was only in 1976 that provincial freedoms over discretionary use of forest and wildlife reserves was curbed by the 42nd Amendment to the Constitution which annexed forests and wildlife from the State list to the Concurrent list. Thus, over 1980.84, the number of national parks increased from 19 to 52 and over 30 per cent of protected areas in 1995 comprised areas taken over after 1983. In the course of these developments, little focus remained on the vexed issue of local rights. While policy formulations like WPA72 and FCA88 had conceded the importance to conservation strategy of improving socio-economic conditions among forest fringe people, harsh measures came to be increasingly adopted to stop the felling of trees in ecologically designated areas.

Current manifestations of conservation conflicts are seen under the increasing economic pressure following economic liberalisation in 1991 to denotify core areas of certain protected and reserved forests to pave the way for mining and resort leases, which amounts to the expropriation of local forest rights under the WPA72 being used to the benefit organised commercial interests. Another emerging conflict that has led in part to concessions through Joint Forest Management [JFM], concerns protests from local populations denied the right to their traditional livelihood while access is allowed to commercial forestry and other allied interests. The number of people living in and around protected areas in India is variously estimated at around 4.5 million. JFM involving them ventures a change from pure preservation to conservation by a willingness to invest in ecologically sound development at the periphery of protected areas in exchange for further protection of biodiversity in their inner cores.

In summary therefore, the conservation debate and strategy in India has moved from the phase of conservation through bureaucratic intervention to enlisting support from forestfringe residents by generating employment through resource-efficient use of natural resources. The point of common agreement is that reworking of man-forest relationships is the order of the day, and that conservation has to be accomplished at the grassroots, and not by bureaucratic means. Stabilisation of shrinking biodiversity therefore requires urgent attention to problems of people sharing the habitat.

Forests in the Darjeeling Hills

At the time of their acquisition by the British, the Darjeeling hill areas (then called British Sikkim) were largely uninhabited and covered with forests. Forests to the east of the Tista were found to be in relatively poor condition due to the greater degree of rural settlement there by the indigenous Lepcha people who followed Swidden agricultural practices. Extensive forest fires were often reported in the outer hills and along the Tista and Rangit valleys which often originated in the uncontrolled spread of 'slash and burn' fires. The British notification of reservation of forests in the Darjeeling Division under the first Indian forest Act of 1865 arose out of the need for conservation of timber and also to eliminate the prevalent practice of swidden agriculture. By virtue of a gazetted notification in 1871-72, 186.48 sq km (72 sq mi) of hill forests were notified as Reserve Forests, and 1986.52 sq km (767 sq mi) of primary sal (Shorea robusta) forests in the ceded Bhutan Duars were notified as Open Government Forests.

The Darjeeling and Jalpaiguri Forest Divisions, comprising areas of 274.54 sq km (106 sq mi) and 334.11 sq km (129 sq mi), respectively, were constituted under Dr. W.Schlich who took over as Conservator of Forests in 1872-73. An inspection tour of the Singalila forest extending upto 12,000 ft. was made by Gamble, who suggested the retention of natural forests there for stabilisation of climate, water sources and to prevent landslips from occurring on the high-degree slopes. Addition of the Apalchand Reserves to Jalpaiguri Division and reservation of nine forest blocks to the present KCalimpong Division over 1875-77 expanded the areas of the Darjeeling and Jalpaiguri Divisions to 416.99 sq km (161sq mi) and 1010.10 sq km (390 sq mi) respectively. The Indian Forests Act (1927) subsequently designated a part of the forest areas as protected forests. Since 1879, the areas notified under forests have remained more or less stable, although marginal additions took place under the Estate Acquisition Act (1953) and transfers of *khasmahal* forests and surplus forests on tea-leased lands. Under the British and for some time after their departure, the primary official purpose for working forests in the two Northern Divisions was the production of timber for railway sleepers, which averaged over 2,000 tons annually between 1874-1960.

Timber Extraction and the Beginnings of Depletion

In the beginning trees exeeding on particular grith were sold under a permit system. Indian forestry was completely new at that time. The initial methods did not prove fruitful. The impact of the system was decimation of all the best species and consequent accumulation of defective or otherwise poor quality species and specimens in production forest areas, quite the antithesis of sound silvicultural practice. Exploitation of the Darjeeling forests commenced in 1884 primarily to supply railway timbers and to meet the fuelwood needs of tea labour.

With the establishment of sounder forest management under recommendations of Brandis in 1878 as later modified by Schlich, the working practice in hill forests gradually changed over to selective felling at altitudes above 7500 ft. and mostly clear-felling below these levels. Monoculture gradually entered as the practical solution for improvement of commercial forest quality, and spelt the doom of broadleaf stands in many naturally forested areas. The principles of economic forest management evolved since Independence were to provide forest-based industry with forest resources as inputs and to develop forestry support for the rural economy. A major change in forestry practice in the Darjeeling hill areas as compared to the colonial period was its reorientation towards production forestry aimed at maximisation of revenues.

The low ratio of forest cover in West Bengal to burgeoning timber and fuelwood demands in the state sparked off another major reversal of British forestry practices in the high altitude forests by opening them for production forestry through the West Bengal Forest Development Corporation [WBFDC] which had been established for the purpose under the S. S. Ray ministry on 2 November 1974, and to which an area of 832 sq km of forests was transferred on Government lease from the Darjeeling and Kalimpong Forest Divisions. The intention behind the transfer was to bring around 4500 ha. Of high altitude forest reserves under a 30-year production cycle, primarily to serve the needs of wood-based industry in West Bengal which then faced an estimated shortfall of between 39-48 thousand cum. The principles to be followed were those of commercial forestry, with the corporation also being charged with reforestation/afforestation of production areas and other wastelands.

Because of the higher commercial offtake envisaged, the focus now shifted from. hardwood to softwood extraction. A consequence of the shortening of the production cycle from 50-60 years for timber hardwood species like teak and sal to 30 years for quick-growing softwood species like eucalyptus to serve the needs of plywood and matchwood industries was a restocking of production forest areas with non-endemic tree species. Another factor in deforestation resulting from the expanded working of hill forests was consistent failure to meet replantation and reforestation targets, as evinced in several annual reviews on the Darjeeling Hill Areas Annual Plans in the Seventies and Eighties, with shortfalls ranging from 50-75 per cent of targets. The usual plea for such poor performance was the financial constraint on implementing a large-scale replantation programme following accelerated felling , because of high establishment and operational costs governing the working of the corporation.

Depletions and Urban Energy Need

The main question that still remains unaddressed by forest policy in India is not associated with timber forestry, but instead with the local needs for energy. A model on woodfuel-use and deforestation developed vis-à-vis the growth of settlement extending a parallel model for the Sudan (cf, Digernes 1977) holds important insights into the phenomenon in the Darjeeling hills. The model is outlined schematically in Figure1.

At the initial settlement stages of the settlement-centre C, fuelwood is a collected fuel, rather than a priced fuel and is gathered by the settlers themselves or by a section among them. Collection at this stage is relatively easy on account of the relatively small size of the settlement and proximity of local forests. In the second settlement stage, expanding energy needs and exhaustion of fuelwood supplies in the close periphery of the settlement, lead to emergence of a specialised class or agency that supplies these needs from outer forests, often reducing the bulk of biomass to be transported by converting a part of it into charcoal.

Index

C

D

I

J

K

T

U